formatio

TRADITION. EXPERIENCE.
TRANSFORMATION.

Formatio books from InterVarsity Press follow the rich tradition of the church in the journey of spiritual formation. These books are not merely about being informed, but about being transformed by Christ and conformed to his image. Formatio stands in InterVarsity Press's evangelical publishing tradition by integrating God's Word with spiritual practice and by prompting readers to move from inward change to outward witness. InterVarsity Press uses the chambered nautilus for Formatio, a symbol of spiritual formation because of its continual spiral journey outward as it moves from its center. We believe that each of us is made with a deep desire to be in God's presence. Formatio books help us to fulfill our deepest desires and to become our true selves in light of God's grace.

SPIRITUAL DISCIPLINES
COMPANION

Bible Studies and Practices to Transform Your Soul

Jan Johnson

IVP Books
An imprint of InterVarsity Press
Downers Grove, Illinois

InterVarsity Press, USA
P.O. Box 1400, Downers Grove, IL 60515-1426, USA
World Wide Web: www.ivpress.com
Email: email@ivpress.com

InterVarsity Press®, USA, is the book-publishing division of InterVarsity Christian Fellowship/USA®, a student movement active on campus at hundreds of universities, colleges and schools of nursing in the United States of America, and a member movement of the International Fellowship of Evangelical Students. For information about local and regional activities, write Public Relations Dept., InterVarsity Christian Fellowship/USA, 6400 Schroeder Rd., P.O. Box 7895, Madison, WI 53707-7895, or visit the IVCF website at <www.intervarsity.org>.

All Scripture quotations, unless otherwise indicated, are taken from the Holy Bible, New International Version®. NIV®. Copyright © 1973, 1978, 1984 by International Bible Society. Used by permission of Zondervan Publishing House. Distributed in the U.K. by permission of Hodder and Stoughton Ltd. All rights reserved. "NIV" is a registered trademark of International Bible Society. UK trademark number 1448790.

The parts in this book were originally published as Solitude & Silence © 2003 by Jan Johnson; Service & Secrecy © 2003 by Jan Johnson; Prayer & Listening © 2003 by Jan Johnson; Study & Meditation © 2003 by Jan Johnson; Community & Submission © 2003 by Jan Johnson; Reflection & Confession © 2003 by Jan Johnson; Simplicity & Fasting © 2003 by Jan Johnson; Worship & Celebration © 2003 by Jan Johnson.

Design: Cindy Kiple

Images: Steve Coleman/Getty Images

ISBN 978-0-8308-3523-2

Printed in the United States of America ∞

P	21	20	19	18	17	16	15	14	13	12	11	10	9	8	7	6	5	4	3	2	1
Y	26	25	24	23	22	21	20	19	18	17	16	15	14	13	12	11	10	09			

CONTENTS

INTRODUCING
SPIRITUAL DISCIPLINES
BIBLE STUDIES

Have you ever wondered how God changes people? Maybe it seems as if old habits never change no matter how hard you try. Maybe you've become discouraged with your lack of growth into Christlikeness. You know that you are forgiven through Jesus' suffering on the cross, and you realize that you are totally accepted by God on that basis. This is wonderful. And yet your desire to live in a way that pleases God somehow constantly falls short of the mark.

God desires to transform our souls. This transformation occurs as we recognize that God created us to live in an interactive relationship with the Trinity. Our task is not to transform ourselves, but to stay connected with God in as much of life as possible. As we pay attention to the nudges of the Holy Spirit, we become disciples of Christ. Our task is to do the connecting, while God does the perfecting.

As we connect with God, we gradually begin acting more like Christ. We become more likely to weep over our enemies instead of discrediting them. We're more likely to give up power instead of taking control. We're more likely to point out another's successes rather than grab the credit. Connecting with God changes us on the inside, and we slowly become the tenderhearted, conscientious people our families always wished we'd become. This transformation of our souls through the work of the Holy Spirit results in "Christ in you, the hope of glory" (Colossians 1:27).

God does in us what we cannot do by being good. Trying to be good generally makes us obnoxious because it's so obvious that we're only trying. The goodness doesn't come from within ourselves. When we do succeed at being good, we subtly look down on those who don't do as well. When we don't succeed, we beat ourselves up and despair over our lack of spirituality. Either way, we remain focused on self instead of on setting our hearts on things above.

Connecting with God, then, is important. But what does connecting with God look like? Through the work of the Holy Spirit, we copy Jesus in behind-the-scenes, everyday activities he did to connect with God. As we let these activities become habits, we slowly become "trained" to have the heart of Christ and behave as he did. These activities are spiritual disciplines, also called spiritual exercises or strategies.

How Spiritual Disciplines Work

We connect with God through spiritual disciplines (or exercises or practices, which are specific versions of disciplines). Included in this book are six studies each on eight sets of disciplines: solitude and silence, service and secrecy, prayer and listening, Bible study and Scripture meditation, community and submission, reflection and confession, simplicity and fasting, and worship and celebration. Now and then other disciplines are included as a session within a set, such as: journaling (Reflection and Confession, session 6); practicing the presence of God (Prayer and Listening, session 6); and welcoming the stranger (Community and Submission, session 6).

Many other activities become spiritual disciplines for us as we practice them on a regular basis to "partcipate in the divine nature" (2 Peter 1:4), that is, to bring us into union with God and transformation into Christlikeness. Some of them are written about in the classics of the faith and God will show you many others. Indeed, a spiritual discipline is *anything,* as Henri Nouwen said, that helps us practice "how to become attentive to that small voice and willing to respond when we hear it."[1]

Some spiritual disciplines are activities of *engagement.* For example, in practicing the disciplines of Bible study and worship we engage in those activities in regular, focused ways. Others are disciplines of *abstinence* because we abstain from something. For example, in fasting we refrain from eating or another activity in a regular, focused way. In secrecy we refrain from letting anyone know about our good deeds. When we abstain from a substance or activity this way, we miss it and feel its absence. We have to depend on God more. We also hear our heart better—that part of us that is "deceitful above all things" (Jeremiah 17:9). As we hear our heart, we face our real self and surrender it to God. Disciplines of engagement are like breathing in (we take in good things), and disciplines of abstinence are like breathing out (we let go of things we don't need for a while to die to self and trust in God).

Spiritual disciplines help us in the following ways.

- They build our relationship with God as we acquaint ourselves with the ways of God. (It's possible, of course, to do these disciplines in a legalistic way and never bond with Christ.)

---

[1]Sources for quoted material can be found at the end of the book.

- They build our trust in Christ. Some of the disciplines are uncomfortable. You have to go out on a limb. You try fasting, and you don't die. You serve someone, and it turns out to be fun and enriching.

- They force us to make "little decisions" that multiply. Your little decision to abstain from watching a television show helps you to deny yourself and love others in all sorts of ways.

- They reorganize our impulses so that obedience is more natural. For example, if you have a spiritual discipline of practicing the presence of God, you may learn to automatically pray the breath prayer "Into thy hands" when someone opposes you. Without your realizing it, your opponent is no longer an adversary, but a person God is dealing with or perhaps even speaking through in some way.

- They help us eventually behave like Christ—but this is by God's miraculous work, not our direct effort.

- They teach us to trust that God will do the work in our inner being through the power of the Spirit (Ephesians 3:16). Your spirituality is not about you; it's the work of God in you. You get to cooperate in God's "family business" of transforming the world.

How We Get Spiritual Disciplines Wrong

Spiritual exercises must be done with the goal of connecting, not for any sake of their own or any desire to check them off a list of to-do items. If you read your Bible just to get it done, or because you've heard this will help you have a better day, you'll be anxious to complete the Bible study questions or to get to the bottom of the page of today's reading. But if your goal in Bible reading is to connect with God, you may pause whenever you sense God speaking to you. You'll stop and meditate on it. You may pray certain phrases back to God, indicating your needs or your wishes or your questions. You may choose to read that passage day after day for a month because God keeps using it to speak to you.

After such a session, you will have a stronger desire to connect with God. That "little choice" you made to connect will leave you slightly different for life.

The exercise or discipline is beneficial because it helps you practice connecting with God. If you want to play the piano well or swing a tennis racket well, you have to practice certain exercises over and over. Good baseball players train behind the scenes by practicing their batting day after day, with no crowds watching.[2] That's what spiritual disciplines or exercises are about. If you can hear God in fasting and simplicity, you'll more likely hear God in a board meeting or an

---

[2]This comparison originated from and is expanded in Dallas Willard, *The Spirit of the Disciplines* (San Francisco: Harper & Row, 1988), p. 3.

altercation with a recalcitrant teen when passions run high. In life with God, we get good at connecting on an everyday basis by devoting time to developing the skills needed.

How Do These Studies Work?

These studies examine examples, methods and results of connecting with God through prayer and practicing God's presence. One question in each of the six studies calls for actual praying to be done in the session. Look for these questions and use them. This will demonstrate the pattern that Bible study leads us to respond to God, especially through prayer.

Each session includes several other elements as well.

Turning Toward God presents discussion (for groups) or reflection questions and exercises to draw us into the topic at hand.

Hearing God Through the Word draws us into a study of a related passage of Scripture with questions that connect it to life and invite us to reflect on what God is saying. A leader's guide is printed in the back of each of the eight sections, providing more helps for leaders and study notes for specific questions.

Transformation Exercises are activities or thoughts to experiment with in order to experience the spiritual exercise studied. Perhaps you'll read the exercise and think it's too elementary or too difficult for you. Adapt it as needed. Or maybe you think you can guess what you'll experience, so you don't have to do it. The point is to experience it. Go ahead and try.

If you are leading these studies in a group, you will find further suggestions in the appendix, "Guidelines for Leaders."

What Order Is Recommended?

You might wonder, *With what set of studies should I begin?* If you want to do several of the eight sections, don't feel that you have to follow the order in the book. Generally, it's good to start with "Solitude and Silence" because those two disciplines are foundational, but many people begin with "Prayer and Listening." If, however, one of the other six sections interests you more, start there. God may be nudging you in that direction, so follow it.

If you are leading a group, to make this decision pray about your potential group members and see what comes to you. Keep in mind two things:

- the personalities of your probable group participants

- that solitude and silence are the basic disciplines and—ideally—should be the first section to study, but that won't work for everyone

If potential participants are unfamiliar with spiritual formation, you might want to begin with "Prayer and Listening" (the most popular topic) and then ask the group to choose the next section to study.

Consider whether potential group participants are introverts or extroverts. (Where do they get their energy and renewal—from being alone or being with peo-

Introverts	Extroverts	Either/Both
Solitude & Silence	Community & Submission	Simplicity & Fasting
Prayer & Listening	Worship & Celebration	
Reflection	Confession	
Secrecy	Service	
Study & Meditation		

ple?) If you have some extroverts, be careful not to follow one introvertish topic with another. This sends a message that spirituality is only for people who sit quietly in corners—Jesus was not like that! If you think you'll do more than two studies, move back and forth between disciplines that are easier for introverts or extroverts. Here's how I designate them.

Also, if your group struggles with being transparent, hold "Reflection and Confession" until later in the order of studies, although these topics are very important and will build community in a valuable way. ("Reflection and Confession" also makes an excellent personal retreat. See below.)

Once you figure out the order you want to do them in, don't be afraid to change if so led.

Using These Studies in Retreats

Do the studies at your own pace, and do not rush them. Allow enough time to do the transformation exercises as well. Don't feel you have to do all the studies. In fact, you may wish to focus only on one discipline and use only those studies.

A group wishing to explore certain disciplines can also use one of these studies the same way. Be sure to allow time for participants to do the transformation exercises. Some exercises may be done as a group. Others may be done individually, with group members reporting back to each other about how they heard God during the exercise.

For either type of retreat, allow plenty of time for pondering. May these studies help you move a few steps closer to living your life in union with God.

Section One

SOLITUDE & SILENCE

Solitude and silence are disciplines of abstinence. We abstain from being with people and from noise. This means we cannot accomplish the things that make us feel worthwhile (especially completing that to-do list), and we rest in the fact that we are of great worth to God, even when we do nothing. We surrender the need to talk and to fill the empty air with clever thoughts. In the absence of all this puzzling and planning, wheeling and dealing, we meet our true selves. Often this is not pretty. Thoughts we never knew we had come to the surface.

To take time for silence and solitude means we assume that God wants to speak to us and relate to us in a personal way.* This is such a stretch for those of us accustomed to prayer being an exercise in non-stop talking. Instead, we learn to converse with God and hear God—first in the solitude, then in all of life.

---

*For instruction on this, see my book, *When the Soul Listens* (Colorado Springs: NavPress, 1999).

1

EXAMPLES OF SOLITUDE

Jesus' Personal Getaways

MARK 1:21-39

If you picture Jesus' day-to-day life, it's easy to imagine him among crowds of people who were trying to get his attention or listening to him as they sat on a hillside. Yet one of the central pictures of Jesus in the Gospels is the solitary figure going off to be alone with God.

Some may wonder why Jesus would need a pattern of private getaways while living on earth as a human being. Hadn't he already spent eternity in fellowship with the Father? This puzzled even the disciples, who are portrayed in the Gospels as having to find Jesus when he had gone away to pray. People have said he did it primarily to set a marvelous example for us today. But his urgency and frequency hint at something better—he sought solitude simply because he longed to be alone with God.

Another startling dimension of Jesus' pattern of solitude is that he took time alone in spite of being a "people person." Unlike John the Baptist, Jesus was not a loner living in the desert. He attended parties, surrounded himself with an entourage of disciples and mixed constantly with crowds. Jesus loved to be with people, and he loved to be alone with God.

Turning Toward God

What moments of aloneness have you enjoyed at any time in your life? Swinging on a swing set in a park as a child? Taking a shower as a teen? Commuting to work without the ringing of the telephone?

In the past, how have you felt during times alone with God?

- awkward   • bored

- hopeful   • confused

- this is for sissies   • this is for loner types

- nurtured   • such times are too loose

- dutiful   • such times are too rigid

- this is for *spiritual* people   • can't get enough of it

- other:

Hearing God Through the Word

Read Mark 1:21-34.

1. If you had been Jesus, what activities recounted here would have exhausted you?

    Which ones would have exhilarated you?

2. What emotions might you have felt after healing Simon's mother-in-law? (Keep in mind that Simon Peter could have been called Jesus' best friend.)

Read Mark 1:35-37.

3. Consider your own pattern of sleep after an exhausting day of service. Why do you suppose Jesus did not sleep late the next morning?

4. Since it was still dark when Jesus left the house, what inconveniences (such as dampness) might he have experienced in getting off to a solitary place?

What does this tell you about Jesus' desire to have solitude?

_____

5. Why is it important to stop and reflect with God after hectic times of service? How do you usually debrief or clear your head after such times? (Do you talk with a friend? take a walk? engage in vigorous exercise? go to a movie?)

_____

6. If you had been Jesus, what topics relating to the day before would you have prayed about?

"Turn your

loneliness into

solitude and

_____

your solitude

7. What do you find inconvenient or uncomfortable about solitude and silence?

into prayer."

ELISABETH ELLIOT

Read Mark 1:38-39.

_____

8. How did Jesus respond to being found and interrupted? How do you explain this, especially his statement "That is why I have come"?

_____

9. How does this passage encourage you to understand the helpfulness of time alone with God?

10. What do you think is the difference between solitude and loneliness?

11. If you were to have a personal retreat day or morning, where would you go and what would you do?

"In silence, God

pours into you a

deep, inward love.

This experience

of love is one

that will fill and

permeate your

whole being. [It]

is the beginning of

an indescribable

blessedness."

JEANNE GUYON
(WHO SPENT MORE
THAN TWENTY YEARS
IN PRISON AND EXILE)

Transformation Exercises

Experiment with one or more of the following.

- Reread Mark 1:21-39. Which moment in this story speaks most to you? Sit and imagine yourself in that moment. What about that moment would you like to integrate into your life?

- Walk around your bedroom, apartment, house or backyard. Where could you sit with no distractions? What could you do to make it easier to focus in that place—move a bench or rocking chair there? turn a chair toward a window?

- Start a file folder for a personal retreat day. Place a blank sheet of paper in it. As you move through your days, write on that sheet any passage of Scripture that begs to be pondered. Toss in the folder any magazine articles that you'd like to ponder. Next to the folder, set books through which God has spoken to you in the past.

- Think back to a recent day full of service (or a week-by-week program you're involved in). Pray about this time of service, commenting to God on what startled you or pleased you. Ask God to offer other insights regarding the day.

- If you already spend a lot of time on your own, seek out a different place of solitude away from your usual habitat, such as a public park or walking down a quiet street.

2

EXAMPLES OF SOLITUDE

Jacob's Transformation

GENESIS 28:10-22; 32:22—33:3

Sometimes we stumble upon solitude, and other times we intentionally create it. Two events in Jacob's life illustrate this. In the first, Jacob stumbled upon the presence of God in a solitude that was forced upon him as he fled from his brother's threats of murder. In the second scene, Jacob chose solitude (to scheme, or to hear from God?—we don't know). And God "showed up" in an unforgettable way.

In both solitary scenes, Jacob was haunted by fear of his brother Esau. Jacob had lied to his father to get a blessing intended for his brother (following the instructions of his mother, who most likely thought she was acting in accordance with God's prophecy in Genesis 25:23). That was why Jacob fled. The second occasion was Jacob's homecoming—would Esau still be angry?

Jacob's encounters with God in solitude show us how solitude is not just for the supposedly spiritually elite. Even remorseless people find help in solitude. For Jacob, these encounters and others became stepping stones to a life devoid of manipulation and full of love for God and purpose in life.

Turning Toward God

What usually causes someone to say, "I need to be alone to think"? When, if ever, has God met you in solitude around a specific challenge in your life?

Hearing God Through the Word

Read Genesis 28:10-22.

1. What promises and reassurances did God give Jacob during Jacob's dream at Bethel (vv. 13-16)?

"We in our

'existence as

usual' are like

2. Why would a person who has lied and manipulated as Jacob had need to hear this message?

Jacob, wearily

asleep on our rock

in our own desert

3. When have you thought, "Surely the LORD is in this place, and I was not aware of it" (v. 16)?

ravine. Jacob

went to sleep

in his sorrow,

alienation, and

Read Genesis 32:22—33:3.

loneliness, seeing

4. What was clever about Jacob's strategy of making sure Esau would see his family (long-lost relatives) and his many possessions before Esau faced Jacob himself?

only the physical

landscape. In

his dream—or

was he only then

5. The prophet Hosea later described Jacob's struggle this way: "He struggled with the angel and overcame him; he wept and begged for his favor" (12:4). What does that add to this picture?

truly awake?—he

beheld the

commerce of God,

and awakening

6. A common experience in solitude is to recall a certain person who is an adversary or challenger and criticize that person. If we consciously invite God's presence, a shift may occur. God confronts *us* about our character or our need to die to self and trust God completely. How would this shift change the way we pray in solitude? Give some examples below.

cried out:

'Surely . . .'"

DALLAS WILLARD

Prayers of a Person Who Fears Someone or Opposes Someone	Prayers of a Person Who Is Being Confronted by God

What does this reveal to you about how you might pray differently?

_____

7. Considering Jacob's character, why was it appropriate for God to appear as a wrestler to Jacob?

_____

8. The "man" renamed Jacob "he struggles with God" (Israel) instead of "deceiver" (Jacob; Genesis 27:36). If God were to rename you (based on a positive change in your character), what would you like your new name to be?

_____

9. How was having a limp in his leg an appropriate memento for Jacob/Israel? (We don't know if the limp was lifelong or temporary.)

_____

10. How did God remedy the situation with Esau without Jacob's having to manipulate it?

"They will question you saying, 'What are you looking for, what do you want?' To all of them you must reply, 'God alone I see and desire, only him.'"

THE CLOUD OF UNKNOWING

11. If you ventured into solitude, which of Jacob's solitary experiences might yours more closely resemble—Jacob's first one of encouragement and comfort or Jacob's second one of being challenged? Which one do you need most? Which one do you think *God thinks* you need most? Why?

---

12. How did God use solitude to transform Jacob's soul? In what ways do you hope the practice of solitude might change you?

Transformation Exercises

Experiment with one or more of the following.

- Imagine Jacob lying beside the Jabbok River, which was about thirty feet wide and hip-deep. It probably made some bubbling or swishing sounds and was very calming to Jacob that night. Are there certain sounds that help you in your practice of solitude—for example, sitting by a river or ocean, listening to wordless music, tuning in to bird calls or wind chimes?

- Journal regarding your character flaws and the way God has been leading you to change your character. Start by listing them on the left side of the paper. Then to the right of each one, list a form in which God might appear to you in a dream or in your thoughts. Choose a form that would correspond to your flaw, as a wrestler corresponded to Jacob's flaw of manipulation. For example, if one of your character flaws is self-pity, perhaps God might "appear" to you in the form of a mourning dove or a whining child.

- Pray, offering two requests, as Jacob did as he wrestled with the "man" (to bless him; to tell him his name). Let one include the new name you think God would like to give you. Interact with God in prayer about this.

"It requires a lot of inner solitude and silence to become aware of these divine movements. God does not shout, scream or push."

HENRI NOUWEN

3

ACTIVITIES IN SOLITUDE

Delighting in God

PSALM 37:1-11

Many people view God primarily as a problem solver, the Great Therapist in the Sky. When this is true, we use psalms to soothe ourselves in times of trouble. As we learn to love God for who God is, we enjoy God more. We learn the important skills of waiting on God, being still before God and delighting in God, meaning that we love God, are thrilled by God, and can't keep our minds off God.

This new attitude changes the way we approach passages such as the well-known verses of Psalm 37. Before, we may have thought that if we delighted ourselves "in the Lord" (paid some spiritual dues of praise), God would give us the desires of our hearts (an upbeat attitude, an attractive body, a car that never breaks down). We delighted in the Lord to get God to give us stuff. But as we instead learn to treasure the person of God, God becomes the desire of our hearts.

Psalm 37 is often considered a comfort psalm, but it also shows us concrete ways of trusting God: delighting, waiting and being still. These are a few of the how-to techniques of solitude. Learning them ensures that our solitude and silence with God are not empty. Waiting on God and being still is not a tiresome ordeal for the super holy. It is full of interaction with God. We can look forward to it with expectant alertness.

Turning Toward God

What do you find particularly satisfying or meaningful in life?

Hearing God Through the Word

Read Psalm 37:1-6.

1. Based on the commands in verse 1, what did the psalmist assume his hearers were going through?

"Center all your

attention and

desire on [God]

and let this be

the sole concern

of your mind and

heart. Nourish in

your heart a lively

longing for God."

THE CLOUD OF
UNKNOWING

2. The command to "dwell in the land" implies that the hearers expected the worst and planned to run away from the evildoers. What does the psalmist say they should do instead (v. 3)?

3. If you were to "delight in the LORD," what aspects of God (what God is like, how God acts, evidence of God) would you treasure?

4. Imagine that you know some people who obviously delight in the Lord. Why would it be easier to see goodness (righteousness) in them or to see the justice of their causes (v. 6)?

5. Why would it be easier for a person who is fully committed to God to delight in God, wait on God and be still before God?

Read Psalm 37:7-11.

6. What are some practical ways you can still yourself before God when you're irked that wickedness seems to be winning?

7. What is the wisdom behind the spiritual adage, "When in doubt, wait"?

8. In what situations do you need to walk away in order to refrain from a display of anger?

9. Many times it seems that those who "possess the land" (RSV) or "inherit the land" (NIV) are the ones who have grabbed it successfully. But what sorts of people does this passage say will actually secure the land?

10. Find the two places in verses 1-11 in which the word *enjoy* occurs. What attitudes or actions bring on enjoyment?

11. How do you think a person who has learned to wait on God, delight in God and be still before God would be different from others?

12. Reread Psalm 37:1-11 aloud slowly. Which word or phrase is most meaningful to you? Why? What does that phrase tell you about how you want to connect with God?

"For the man or woman who has come to know and love the Lord God in the depths of such intimacy, the times of solitude are the most precious in all of life. They are a rendezvous with the Beloved. They are anticipated with eagerness. . . . Gentle interludes with [God] alone are highlights of life."

PHILLIP KELLER

"When Thou dost knock at my heart's door, let me not keep Thee standing without but welcome Thee with joy and thanksgiving."
JOHN BAILLIE

"We need to find God, and he cannot be found in noise and restlessness. God is the friend of silence. . . . We need silence to be able to touch souls. The essential thing is not what we say, but what God says to us and through us."
MALCOLM MUGGERIDGE

Transformation Exercises

Experiment with one or more of the following.

- Sit in a quiet place and read the following verse:

  The LORD your God is with you,
      he is mighty to save.
  He will take great delight in you,
      he will quiet you with his love,
      he will rejoice over you with singing.
  (Zephaniah 3:17)

  What song do you need for God to sing over you?

- Extend the palms of your hands out in front of you. Imagine that in your hands you hold someone who irks you or a troublesome situation. Illustrate what this passage has urged you to do with these troubling situations by moving your hands in some way. (Some examples: dumping out their contents, tossing away the contents, gently putting the contents down somewhere safe and walking away.) What is God urging you to do?

- Try doing a physical activity such as taking a walk or riding a bike or gardening and in some way delighting in God at the same time. Don't try too hard or worry about doing it perfectly. Just try it. When your mind wanders, pull it back gently to God's goodness in your life.

- Study the connections between waiting and hoping as they are linked in passages such as Psalm 33:20; 130:5-7; Lamentations 3:24-25; Romans 8:23-25. How are waiting on God and hoping in God related? What does this tell us about the nature of waiting on God?

4

ACTIVITIES IN SOLITUDE

Resting in God

ISAIAH 30:15-22

Let's say you decide to sit for a few minutes in solitude and silence. To most people this signals one thing—sleep! If drowsiness doesn't overtake you, another obstacle looms: the list of all the things you should be doing. (You can put them to rest by jotting them down on a pad.)

It's never surprising when the first few minutes of quiet prayer or the first hours of a private retreat must be spent ushering distractions to the door. You may have noticed that an entire "distraction committee" lives in your head. Members of this committee vary but often include

- *Looking Good Kid,* who says to you: "Excel! Be smart! Look great! Achieve, achieve, achieve!"

- *Rescue the World Crusader,* who says to you: "Help folks to the extreme, even if they don't want it."

- *Critic,* who scolds you and evaluates everyone around you, saying, "Why aren't they doing what's right or what you want?"

- *Leisure Junkie,* who says to you: "How long until your favorite TV program? Why don't you stop and get a doughnut, or ten doughnuts?"

Inviting these inner committee members to leave (a gentle approach works best) is a primary skill needed to hear God in solitude and silence. What we're aiming for is silence within, quietness in the soul.

Turning Toward God

When your mind is racing with thoughts, what are they usually about? What do you do to quiet these thoughts?

"When you come

to the Lord, learn

to have a quiet

mind. Cease from

any self-effort.

In this way, God

himself can act

all alone," wrote

JEANNE GUYON.

Wise souls will

find it a relief

to no longer

be "pleasantly

attached to their

own efforts."

Hearing God Through the Word

In this session's passage Isaiah prophesies to Judah, a nation in the midst of crisis. Assyria was threatening to overrun Judah. Would the people of Judah turn to God for help or put their confidence in human help (particularly Egypt)? They were full of hurry and panic. God told them to rest, to be quiet and to wait. Then they would hear God.

Read Isaiah 30:15-17.

1. What means of finding salvation and strength does Isaiah recommend?

2. How are these means the opposite of what a panicked person often does?

3. What kinds of things does a person of quietness and trust "put to rest"?

4. What evidence of panic do you see in the lives of the Judeans (vv. 16-17)?

5. Think of a situation that usually rouses panic in you. If you took time to rest and be quiet before God (or habitually did so and therefore your response would come from that), how would you respond differently?

Read Isaiah 30:18-22.

6. What do these verses tell us about how God feels about us—even when we panic?

7. How can the assurance that God loves to show grace and compassion and to bring about justice make us more likely to wait on God?

8. What does Isaiah say would be God's response to the people's cries for help (vv. 19-20)?

9. In what ways do you experience the phenomenon described in verse 21?

    ___ remembering the words of helpful teachers

    ___ receiving holy nudges through a sense of rightness, based on what you've been taught

    ___ hearing God within the heart

    ___ other:

"I am becoming aware that with words ambiguous feelings enter into my life. It almost seems as if it is impossible to speak and not sin."

HENRI NOUWEN,
AFTER SPENDING
THREE MONTHS
AT AN ABBEY
WHERE SPEECH
WAS LIMITED

10. What specific form of obedience did Isaiah prophesy would occur if Judah heard God as described in verse 21?

11. Why would a life of constantly hearing God (as described in v. 21) make people want to give up whatever distracts them from God?

12. How can quietness and rest help us hear God?

"Silence—how I detest [it]! Ever since our Father entered Hell, all has been occupied by Noise—Noise which alone defends us from silly qualms, despairing scruples, and impossible desires. We will make the whole universe a noise in the end."

UNCLE SCREWTAPE,

A SENIOR DEVIL COUNSELING A JUNIOR DEVIL IN C. S. LEWIS'S *THE SCREWTAPE LETTERS*

Transformation Exercises

Experiment with one or more of the following.

• Reread Isaiah 30:15-22 and pick a phrase that describes the kind of life you'd like to have. Repeat that phrase to God, and sit quietly in God's presence and enjoy the prospect.

• Journal your own down-to-earth paraphrase of Isaiah 30:15-22. Rephrase verse 15 as needed. Then rewrite verses 16-17 inserting your sources of hurry and panic. Rephrase verse 18, and replace verses 19-20 with what you believe might be God's response if you waited on him. Rephrase verse 21, then replace verse 22 with an act of radical obedience that might result.

• Sit for a while in silence and ask God this question: What do I need to know? Don't force an answer, but wait quietly. If nothing comes, simply enjoy God, focusing on what you love most about God when distracting thoughts come.

• Try being silent for a period of time as you go about your business (a whole hour, a whole morning, a whole day). If your situation requires you to speak, say as little as possible. Try going without any background noise such as a radio or television. If you think this will bore or isolate you, keep a Bible open to Isaiah 30:21 and read it occasionally.

5

RESULTS OF SOLITUDE

Hearing God's Surprises

1 Kings 19:1-18

After her daughter died, my friend began making a silent retreat every year. Each time she gained amazing insights and experienced spiritually uplifting moments. But in the fourth year, her retreat seemed dry. She read Scripture as usual, but she felt disappointed and let down. Four odd things came to mind. She needed to eat properly (instead of snacking so much), get more exercise (besides her old routine), get more sleep and stop trying to get sleepy by watching so much TV late at night. She wrote these things down and waited for more. Nothing came—where were the "spiritual" insights?

After the retreat, she felt disappointed, but she implemented those four changes, one at a time. She found that her perspective changed in amazing ways. "I realized my spiritual part was not a separate part of who I am," she said. "God is concerned with every detail about me." With these changes, she found it easier to receive from Scripture and to sense God's presence.

This is a common experience with God. In solitude God "shows up" in surprising ways, often with uncommonly practical insights. In this passage Elijah has similar experiences in solitude with God. After Elijah infuriated Queen Jezebel by upstaging her false prophets and calling down fire from heaven, she threatened him with death. Fleeing from her, Elijah was greeted with God's tender practicality and brilliant ability to show him what he needed to know.

Turning Toward God

Share an experience of being surprised by God.

Hearing God Through the Word

Read 1 Kings 19:1-8.

1. Why does Elijah flee to the desert and on to Mount Horeb? What is he seeking?

2. What sorts of character traits are formed in a person who relies so heavily on the protection, guidance and companionship of God?

3. How did the angel choose to respond to Elijah's hopelessness (vv. 5-8)?

Read 1 Kings 19:9-18.

4. Why do you think the all-knowing God would ask, "What are you doing here, Elijah?"

5. Which of the following attitudes do you detect in Elijah's response?

    ___ wishing God to be honored

    ___ whining about his state

    ___ self-righteous in his actions

    ___ self-pitying in his aloneness

___ wishing a carnal vengeance on the idolaters of Israel (possibly a showy one such as more fire falling from heaven, see 1 Kings 18:38)

___ rebuking God for allowing such miserable circumstances to continue

___ others:

6. How does God's "gentle whisper" (v. 12) compare with Elijah's previous experiences with God (1 Kings 18:24, 38) and Moses' experiences in this same place (Exodus 33:21—34:10)?

7. How do you respond to God's choice to use the "gentle whisper" to communicate with people?

8. What do you learn about human encounters with God in solitude from the fact that after God spoke in the gentle whisper, God repeated the same question to Elijah, and Elijah gave the same answer (vv. 9, 13)?

9. What do you make of God's belated comment about the many people in Israel not devoted to Baal, though Elijah had insisted he was the only faithful one left (v. 18)?

10. What do you learn about solitude with God from God's practical instructions to Elijah in verses 15-18?

"The longer I walk in faith and consistently acknowledge my beloved Spouse by waiting on Him in silence, the more I 'hear' Him and sense His leading in the details of everyday life. Now, instead of agonizing over every situation, I rest in Him, aware of His involvement in the myriad of daily decisions, and excited beyond imagination about each new day as it unfolds."

BILL VOLKMAN

11. If you were to run off to be with God in a place of historic holiness (as Mount Horeb was), what do you think (or hope) God would offer you?

___ rest

___ nutritious food

___ conversation

___ opportunities to release honest thoughts and feelings

___ ideas for future service

___ ideas for whom you need for companionship

___ other:

Transformation Exercises

Experiment with one or more of the following.

- Imagine a tempest, earthquake or fire in the terrible solitude of a mountain pass. Journal or talk with a friend about how you would have felt during this natural phenomenon (breathing hard, covering your face, hiding in the dark of the cave). Then write or tell about how you would have responded to the gentle whisper.

- Choose a specific place where you love to be alone. Plan a time when you can be there for a while.

- Sing a song about solitude (such as the hymn "In the Garden") as you are driving, or hum it quietly while riding the bus.

- Figure out all the details that would need to be addressed in order for you to have a few hours alone somewhere. For example, find out when people in your household will be out (or could be, or could take others with them) or when a certain solitary place is available.

6

RESULTS OF SOLITUDE

How God Changes You

JOHN 15:1-16

Folks sometimes view solitude and silence as me-myself-and-I practices. They think, *You do this to make you feel warm and close to God.* But besides helping us enjoy God's presence, a steady habit of solitude and silence changes the way we behave toward others. The two great commandments are inseparable: to bask in the love of God results in a quiet but powerful love for others (Matthew 22:37-39).

When I first began having snatches of solitude, I found myself feeling grouchy when my kids interrupted. Or when I returned from times of solitude, I dreaded the noise and chaos. It took practice to let this sense of God's nearness flow back into the clamor of family life.

Yes, there's a shift when we move from the peacefulness of solitude to the chaos of relationships, but solitude affects our relationship with God *and* our relationships with others. In solitude God speaks to us about the people we love (and those we don't) through prayer, Scripture reading, journaling and so on. God draws us toward them. God uses solitude and silence to change us—we bear fruit, obey difficult commands and offer others selfless, Christ-driven love.

Enjoy this peek at a discourse in which Jesus explains that as we do the connecting, God does the perfecting. As we abide in Christ, we bear fruit of loving obedience. This bonds us as friends of God, and the abiding becomes more automatic.

Turning Toward God

Why is it sometimes easy to feel that we love God but still be a little annoyed with someone in our life?

Hearing God Through the Word

"The sole purpose

of solitude is

knowing God,

and those who

know God will

care for God's

children. . . . It is

out of solitude,

out of being

authentically

present to God,

that the deepest

care for God's

creatures comes."

DAVID RENSBERGER

Read John 15:1-10.

1. The dual theme of John 15:1-10 is "to abide" (NRSV, NKJV, or "remain," NIV) and "to bear fruit." Consider what it means to abide or remain in Christ. What would abiding look like in your life?

_____

2. What does "bearing fruit" mean in this passage?

_____

3. If God were to use solitude and silence to prune your soul, what challenges might God present to you in the quiet atmosphere of overflowing love?

_____

4. If God were to use solitude and silence to cultivate your spiritual life, what truths might God want to make real to you—because you don't fully accept them with all of your being? (Here are some ideas to get you started.)

___ You are loved, no matter what.

___ Knowing God is delightful; he says, "Taste and see that I am good."

___ God has a redemptive purpose for your life.

___ Other:

5. For obedience (loving enemies, caring for the havenots, telling the truth) to be possible, what needs to be in place in our lives (vv. 5-6)?

_____

6. If a person abides in union with God, why might their prayers normally be answered "yes"?

_____

7. What personal insight about obedience and survival does Jesus give us about himself (vv. 9-10)?

Read John 15:11-16.

_____

8. What results occur for the person who lives in union with God?

_____

9. In what way is the battle to love others waged in solitude and silence on one's knees?

_____

10. What reasons might we give for hesitating to think that God would ever call a human a "friend"?

How could we answer those doubts?

_____

11. If you had a personal retreat day (or "Friendship Day with God"), what pitfalls (obstacles to be pruned) might trouble you?

___ I would structure it so much that I would have a difficult time hearing God.

___ I would put off doing it.

"Solitude molds self-righteous people into gentle, caring, forgiving persons who are so deeply convinced of their own great sinfulness and so fully aware of God's even greater mercy that their life itself becomes a ministry."

HENRI NOUWEN

____ I would goof off all day.

____ I would fill the day with tasks from my to-do list.

____ Other:

12. What format for solitude and silence works best for you? (Taking a walk? Going to a retreat center?) How, if at all, are you motivated to expand that?

Transformation Exercises

Experiment with one or more of the following.

- Describe in your journal a mental picture or a sensory image that would represent what it means to abide in God. Or make a photo album or video diary of these images. Here are some examples.

    God singing or humming over you, perhaps rocking you (Zephaniah 3:17)

    squatting in the shadow of God's wings (Psalm 36:7; 63:7)

    riding behind God on a majestic horse on behalf of truth, humility and righteousness (Psalm 45:4)

    drinking from and romping in God's river of delights (Psalm 36:8)

    gazing on God's beauty; dwelling in God's house (Psalm 27:4)

- Set aside a period of time for silence and solitude. Pray for someone who is difficult or who has opposed you. Ask God to show you this person's heart.

- Think forward to a conversation you'll be having (lunch with a friend, a break at work, after dinner with your child). Purpose that for five minutes you will be "slow to speak and quick to listen." You will drink deeply from that person's words, without jumping ahead mentally to what you want to say next or what your opinion is of what they're saying.

- Take a hymnal, sit in a swing and sing all the hymns you can find that have the word *abide* in them. You can start with "Abide with Me" or "Beneath the Cross of Jesus."

"Without a certain element of solitude there can be no compassion because when a man is lost in the wheels of a social machine he is no longer aware of human needs as a matter of personal responsibility. . . . Go into the desert, not to escape other [people] but in order to find them in God."

THOMAS MERTON

STUDY NOTES FOR
SOLITUDE AND SILENCE

Session 1. Examples of Solitude

Jesus' Personal Getaways

MARK 1:21-39

FOCUS: When Jesus, Son of God yet very active human, came to earth, he spent time in solitude and silence with God.

Turning Toward God. Use one or both of these questions to warm up participants to this topic. In the second question, it may help to own up to your shortcomings by telling of your limited ideas about solitude.

Question 1. Many of these activities may have exhausted Jesus: having people hang on to every word because he taught with such authority (being popular can be exhausting!); the physical exhaustion of teaching so authoritatively; the shock of being interrupted by a screaming possessed man; the dismay of being identified so well so publicly so early in his ministry; the demands of having the "whole town gathered at the door"; the grief at seeing so many people who had been ravaged by disease and demonic possession; the pressure of keeping those demons quiet about his identity.

Question 2. Consider these possibilities: the tears and emotionalism of Simon's mother-in-law and her family, whom Jesus may have known very well since he often stayed in Capernaum; the solicitous gratitude Peter may have felt and kept expressing.

Question 4. Other inconveniences might have

been not disturbing anyone (or being detained) as he left the house; finding his way in the dark; being cold and shivering because the sun wasn't yet shining; perhaps being very hungry if he left without eating anything.

Question 5. Often we don't reflect because we're so tired. Yet reflection time can be fun—praising God and expressing those "Gee whiz!" feelings; expressing questions of fear and uncertainty; offering prayers for ongoing healing in people's lives.

Question 6. Possibly Jesus prayed for people's ongoing healing. He may have prayed for the discernment of Peter and the other disciples upon receiving a very personal miracle. Since word of him was spreading through his home region of Galilee, he may have prayed for his precious home folk and the many world travelers who passed through along the trade routes of Galilee. Maybe he prayed for friends and neighbors in Nazareth. Or perhaps Jesus let himself be filled up with the love of God—which would have made him more energetic and ready to serve, as shown in the text.

Question 7. If you wish, refer back to the second question in "Turning Toward God" for ideas. If participants identified with some of those responses, probe more deeply into them.

Question 10. Solitude is the glory of being alone, while loneliness is the pain of being alone. Solitude is being alone with God, so it is not lonely.

Question 11. Listen without commenting. Many people try to be very structured when taking a re-treat day, which is not a good idea, but that will be discussed later. Most people feel pretty lost if someone suggests they take a personal retreat. Allow them to express that feeling.

Session 2. Examples of Solitude

Jacob's Transformation

GENESIS 28:10-22; 32:22—33:3

FOCUS: In solitude and silence, Jacob finally stopped trying to manipulate God and became Israel, who loved God and gave himself to God's purposes. Even very unregenerate people find help in solitude.

Question 1. In the dream, God gave Jacob a "do-ing" promise—that his descendants would become a great nation that would bless the entire world (through Jesus)—and a "being" promise—that God would be with him and keep him safe.

Question 2. Jacob needed God's protection, and he needed to know his life had purpose even though he had displeased his brother. Even though he began his pattern of manipulation by simply obeying his mother (and she had acted on divine insight; see Genesis 25:23), he apparently developed a penchant for manipulation that would meet its match in his uncle, Laban.

Question 4. Jacob created safety for himself by putting women and children in front of his rugged, brawny brother. Genesis 32:13-22 describes Jacob's presents to his brother and how he planned to impress him with his possessions.

Question 5. This "wrestling match" was more than physical. Jacob wept—a strong show of emotion. He begged for favor, apparently giving up (finally) ideas that tricks or schemes would save him this time.

Who was "the man"? Some say this was an angel, as identified by Hosea (12:4). Others believe it was Jesus because of Jacob's words "because I saw God face to face" (Genesis 32:30).

You might ask participants to consider how anyone could overcome a supernatural being. Theologian H. C. Leupold explains this: "This statement does not impugn God's omnipotence, but it does effectively portray the power of prayer. . . . As the will of man learns ever more perfectly to submit to God's will, God can no longer 'prevail' against such a one."[1] Jacob's "winning" may have been not a power match but a spiritual victory enacted in physical terms to give Jacob the lifelong encouragement he would need.

Question 6. Instead of begging for God to make our situation okay or wreak vengeance on a person, we ask God to search our hearts, give us grace and lead us in the right path (Psalm 139:23-24).

Question 7. Wrestlers manipulate arms and legs, and Jacob had been manipulating people. A wrestler, then, appealed to Jacob's character and drew him in.

Question 8. If you wish, lighten the tone by re-wording the end of the question with, "What would your mother or your roommate or your spouse like for that new name to be?"

Question 9. A limp is a sign of weakness. Weak-

---

[1]H. C. Leupold, *Exposition of Genesis* (Grand Rapids: Baker, 1976), 2:877.

ness is something a clever manipulator (such as Jacob used to be) would never want. But based on the way Jacob's character exhibited greater trust after this, this weakness apparently created a powerful dependence on God in this patriarch of Israel.

Question 12. Through solitude, God communicated to Jacob that he would use him in spite of all the chaos and even horror (potential fratricide) in his family. This built endurance. In the second solitary interlude, God interacted with Jacob in a tangible and believable form, providing Jacob with the peace he was going to need to steer a brood of sons who would become heads of the twelve tribes—deceiving each other and helping each other.

Session 3. Activities in Solitude

Delighting in God

PSALM 37:1-11

FOCUS: Solitude is not empty but full of expectant alertness. We enjoy God by delighting in God, waiting on God and being still before God.

Turning Toward God. This could be anything from eating chocolate to attending a professional basketball game. Comment on anyone in whom you see that glow. You might even say that this session is about having that sort of anticipation for God.

Question 1. Apparently evildoers were inhabiting Israel or threatening the Israelites. From the moment the Israelites moved into the Promised Land, there always seemed to be people threatening their claim: the remaining Canaanites; the Philistines (and Midianites and Edomites and so on); and finally Assyria and Babylon. The land was the Israelites' sign of promise, and they feared losing it.

Question 3. Some possibilities for delighting in God: being thrilled and preoccupied with God's great love for us, God's thinking us up before time began and planning for us to be "holy and blameless" (Ephesians 1:4-6), God's work in na-

ture, God's work in others.

Question 4. According to Franz Delitzsch, "he who finds his highest delight in God, cannot desire anything that is at enmity with God," and that person's will is thoroughly blended in love with God's will.[2] Those who delight in God are focused on God and not on themselves. Such selflessness makes it easier for people to see righteousness in them, not self-righteousness. This often promotes nonadversarial encounters, which are more convincing than a competitive approach to others.

Question 5. We know that the actions of delighting in God and committing our ways to God are linked because Hebrew poetry isn't about rhyming but about parallelism—saying the same things in many different ways, using different images.

"Commit your way" means "roll your way," implying one should dislodge the burden from one's shoulders and lay it on God.[3] This would make it easier to wait and be still.

Question 6. Focusing on a short phrase of Scripture is helpful. So is turning each chaotic thought over to God, sometimes using one's hands as an outward sign. "Palms up" indicates turning the

---

[2]Franz Delitzsch, *Commentary on the Old Testament,* vol. 5, *Commentary on the Psalms* (Grand Rapids: Eerdmans, 1973), p. 12.

[3]H. C. Leupold, *Exposition of the Psalms* (Grand Rapids: Baker, 1972), p. 301.

situation over; palms down invites God to give you back his peace.[4]

Question 7. Rushing ahead is full of hurry and panic. It indicates worry and lack of trust. Trusting and waiting work both ways: a trusting person can wait; a person who chooses to wait will find trust easier.

Question 9. Those who hope in the Lord (v. 9) and the meek (v. 11). In the inverted values of the kingdom of God, advantage is gained by those who wait and hope, not by those who seize control or grab power.

Question 10. *Enjoy* is used in verses 3 and 11. The first requires trusting God (and perhaps not moving around geographically in a search for safety). The second speaks of an inner sense of meekness—not having to control circumstances but being at peace with things as they are.

Question 11. They will live without hurry and panic. They will have an inner posture of patience that will be evident in the way they behave. This will help them fulfill Jesus' second commandment: to love others deeply and truly.

Question 12. After you read the question, explain that you'll read Psalm 37:1-11 aloud slowly and give participants a few moments to respond.

Session 4. Activities in Solitude

Resting in God

ISAIAH 30:15-22

FOCUS: Being quiet before God requires that we get rid of distractions and quiet down the "voices" in our heads.

Question 2. A panicked person often hurries and tries quick solutions without thinking. Repentance, rest and quietness help a person to reflect and see what is needed. Trust helps a person turn situations over to God and find wisdom.

Question 3. People of quietness put to rest thoughts that race through their minds—often these are the agenda of the "inner committee members" mentioned in the introduction.

Question 4. They wanted to flee from trouble quickly on horses. But this panicked response would have overestimated the threat. With only one person threatening, a thousand should not have run off. This would have been an unnecessary overreaction.

The flagstaff phrase refers to desolation. Says commentary writer Delitzsch, "The nation, which had hitherto resembled a thick forest, would become like a lofty pine, standing solitary upon the top of a mountain, and like a flagstaff planted upon a hill."[5]

Question 7. Trust grows as we believe that God will act in compassion and justice. With trust in place, we can wait on God more easily.

Question 8. God would provide the necessary support by answering. Also, the "faithful and well-meaning teachers no longer keep themselves hidden because of the hard-heartedness and hatred of the people."[6] Prophets and teachers of Judah who reflected God's heart would come forth and teach when they saw people crying out to God instead of relying on Egypt. They had been in hiding since the time of Ahaz.

Question 10. They would undertake a radical act

---

[4]Richard Foster, *Celebration of Discipline* (San Francisco: Harper & Row, 1988), pp. 30-31.
[5]Franz Delitzsch, *Commentary on the Old Testament,* vol. 7, *Biblical Commentary on the Prophecies of Isaiah* (Grand Rapids.: Eerdmans, 1969), 2:33
[6]Ibid., p. 35.

of obedience—defiling their idols. Idolatry was the continuous chief sin of the Israelites for hundreds of years.

Question 11. Silencing the voices of the "inner committee members"—all those conflicting ideas—removes primary obstacles.

Question 12. Panicked thoughts and hurried actions make it difficult to hear God, who spoke to Elijah in a whisper (1 Kings 19:12). A person trained in quietness can respond to holy nudges more easily.

Session 5. Results of Solitude

Hearing God's Surprises

1 KINGS 19:1-18

FOCUS: In solitude, God probes us with questions and surprises us not only with answers but with interaction and practical help.

Background. For the context see 1 Kings 18, especially verses 20-46. Jezebel was devoted to the false god Baal and viewed Elijah and the prophets as the cause of the famine the nation had been enduring. Elijah challenged the prophets of Baal to a contest to see which god, Baal or Yahweh, would bring fire down on a sacrifice. God brought down fire on a water-soaked altar in a dramatic way. Elijah then ordered that Baal's false prophets be slaughtered.

Turning Toward God. Let the question settle for a moment and then offer these possibilities: being surprised by God in nature or in the responses of a child to you or a stranger to you.

Question 1. Commentator C. F. Keil insists that Elijah went to the desert "to pour out before the Lord God his weariness of life, . . . not to save his life . . . but to care for his soul, . . . to commit his soul or his life to the Lord his God in the solitude of the desert and see what He would determine concerning him."[7]

Also, Elijah's entire journey is rich in the symbolism of Moses' experiences in the same geographical area. In this same desert, Moses wandered forty years with the Israelites. Keil says that it took Elijah this long "that he might know that the Lord was still the same God who had nourished and sustained His whole nation in the desert with manna from heaven for forty years."[8] Also, Moses spent forty days and forty nights with the Lord, writing the Ten Commandments on tablets of stone (Exodus 34:28).

Question 2. Such a person not only would have confidence but would not be enslaved to wondering what people thought or pleasing the people around him.

Question 3. First, the angel let Elijah sleep. Then, in both encounters, the angel touched Elijah, then urged him to eat. Finally, the angel provided food so nourishing that Elijah traveled forty days and nights on its strength.

Question 4. This question is probably not the scolding rebuke of a parent but simply God's allowing Elijah to express his extreme feelings.

Question 5. All of these possibilities are suggested by one or more commentators. While Elijah seemed to desire to honor God in a pure way, he also seemed to be focused on self. Thus he overlooked his recent encounter with Obadiah,

---

[7]C. F. Keil, *Commentary on the Old Testament*, vol. 3, *I & II Kings, I & II Chronicles, Ezra, Nehemiah, Esther* (Grand Rapids: Eerdmans, 1973), p. 253.

[8]Ibid., p. 255.

in which this devout believer and palace servant revealed to Elijah that he had hidden a hundred of the Lord's prophets in two caves (1 Kings 18:7-15).

Question 6. Elijah had just witnessed God's bringing down fire from heaven on an altar, and he may have wished God would be more fiery with the false prophets and leaders. William Sanford La-Sor translates this Hebrew phrase as "the sound of gentle quietness," or "gentle silence,"[9] while Keil translates it as "a gentle rustling."[10] Keil goes on to say that God wanted to "show [Elijah] that zeal for the honour of the Lord was not in harmony with the love and grace and long-suffering of God." Keil quotes Herder regarding the "fiery zeal of the prophet" Elijah, who "'wanted to reform everything by means of the tempest" but instead learned "the gentle way which God pursues, proclaim[ing] the long-suffering and mildness of His nature, as the voice had already done to Moses on that very spot.'"

Question 7. Those who see God as a fiery being may be surprised and comforted by this. Those who think that God doesn't do much in this world except whisper quietly might need to be reminded of the fire in the previous chapter.

Question 8. Acknowledge all answers, saying that this repetition baffles readers terribly. Some scholars even think the repetition is a mistake! We expect Elijah to have learned from his encounter that God is capable of all kinds of fireworks and will bring justice at the right moment, but God plans to be gentle and patient for now.

Assuming the repetition is not a mistake, we can learn a lot about solitude. First, God uses it to ask us penetrating questions (over and over) that will bring out both our selfless and our selfish motives. Also, we can expect this conversation with God to be a process and not give us instant answers or relief. Solitude is about having a *relationship* with God, and it is the nature of relationship not to be cut and dried.

Question 9. This "gentle reminder" is perhaps the most characteristic activity of solitude. God reminds us of truths we've forgotten, making us uncomfortable except that he does it so gently. (If the reminder does not come in peace, it might not be from God but from a scolding committee member; see session 4.) God could have metaphorically grabbed Elijah by the collar and said, "Look, you self-pitying know-it-all . . ." but God didn't. God met Elijah's needs. God let Elijah talk. God assigned him some important jobs. But God also told him the truth.

Question 10. First of all, God often gives depressed people (such as Elijah) some jobs to do. (God is also practical, providing rest, food and drink—vv. 6-8.) In Elijah's case, these jobs were three anointings. The first two would have excited Elijah because they moved forward the cause of justice, which consumed Elijah. (These kings would discipline Ahab and Jezebel, and therefore defeat Baal worship.)

The third anointing would have given Elijah some relief. This loner prophet would gain some sense of community through his mentoring of Elisha. Elisha's appointment also let Elijah know that his prophetic work would continue. These instructions show how God often gives us concrete ideas that are so creative and God-ordained that we would never have come up with them ourselves.

---

[9]William Sanford LaSor, "1 and 2 Kings" in *New Bible Commentary,* 3rd ed., ed. Donald Guthrie and J. A. Motyer (Grand Rapids: Eerdmans, 1991), p. 345.
[10]Keil, *I and II Kings,* 3:258.

Session 6. Results of Solitude

How God Changes You

JOHN 15:1-16

FOCUS: Those who abide in Christ not only find union with God, but also bear the fruit of love, joy, peace, patience, kindness, goodness, meekness and self-control.

Question 1. *Abide* appears in verses 4 (twice), 6, 7, 9 and 10 (twice). Synonyms for *abide* are *continue, dwell, endure, stand, tarry,*[11] but perhaps the best one is to be "in Christ." This phrase, appearing many times in the New Testament, refers to salvation (Romans 8:1), obedience (being "alive to God" but "dead to sin," Romans 6:11), belonging to Christ's body (Romans 12:5), commitment to the cause of Christ (Romans 16:3, 9), and being sanctified and changed by God (1 Corinthians 1:2). To dwell in Christ involves developing an awareness of God's companionship, often through solitude and silence, which may include Bible reading, prayer, journaling, worship and other practices.

Question 2. Bearing fruit refers to changes in character and behavior (Romans 7:4-5; Galatians 5:22-23; Ephesians 5:9; Colossians 1:10). Love entails obedience (John 14:15, 21, 23). These concepts are inseparable in these discourse chapters. Some have insisted that the fruit a Christian bears is the conversions of new Christians. But the above verses speak of character and righteous conduct as fruit. The "new Christians" view would also deny the allegory of John 15. Branches bear grapes, not other branches. The vine bears the branches.

Question 3. God often challenges us with the need to love certain people more, to work harder, to live with more integrity—to prune our faults and live as Jesus lived. Sometimes God surprises us with a fault no one has brought up for years.

Question 5. Abiding in God must be in place if we are to obey wisely and faithfully. In solitude, we experience an interactive relationship with God, and through this we are drawn into obedience.

Question 6. If Christ and a person are in a mutually abiding relationship, why would the will of the one differ from the will of the other? What could the abiding person want that would be contrary to love, joy, peace and so on? "Their prayer is only some fragment of [Christ's] teaching transformed into a supplication."[12]

It's important that the "answer to prayer" in this verse not be interpreted as a key to getting what we want from God; instead it's a description of the natural outcome of living in union with God.

Question 7. With our postresurrection view, we see in these words Jesus' explanation of how he could go to the cross. These verses are Jesus' "how I did it" story. Jesus remained in the Father's love, no matter what. Scholars J. N. Sanders and B. A. Mastin say it this way: "The reason for Jesus' joy is his obedience to his Father and the love which subsists between them (v.10)."[13]

Question 8. They live a life of Christ's joy (as opposed to frail human joy); they learn to love others sacrificially; they become friends of God (vv. 11-14).

Question 9. In solitude we can pray for others, especially those who irritate us. It can take some extended time in solitude before we stop asking God to eliminate that person from our lives and begin asking God to show us what we need to

---

[11]W. E. Vine, Merrill F. Unger and William White Jr., *Vine's Expository Dictionary of Biblical Words* (Nashville: Thomas Nelson, 1985), p. 1 of NT section.

[12]B. F. Westcott, *The Gospel According to St. John* (Grand Rapids: Eerdmans, 1978), p. 218.

[13]J. N. Sanders and B. A. Mastin, *The Gospel According to St. John* (London: Adam & Charles Black, 1977), p. 340.

know about that person. When we do, God often shows us the needs of our enemies and gives us a heart of love for them.

Question 10. Abraham was called "a friend of God" (Isaiah 41:8; James 2:23). This doesn't mean having a buddy-buddy relationship with God. It is not an ordinary human friendship based on mutuality and reciprocity; it is based on the unending stability of Jesus' choice of me as a friend (v. 16).

We are friends of God, as opposed to being merely slaves. "A slave obeys from fear, and is left in ignorance of his lord's plans. . . . But Jesus throughout his ministry has taken his disciples completely into his confidence."[14] "The relation of the believer to Christ . . . is essentially one not of service but of love."[15]

[14]Ibid.
[15]Westcott, *Gospel According to St. John*, p. 220.

Section Two

SERVICE & SECRECY

Service, as a spiritual discipline, is doing good for others with no thought of ourselves. Although we are commanded to serve others, service also acts as a spiritual discipline as it trains us to be selfless, to get our spirituality beyond our heads and into our hands, to connect with God in everything we do. We connect with God, for example, when as we serve we encounter exasperating situations in which we pray and plead with God for help: How can I love an annoying fellow volunteer? How can I be compassionate toward people who don't deserve it? Service can force us to the edge so our prayer life grows.

Service needs to be deeply rooted in other spiritual disciplines such as solitude and Bible study so we can encounter the heart of God, see how the neediness of people breaks it, and then our hearts can be broken too. By helping others, we become the hands and feet of Christ and experience Christ's power on earth.

But if our service is considered successful, we can become wrapped up in ourselves or in the service. That's why secrecy is a twin discipline of service. We refrain from letting our good deeds be known and keep our service "hidden with Christ in God" (Colossians 3:3). Says Richard Foster, "Hiddenness is a rebuke to the flesh and can deal a fatal blow to pride." Our character is further formed as we become humble and learn to delight with God in the work God does in us.

1

DOING FLOWS
OUT OF BEING

Nehemiah 1:1—2:18

We burn out on service when our *doing* overshadows our *being*. We do good things that good folks are supposed to do without remaining inwardly connected with God. Running on no reserves, we wear ourselves out. But when we stay connected to God through disciplines such as solitude, worship, prayer and community, our inner self is filled and alert. Practicing these disciplines on a regular basis gives us the opportunity to pour our hearts out to God when we are troubled, and our service remains passionate. This back-and-forth process changes us into compassionate, patient people who serve with a full heart.

Turning Toward God

What do you think keeps people from burning out?

Hearing God Through the Word

Nehemiah achieved what anyone would call success. As an exiled Jew who had become a high-level politician in Persia, he found his heart broken by reports of the condition of his homeland. He went on to organize and supervise the rebuilding of the broken walls of Jerusalem in just fifty-two days. He faced opposition from within and without but stayed focused.

Nehemiah's service was God-drenched, flowing out of his ongoing relationship with God. He wept over the destruction of God's people; he prayed with a confessional yet eager heart; he investigated the wretched details himself; and he discussed the problems with powerful people who understood such things.

Read Nehemiah 1:1-11.

1. What did Nehemiah confess in prayer? What did he request?

2. When have you sat down and wept over a situation or cause?

Read Nehemiah 2:1-9.

3. Consider something you are passionate about doing for the good of others. If a rich and powerful person asked you, "What is it you want?" (v. 4), what would you say?

4. What might Nehemiah have prayed specifically while on the spot (v. 4)?

Read Nehemiah 2:10-18.

5. How did Nehemiah respond to opposition?

6. When, if ever, has God put something "in your heart to do for" someone (v. 12)?

7. Which scene in this detailed description of Nehemiah's inspection most holds your attention?

8. What elements of Nehemiah's simple speech made it convincing, so that it elicited a favorable response (vv. 17-18)?

9. People who serve with a sense of *being* have a passion from God, they ponder needs, they go to God for direction, they put outcomes in God's hands. How would such a person's service be different from others'?

"To serve is to be

'a feather on the

breath of God.'"

HILDEGARD
OF BINGEN

10. How does *being* bond you to the heart of God and fuel you for diligent service?

11. Do you need more *being* behind your *doing?* If so, what efforts might deepen your inner resources?

___ asking questions about the conditions of those you'd like to serve (1:2-3)

___ weeping over the need (1:4)

___ praying about the need, including confession, praise and requests (1:4-11)

___ investigating the possibilities for help (2:1-9)

____ investigating the needs in a hands-on way (2:13-16)

____ telling others about what God has put on your heart (2:17-18)

____ other:

Transformation Exercises

Experiment with one or more of the following.

- Take a walk and ask God to help you see what it is God has "put in your heart to do for him."

- Compose a prayer about some service you do. Include confession, praise and requests.

- Journal about what you most admire in Nehemiah, or make a photo album or video diary of images reflecting those qualities. How would you like to be more like him?

- Look at the prayers Nehemiah prayed throughout his service (see Nehemiah 2:4; 4:4, 9; 5:19; 6:9, 14). Choose one to use as you serve.

- Call someone or talk to someone about a cause or concern over which God has been breaking your heart.

"We actually

slander and

dishonor God

by our very

eagerness

to serve

Him without

knowing Him."

OSWALD CHAMBERS

2

JESUS' HEART FOR OTHERS

LUKE 8:26-39

Gate after gate slammed shut behind me. I was frisked. After months of medical tests and background checks, I was walking with a team of Christians to lead a retreat for thirty juvenile felons. For three days I sat at a table with five boylike men who had committed murder or something close to it. If there were throwaway people in the county where I lived, these were they. It took a few hours to stop thinking, *What am I—an average woman wearing a pink T-shirt—doing here?*

Service like this is a boot-camp experience for those of us who don't find it easy to serve with no thought of ourselves. To serve people who can do nothing for us in return trains us in selflessness. Often these are the outcasts and have-nots of society, mentioned over and over in Scripture throughout the Law, the Wisdom literature and the Prophets. The gospel message is just as tough: "How does God's love abide in anyone who has the world's goods and sees a brother or sister in need and yet refuses help?" (1 John 3:17 NRSV). Dallas Willard writes that "possibly *the* most pervasive theme of the biblical writings" is the "transformation of status for the lowly, the humanly hopeless, as they experience the hand of God reaching into their situation."

Turning Toward God

What sorts of "have-nots" do you find most unsettling?

- high school dropouts
- rich

- drug users
- HIV-positive

- brain-damaged
- those with infertility problems
- homeless
- lonely folks in rest homes
- those with unwanted pregnancies
- burned-out folks who no longer go to church
- other:

- incurably ill
- unemployed
- incompetent fellow workers
- emotionally starved people

Hearing God Through the Word

Jesus often served people you and I wouldn't want our children to be around. What's more, he went out of his way to a district that was predominantly Gentile to reconcile one man to God, to his community, even to himself.

Read Luke 8:26-29.

1. Describe the Gerasene man's appearance and behavior.

2. What aspect of this man's appearance and behavior would have been most unsettling to you, had you been present?

3. Why do you think Jesus would spend a whole day or more going across the sea to non-Jewish territory to minister to this one man when there was so much to do elsewhere?

Read Luke 8:30-33.

4. How do you answer the criticism that a just and merciful Jesus would not have allowed a herd of swine to be harmed in this way?

___ The demons deceived Jesus when they caused the swine to die.

___ Jesus granted the demons' request, which gave them temporary amnesty.

___ Jesus was Jewish and Jews didn't raise swine, so he did this to teach those in this predominantly Gentile area how Jews lived.

___ The dramatic stampede served to convince both the man and the town that his cleansing was not a hoax and that the demons would not return.

___ The death of pigs is not as significant as the life of a person.

___ Other:

Read Luke 8:34-37.

5. Compare the appearance and behavior of the man at this point with the way he had appeared when Jesus and the disciples put ashore (vv. 27-28, 35).

Read Luke 8:38-39.

6. Why do you think Jesus told the man to return home?

7. In what way did Jesus show mercy to the man?

8. In what way did Jesus respond to the man's plight with justice?

"The New Testament regularly conjoins love for God with love for one's neighbor, and indicates that the godliness that is pure and faultless is to look after marginalized and powerless people."

ROBERT
MULHOLLAND

9. Based on Jesus' actions, what do you suspect that Jesus prayed for this man?

10. What fears or sins might be gradually overcome if you practiced this discipline of service to the have-nots in your community?

11. Pick a have-not for whom you don't feel much mercy. What would be appropriate for you to pray for that person?

"Let my heart be

broken with the

things that break

the heart of God."

BOB PIERCE

Transformation Exercises

Experiment with one or more of the following.

- Picture yourself as a disciple in the boat sailing to the region of the Gerasenes. Would you have gotten out of the boat? (Scripture doesn't record that any did, although some may have.)

- Do a search in Scripture for the following words: *poor, needy, oppressed, widow, orphan*. Notice how care for them is commanded over and over throughout the Law, the Wisdom literature and the Prophets.

- Discuss with someone what kind of service reconciles people to each other and what sort of service divides people or estranges them from one another.

- Do something kind for someone who is a have-not—deprived in some way. Journal about or discuss what you learn from Jesus through your service.

3

SERVICE TRANSFORMS THE SOUL

JOHN 13:1-17

Have you ever watched someone who embodies love? They don't attack people verbally, nor do they withdraw when someone is obnoxious. They don't try to manage and control people. They know how to love respectfully—to say and do just the thing you need.

How do we become this way? While activities such as praying 1 Corinthians 13 meditatively help, we need to follow up by *doing* love. Practice love through service. Get inside acts of love and find the traps of self-importance. That's how service stretches us and forms us as people. God doesn't need our service; *we* need to serve.

Witnessing selfless service can be transforming too. You forget to breathe as someone gets up and acts generously, saying almost nothing. Your eyes see truth enacted. This sort of parable in action (or street theater, if you will) can create an unforgettable ripple in your memory and change you forever.

Turning Toward God

What is the most outrageous, unthinkable, shocking act of love you have witnessed in person, read about or seen on film?

Hearing God Through the Word

One example of outrageously humble service is when the disciples' Master and Teacher dressed down and behaved like a common slave to wash their feet. This unthinkable act (a Jewish pupil could be expected to wash his master's feet, but not vice versa) broke through their disdain for drudgery. No doubt this jolt of cold water changed them forever.

Read John 13:1-3.

1. What do these verses tell us about the mood and setting of this Gospel episode? (Casual or formal? Heartfelt or laid-back?)

"In Jesus' life

prayer and

action follow

one another in

a rhythm which

seems as constant

as the inhaling

and exhaling of

breathing."

THELMA HALL

2. Verse 3 reads like identity statements for Jesus. Rephrase them to create identity statements for yourself, using the unfinished phrases in the right column.

Jesus knew that the Father had put all things under his power.	I know that God has . . . [regarding me]
Jesus knew that . . . he had come from God and was returning to God.	I know that I . . . [regarding origins and future]

3. How does knowing who you are in the life of God (as Jesus did) make doing humble acts of service more appealing?

Read John 13:4-5.

4. Put yourself in the place of a disciple. Describe your emotions as Jesus

did these six specific actions, apparently without saying a word:

got up from the meal

took off his outer clothing

wrapped a towel around his waist

poured water into a basin

washed his disciples' feet

dried them with the towel that was wrapped around him

5. As Jesus dried their feet, we can imagine how the towel became an extension of his arms and hands—of his love. What object is an extension of you to be used gently, pliably and skillfully to serve others—a car? your hands? a serving spoon?

"Intimate union with God leads to the most creative involvement in the contemporary world."

HENRI NOUWEN

Read John 13:6-11.

6. Why do you think Peter tried to manage and control the situation by saying, "You shall never . . ." and "Not just my feet . . ."?

7. Jesus moved the conversation from the concrete act of footwashing to the spiritual life. Verse 10 could have many layers of meaning. Which meaning best addresses the spiritual issues you're currently dealing with?

___ Jesus wants to wash you clean of your tendencies toward spiritual deadness, but you keep resisting.

___ Jesus is telling you what discipleship looks like (service), but you, like Peter, keep dictating what you want discipleship to look like.

___ God wants to lead you in your spiritual life, but you are more interested in what people say it *should* be like. You need to stop and listen and receive from God.

___ Other:

8. What inner responses to Jesus' behavior may Judas have had, especially when his own feet were being washed?

"*The grace of humility is worked into our lives through the discipline of service.*"

RICHARD FOSTER

Read John 13:12-17.

9. When Jesus asked the disciples, "Do you understand what I have done for you?" he was asking them to think more deeply (v. 12). Review a current situation in which you believe God has shown you some truth. Consider now whether God wants you to think more deeply about it.

10. How does serving others transform a person ("Now that you know these things, you will be blessed if you do them," v. 17)?

11. Who, if anyone, has served you, but also taught you something in the process?

12. In what ways could you serve those you're "discipling" (spiritually mentoring) or those who look up to you in some way?

Transformation Exercises

Experiment with one or more of the following.

- Hold a towel in your hands. As you look at your hands and feel the towel's texture, ask God how you can selflessly serve someone who looks up to you—how you can serve with humility and without getting a lot of credit.

- Be a storyteller. Make up a story about a criminal or obstinate child and how that person is changed by serving someone or being served.

- Look at the people you interact with everyday. Observe what menial, foot-washing type tasks they bemoan. Then quietly do one of these tasks for them while they're not looking.

- Pick a word or phrase from this passage (perhaps "showed them the full extent of his love" or "you will be blessed if you do them"). For several minutes, sit in that phrase. Don't think about anything much, except the love of God or God's grand design to transform your soul.

4

THE PERIL OF THE
HYPOCRITICAL HEART

MATTHEW 23:1-37

Serving others can make you or break you. Working hard to help others can train you in compassion and selflessness as no other discipline can—if you stay connected with God. Otherwise your diligent efforts can become self-serving. As people appreciate you, your insecurities take over and you start trying to prove yourself. You use your helpfulness to gain religious respectability so that others look up to you.

If you harbor a need to be right, serving can become your war machine. You serve not with a heart for others but with your own agenda, leading people not to God but to your own ideas. You'll be meticulous with taking care of the details—but not offering mercy and justice.

Perhaps you avoid these shortcomings but allow service to become a series of benevolent outward actions. Getting the job done becomes the goal, and you disregard the heart of those you serve, those you serve alongside and even your own self. You're eager to guide others, but you guide them to good works, not to following God. Without realizing it, you become hypocritical because your service is about you, not about God.

Turning Toward God

Why is it so easy to become self-congratulatory when serving others?

Hearing God Through the Word

These were the faults of the Pharisees, some of the hardest workers in God's kingdom. They longed to restore the nation of Israel to a God-obedient nation. But their brand of righteousness focused on outward actions only, not on having a just and merciful heart.

Read Matthew 23:1-12.

1. What behaviors did Jesus confront the Pharisees about?

"Every one of the

seven 'woes' is

an exclamation

2. We find fault with the Pharisees, but it's true that when you're serving tirelessly, it's tempting to focus on self instead of being devoted to God. Why?

like the 'blessed'

in the Beatitudes.

It is not a curse

that calls down

3. Reread Matthew 23:8-12. Pretend for a moment that a Pharisee is sitting next to you and wants your advice. What would you say to help him see the astonishing truth that "the greatest among you will be your servant" (v. 11)?

a calamity but

a calm, true

judgment and

verdict rendered

by the supreme

Read Matthew 23:13-22.

4. How do the three "woe to you" statements in the passage show these Pharisees to be hypocrites?

- they "shut the kingdom of heaven in men's faces" (v. 13)

- "travel over land and sea to win a single convert" (v. 15)

- swearing by the temple, but not the gold of the temple (v. 16)

Judge himself."

R. C. H. LENSKI

5. The Pharisees served diligently but harbored their own agenda. How do we keep from serving others while also serving our own hidden agenda?

6. What is at the root of our splitting hairs or focusing on technicalities when we serve others (as the Pharisees did with oaths)?

Read Matthew 23:23-28.

7. What important issues did the overscrupulous behavior of the spice-rack-tithing Pharisees cause them to overlook?

"O God, grant that

what I

give may be   *Read Matthew 23:29-37.*

given without   8. In what way did these Pharisees overestimate their goodness (vv. 29-36)?

self-congratulation,

and without

thought of praise   9. How did Jesus speak these very difficult truths in love to the Pharisees (v. 37)?

or reward."

JOHN BAILLIE

10. Which hypocritical attitude, if any, do you find most difficult to avoid when you are serving others?

___ trying to prove yourself (wanting religious respectability; thinking about how you look; wondering if people notice your good deeds)

___ needing to be right (having your own agenda; leading people to your ideas rather than to God; being overly scrupulous about small things; not ever pondering the goals of mercy, justice or faithfulness)

___ rationalizing your behavior (splitting hairs; getting by on technicalities)

___ letting service be about outward acts only (being concerned only about getting the job done; overlooking how God is working in those you are leading)

___ being eager to guide others but treating them disrespectfully (not asking people what they need but assuming you know more than those you're serving)

___ other:

---

11. When we're in the middle of serving others and we realize we have some of the above attitudes, what can we do to find help from God?

---

12. What can we do on a regular basis that would help us stay away from hypocrisy and move toward humble, respectful service?

Transformation Exercises

Experiment with one or more of the following.

• Go to the room or place where you serve when no one is there. Sit quietly and pray a prayer such as this one by John Baillie: "O holy One, let the fire of Thy love enter my heart, and burn up all this coil of meanness and hypocrisy, and make my heart as the heart of a little child."

• Take pictures of those you serve (with their permission), and keep them in your Bible. Pray for them daily. If possible, weep for them.

• Journal about possible needs to prove yourself or to be right. Be brutally honest about how you use service to feel better about yourself.

• Talk with someone who seems to serve in a truly selfless way. Ask casual questions such as "Why do you like being involved in this service?"

"Our relationships with others are not only the testing grounds of our spiritual life but also the places where our growth toward wholeness in Christ happens."

ROBERT MULHOLLAND

- Reread John 13:1-17. Imagine Jesus tenderly washing your feet and loving you dearly. Then imagine Jesus washing the feet of those you serve. See yourself holding the towel for Jesus and handing it to him.

5

SECRECY AS A DISCIPLINE

MATTHEW 6:1-8

You probably have never blown a trumpet to draw attention to a good deed you've just done. But maybe you've mentioned it subtly in ordinary conversation. Or if you have blown a trumpet, it was only to encourage someone: "I've been praying for you every day . . ."

We don't think we're trumpet blowers until we agree not to tell anyone about the good thing we just did. Then our need to announce our goodness overwhelms us.

In the discipline of secrecy, we do not tell, hint or cause our good deeds to be known. This quiets our desire for admiration or even the mere attention of others. Before you dismiss this discipline as too ascetic or legalistic, hear the words of one who practices it. Elaine Prevallet writes:

> When I was in the novitiate, in my early twenties, I decided to do one small act of kindness each day that was completely unknown to anyone. So I would keep my eyes peeled for something helpful I could do that no one would see. I wanted to be absolutely sure that I was doing it for no one but God, whom I loved with a kind of simple and quite passionate fervor. I made beds, or turned them down. I folded clothes, I tidied. At least one a day, and no one knew. That very infinitesimal act each day gave me enormous joy. It gave me a kind of inner excitement to do this only for God: a secret between me and God. It kept me alert to the small needs of others; maybe it provided spontaneity and creativity in an otherwise highly regimented situation.

Turning Toward God

Imagine yourself in the place of the person above, doing a good deed in secret every day. What might you want to say to God in the midst of this—words of joy? of desire to be noticed?

"The Christian

who is truly

intimate with

Jesus will never

draw attention

to himself but

will only show

the evidence of a

life where Jesus

is completely in

control."

OSWALD CHAMBERS

Hearing God Through the Word

Read Matthew 6:1-4.

1. What rewards do we miss when we do good deeds to be seen by others?

2. How do you explain the odd phrase "do not let your left hand know what your right hand is doing"?

Read Matthew 6:5-8.

3. What appears to have been in the heart of these people praying in the synagogue? What did Jesus say they were thinking?

4. What are the advantages of praying in secret (with no listeners) over praying aloud while others listen?

5. How do you respond to the idea of not being concerned whether others know you pray for them?

6. Look back through the first eight verses of this chapter and find
    the word *secret*. What similarities do you notice about the words
    around it?

---

7. What do you learn about the hidden life with God from the verses
    below?

    "For you died, and your life is now hidden with Christ in God"
      (Colossians 3:3).

    "All my longings lie open before you, O Lord; my sighing is not hid-
      den from you" (Psalm 38:9).

    "You are my hiding place;
       you will protect me from trouble
       and surround me with songs of
          deliverance" (Psalm 32:7).

      "Because you are my help,
          I sing in the shadow of your wings" (Psalm 63:7).

"The discipline of

secrecy will help

us break the grip

of human opinion

over our souls and

our action."

DALLAS WILLARD

---

8. What would it be like to serve alongside people who didn't want
    credit for doing good or who weren't concerned about what others
    thought of their service?

---

9. How is the discipline of secrecy helpful in connecting with God?

---

10. What fears or sins might we slowly overcome through practicing
    this discipline of secrecy?

---

11. What are some deeds that can actually be done in secret?

Transformation Exercises

Experiment with one or more of the following.

- Do a good deed without letting anyone find out. Then journal about how it feels. Does it feel good because you've done something "undercover"? A little empty because the person doesn't even know how much you loved them in order to do it? Freeing because you are trusting God to do the good work since you aren't in the middle of it?

- Consider a situation in which you are often in competition with someone. When you are next there, go out of your way to avoid mentioning a recent accomplishment. Instead notice one of theirs and comment.

- Reread all of Matthew 6, noticing the three religious activities that Jesus said people did to receive credit from others (giving, praying, fasting). Imagine that you are composing a version of chapter 6 for today's world of churchgoers. Choose three religious activities that people do to receive credit from others (although many do them with pure motives). Ponder what those items might be. Ponder how you are sometimes tempted to do them so that others will notice.

6

SIMPLE, UNPRETENTIOUS SERVICE

LUKE 10:25-37

Ever take a deep breath, grimace and think, "Gee, now it's time to serve"? As we serve in selfless ways, we stop thinking that. Instead our service becomes automatic and unplanned. We mow the widow neighbor's lawn after we do our own. We make or purchase two dishes of food and take one to an ailing friend. We gladly spend Saturday visiting someone in prison instead of going to the movies.

Jesus painted a picture of someone whose service came so naturally that he didn't hesitate. His left hand reached out and helped before his right hand had time to question whether it was wise. This fictional but nevertheless authentic Samaritan didn't have to "go somewhere to serve God" (as perhaps the priest and Levite were doing); he served everywhere he went and in everything he did.

Simple, unpretentious service is foreign to some traditionally religious people. We weigh, plan and program our service, self-conscious about how we look and what people will think. The Samaritan saw a need, took pity on the suffering man and put the guy on his donkey.

Turning Toward God

Think of who you would hope to be the *last* person needing your help. Don't reveal that person's identity. Instead tell the group why it would be so difficult to stop to help this person.

Hearing God Through the Word

As you examine this parable, look at the heart of the storyteller, Jesus. Why did he choose to shock his listeners with his hero's ethnicity? What many things does this uncomplicated hero do right? What truths did Jesus want to impart? What truth do you need to hear?

Read Luke 10:25-37.

1. What questions do you find in this passage? What commands do you find in this passage?

"We may grow

into closer love

with God by

widening into

His interests,

and thinking

His thoughts

and sharing His

enterprises."

FRANK LAUBACH

2. Focus on Luke 10:25-29. Based on this text and the text of session 4 (Matthew 23:1-37), what seems to have been the motive behind the lawyer's second question, "Who is my neighbor?"

3. Why do we sometimes respond to the command to love by thinking of reasons why others may not deserve our love, want it or benefit from it?

4. While the English word *neighbor* makes us think of next-door neighbors, the Greek word meant anyone who was near you or anyone you had something to do with. With that in mind, whom might you regard as a neighbor that you might otherwise overlook?

5. Reread Luke 10:30-37. How did the religious folks behave toward the beaten man? What possible reasons might they have had for their behavior?

6. Step into Jesus' shoes as storyteller. Who is a "Samaritan" in relation to you? (Perhaps a member of an ethnic group, an adherent to another religious tradition or a member of a corporate community that was unfair to you.)

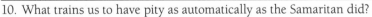

7. Describe the care the Samaritan gave the beaten man.

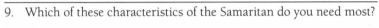

8. Put yourself in the place of the wounded traveler—a Jewish person, no doubt. If you were conscious, would you have cooperated with the Samaritan or begged him to pass you by?

"A New

Testament saint

is not one who

9. Which of these characteristics of the Samaritan do you need most?

___ He helped without being asked.

___ Without fanfare, he did a simple task that presented itself to him. (No fundraisers or newspaper articles.)

___ He used the resources he had—his donkey, his money.

___ He was generous with the person he asked to help him (the innkeeper), not asking for a discount for charity work.

___ He didn't make a big deal out of it, thinking he had to stay by the man's side every minute.

merely proclaims

the gospel, but

one who becomes

broken bread

and poured-out

wine in the hands

of Jesus Christ

for the sake of

10. What trains us to have pity as automatically as the Samaritan did?

others."

OSWALD CHAMBERS

11. In what way, if any, do you need to be more like the Samaritan?

Is there any time soon in which you can put this into practice? If so, when?

"When we are

used as broken

bread and

poured-out wine,

we have to reach

a level where

all awareness

of ourselves and

of what God is

doing through

us is completely

eliminated. A

saint is never

consciously a

saint—a saint

is consciously

dependent on

God."

OSWALD CHAMBERS

Transformation Exercises

Experiment with one or more of the following.

- Look for an opportunity to help someone without hesitation or fanfare.

- Read the parable again and compose a prayer for yourself.

- Compare and contrast Jesus' response to the expert in the law with his response to the rich young ruler (Mark 10:17-22); both asked the same question. How did Jesus address the spiritual state of each questioner in these passages and elsewhere?

- Recast the parable in your own terms by substituting a road or neighborhood dangerous to you; a person generally despised or excluded because of financial status, profession, ethnicity, disability or disease. Put yourself in the place of the victim. How do you feel waking up to find that this person helped you? What questions might you ask when that person comes by to pay your hotel bill? Refine ideas discussed in the group.

STUDY NOTES FOR
SERVICE AND SECRECY

Session 1. Doing Flows Out of Being

NEHEMIAH 1:1—2:18

FOCUS: The discipline of service flows out of constant companionship with God.

Question 1. Nehemiah confessed that the Israelites (including himself) had sinned (v. 6) by acting wickedly and disobeying the commandments (v. 7).

Nehemiah requested God's attentive ear (vv. 6, 11), that God remember the promise that although Israel would be exiled, God would gather them again if they returned to God (vv. 8-9), that God give him favor with the king of Persia (v. 11).

Mention also that Nehemiah praised God as the great God of heaven who keeps the covenant (v. 5) and is the mighty Redeemer (v. 10).

Question 4. Based on the circumstances and Nehemiah's previous prayer, he probably asked for God's favor with the king (1:11). This on-the-spot praying was one of Nehemiah's secrets for keeping his *being* in tact. In the midst of construction work, political tricks and compelling speeches, Nehemiah prayed (see Nehemiah 2:4; 4:4, 9; 5:19; 6:9, 14).

Question 5. The narrator (probably Nehemiah) is almost comical. Nehemiah didn't respond to or comment on the opposition. He simply said, "I went to . . ." He did, however, protect his plans.

He chose to inspect the walls under the cover of night. Ever the savvy politician playing his cards close to his chest, he didn't reveal his plan to rebuild the walls even to the Jewish leaders.

Question 7. The narrator could have said simply, "I inspected the walls," but instead he provides details of the inspection, as if to emphasize Nehemiah's intensity and to inspire us to look closely at the needs around us.

Question 8. Even though Nehemiah was the newcomer, he said *us* and *we*, not *you* (as in "you losers who let this destruction occur"). Also, he gave them the encouragement that resources were coming from the rich king of Persia. The outline is simple. He walked them through his journey: heartbreak at discovering the condition (v. 17), his resolve to rebuild (v. 17), his acquisition of resources (v. 18).

Question 9. The focus is on doing God's work, not being successful. They do their work with the love and mercy of God. The end does not justify the means.

Question 11. Ask those who do feel they have sufficient *being* to tell what has helped them keep their inner resources filled.

Session 2. Jesus' Heart for Others

LUKE 8:26-39

FOCUS: Jesus went out of his way to offer mercy and justice to have-nots.

Turning Toward God. Encourage group participants to offer possibilities for the last blank, "other."

Question 2. Before having group participants answer, have someone read an additional description in Mark 5:3-5: "No one could bind him any more, not even with a chain. For he had often been chained hand and foot, but he tore the chains apart and broke the irons on his feet. No one was strong enough to subdue him. Night and day among the tombs and in the hills he would cry out and cut himself with stones."

Question 3. While many people were healed because they interrupted Jesus as he was on his way somewhere, Jesus seemed to choose this deliverance from a great distance away. With just three short years to plant the plan of redemption, this one person mattered a great deal. God's love often baffles us. The high achievers in your group will be relieved to see that this deliverance did end up benefiting the whole area of Decapolis, a predominantly Gentile area (v. 39; Mark 5:20), so Jesus did optimize his time after all.

Question 4. The most probable answer is the fourth one. Both Legion and the townspeople were bound to have doubts about his deliverance. The stampede showed that the demons did not vanish into thin air. The people not only saw and heard them destroyed but probably tasted their dust.

Question 5. Although he looked and acted very differently, he still lingered at Jesus' feet.

Question 6. We need to be reconciled to God, but also to those around us. "Therefore, if anyone is in Christ, he is a new creation; the old has gone, the new has come! All this is from God, who reconciled us to himself through Christ and gave us the ministry of reconciliation" (2 Corinthians 5:17-18).

Question 10. Encourage participants to come up with their own ideas, but here are some possibilities: we might find ourselves going from pride to humility, from fear to courage, from apathy to charity, from laziness to diligence of faith, from selfishness to love.

Session 3. Service Transforms the Soul

JOHN 13:1-17

FOCUS: Serving selflessly in the style of Jesus transforms people. Prepare your own answers to question 2 ahead of time so you're ready to read them for the discussion. Have pens or pencils available, if needed, to allow participants to tinker with their answers on paper.

Question 1. If members don't comment on the phrase "the full extent of his love," ask how this adds dimension to the scene.

Question 2. Read verse 3 aloud again. Then read your examples. Give group participants time to think for a minute. Offer pens or pencils as needed.

Question 4. John describes these actions with cinematic detail, as if they were directions in a screenplay. They must have made quite an impression on him.

Question 6. Like Peter, we may resist being served. But Jesus wants others to serve us, to enrich us and to teach us how to serve.

Question 7. Reread verse 10 for the group and ask how many chose the first answer, then the second, and so on. Those who chose the first answer may be interested to know that many say that the washing is a symbol of baptism.[1] Those who chose the second answer may be interested in R. C. H. Lenski's insight: "Water is said to be a symbol of sanctification through the Holy Spirit, hence washing symbolizes the cleansing and refreshing of the Spirit."[2]

Question 9. If you wish, ask group participants to shut their eyes. Say, "Let Jesus ask you, 'Do you understand what I have done for you?'" Give them a few moments of silence and then ask them to open their eyes and share with the group anything that came to them. Lenski suggests that Jesus had several messages for the disciples. "His action in washing their feet is not a mere rebuke to their pride [because they should have been the ones washing his feet!], it is an example of true love . . .

that is ready to render the lowliest kind of service to others. He is not concerned in humbling them [only] but [also] in making them like himself so that they may be truly blessed and happy (v. 17)."[3] In other words, Jesus was inviting them to have their lives transformed.

Question 10. Even one instance of obedience (such as service) means you are never the same. You have experienced God in some way, and in order to disobey the next time you have to move backward away from good. Obedience and participation in spiritual disciplines opens you up to great possibilities of transformation because the "*hope* of glory" is experiencing "Christ in you" (Colossians 1:27).

Question 12. Jesus served those he discipled. That's part of what discipleship looks like.

Session 4. The Peril of the Hypocritical Heart

MATTHEW 23:1-37

FOCUS: Service can become hypocritical and self-congratulatory when we focus on ourselves instead of on being devoted to God.

Question 1. They didn't practice what they preached. They tied heavy loads on people with their rules. They did everything "for men to see," choosing important seats and fancy titles. Jesus was indicting Pharisees in general, but Pharisees were thought of as the "good guys" spiritually. They wanted to do what was right. They tried hard. Some of them even became disciples of Jesus. We can learn so much from their mistakes.

Question 2. You become wrapped up in what you're doing, thinking and hoping. In your busyness and fixation on getting things done, devotion to God drops away. As you become weary, you think maybe you deserve a little reward so it's

okay to grab the chief seats and honored titles. If the need is great, you may feel you have to jump in and *do*. You may even become paternalistic, thinking that you know what is best. Instead of asking folks how you can help meet their needs, you think you know what they need and you do it for them.

Question 3. You might follow up with this question: What did the Pharisees need to understand?

Question 4. Before considering each "woe," read the historical background below. Then ask the question again.

Verse 13 background: The Pharisees insisted that others obey their meticulous rules and regulations. You might make a comment to the group like: "See verse 23 also. They pretended to dispense truth, but they didn't."

[1]J. N. Sanders and B. A. Mastin, *The Gospel According to St. John* (London: Adam and Charles Black, 1977), p. 307.
[2]R. C. H. Lenski, *The Interpretation of St. John's Gospel* (Minneapolis: Augsburg, 1943), p. 918
[3]Ibid., p. 924.

Verse 15 background: The Pharisees spent a lot of time convincing "God-fearers" (people who accepted Jewish moral law and worshiped God but took no part in ceremonial law) to participate in their ceremonies. A possible comment to the group would be that the Pharisees worked at turning God-fearers into Pharisees. They were "not really seeking to lead men to God, they were seeking to lead men to Pharisaism."[4]

Verse 16 background: There were two kinds of oaths. One kind could never be broken (swearing by the gold of the temple), but another kind had loopholes and could be legitimately broken (swearing by the temple). You might point out to the group that the Pharisees often took oaths to impress people, but they were the second kind of oath that gave them wiggle room to get out of it. So they deceived others and were not sincere after all.

Question 5. Examples of serving with a hidden agenda include wanting a mentally disabled person to make great developmental progress; wanting a homeless person to have a home because that's what "normal people" do; teaching so that students in your class think as you, their teacher, think.

Serving with a hidden agenda makes us controlling, and controlling people do not generate trust or compassion. If we offer our service to God with no thought of results or outcomes, it's easier to serve others with respect and compassion.

Question 6. The Pharisees intended to deceive by taking oaths they knew they could get out of. Sometimes we split hairs because we lack real, deep compassion. (*I'll help him—because he deserves it—but not her.*) We ask if we have to forgive people who aren't repentant and don't ask or want

to be forgiven. We differentiate between the deserving poor and the undeserving poor, although Jesus never did. We wonder if it's okay to flirt with someone who is married.

Question 7. Justice, mercy and faithfulness. Compare this with Micah 6:8 and Zechariah 7:9.

Question 8. The Pharisees were like folks who say, "If I had been Adam or Eve, I wouldn't have eaten the fruit." They had no humility, no sense of "there but for the grace of God go I."

Question 9. Verse 37 reveals that Jesus spoke with a heart of parental love, wanting to draw the Pharisees close and help them change. Luke 19:41 shows him weeping over Jerusalem, the stronghold of the Pharisees. Even the word *woe* encompasses not only "wrath, but also sorrow; anger from a heart of love."[5]

Question 11. Ceasing to serve is warranted only in extreme cases. Usually spending time in solitude and silence is helpful because it helps us hear our heart and clear it before God. Confessing our wrong attitudes to someone else (the disciplines of community and confession) and being accountable can help, as well as asking that person for prayer. Serving alongside someone whose motives are more selfless helps. Making a point of praying diligently for those we serve—perhaps keeping photos of them in ready view—reminds us that service is not about us.

Question 12. Pray for our attitudes. Practice serving others in humble ways without looking for credit. Talk regularly with anyone you serve to find out what they truly need so your service can be appropriate. Whenever possible, put those you serve in the power-up position by asking them for help, as Jesus did when he asked the Samaritan woman to help him get some water to drink (John 4:7).

---

[4]William Barclay, *The Gospel of Matthew* (Philadelphia: Westminster Press, 1958), 2:321.
[5]Lenski, *St. John's Gospel*, p. 319.

Session 5. Secrecy as a Discipline

MATTHEW 6:1-8

FOCUS: Service done in secret can purify our motives and teach us to respond to God sincerely.

Question 1. Verses 1 and 4 do not stipulate that the reward is only in the hereafter. We miss a level of intimate partnership with God here and now. We miss opportunities to live for that Audience of One—God—instead of playing to the crowd.

Question 2. Jesus used the hands to represent different parts of one's self, playfully suggesting that we can keep something so excessively secret that one part of our mind or will may not know what the other part is thinking or choosing. His figure of speech also speaks of goodness that is automatic and unselfconscious: "The kind of people who have been so transformed by their daily walk with God that good deeds naturally flow from their character are precisely the kind of people whose left hand would not notice what their right hand is doing. [They] do not have to invest a lot of reflection in doing good for others. Their deeds are 'in secret' no matter who is watching, for they are absorbed in love of God and of those around them. They hardly notice their own deed, and rarely remember it."[6]

Question 4. Prayers that are unheard and unknown by others allow us to be honest, and so they help us better connect with God. Secret prayers are not thinking about whether others know they're praying or how they sound to others.

Question 5. While it is often appropriate to encourage others by letting them know you are praying for them, we need to look at our hearts. Are we using it as a subtle means of self-congratulation? What if I could simply listen to a struggling person speak without rushing to say how much I've been praying for them?

Question 6. The phrase "who sees what is done in secret" appears twice and suggests a hidden partnership with God.

Question 7. In the first one, hiddenness is the result of obedience as we set our hearts and minds on Christ. The other three refer to the intimate nature of our relationship with God. We have secrets with God that no one else knows about.

Question 8. Such people make excellent partners because they aren't competitive or defensive. They also aren't swayed by opinions but will seek God with you.

Question 9. We rely only on God for attention and credit. We don't look for others' approval or worry about disappointing others or worry about not being successful. That helps us focus further on God.

Question 11. Help to give each other ideas because this concept is quite foreign to our way of living.

Session 6. Simple, Unpretentious Service

LUKE 10:25-37

FOCUS: Christ's servants help others in uncalculated, unpretentious ways.

Turning Toward God. Since slipping and saying the person's name is a possibility (which will distract from the point of the question), you may want to ask group participants to use "Person X"

---

[6]Dallas Willard, *The Divine Conspiracy* (San Francisco: HarperSanFrancisco, 1998), p. 192.

when referring to the last person they'd want to see needing their help.

Question 1. The expert in the law asked two questions, one about inheriting eternal life and another about the identity of the neighbor he had to love. Jesus asked him two questions, one about what the law said was required for eternal life and which of the three men was a neighbor. Jesus gave the same command twice, to love (vv. 28, 37). He told the expert to do the command and to imitate the fictional Samaritan who obeyed the command.

The command to love (which Jesus expresses first in words, then in story) is so simple. We are to *do* it. But we question it while Jesus says simply to do it. That's what this encounter between Jesus and the expert is about. It's what the parable is about.

Question 2. Besides wanting to trip Jesus up (v. 25), the lawyer engaged in hair-splitting and technicalities (discussed in session 4 in regard to binding oaths and *really* binding oaths, Matthew 23:16-22), as if to ask, "Yes, but *who* is my neighbor." "The Pharisees restricted the term *[neighbor]* so as to exclude not only Gentiles and Samaritans, but also publicans and those who shared not their own peculiar views [folks Jesus ate with]."[7]

Question 3. Loving others is difficult. We think of so many reasons we should not have to forgive or help—at least not certain persons who have harmed us! We can love only as we grow and respond to the power of the Holy Spirit in our lives.

Question 5. Consider reasons that might have occurred to the lawyer and the listeners standing around him. The priest and Levite must have had good reasons because they disobeyed the Law, which called for them to be merciful and helpful (Exodus 23:4, 5; Deuteronomy 22:1-4).

Question 6. Who were the Samaritans? In Old Testament times, the Assyrians invaded the northern kingdom of Israel, scattered most of its inhabitants and brought there other nations they had captured. The Israelite remnant intermarried with these other peoples, resulting in a mixed race with a mixed religion. The Jews who returned from captivity (from the southern kingdom of Judah) went on to become the New Testament Jews, who despised these mixed-blooded Samaritans. "For the Jews generally, at that time, we could say that 'the only *good* Samaritan was a dead Samaritan.'"[8]

Question 7. Note that the Samaritan, filled with pity, bandaged the man with his own hands, using his own oil and wine, his own donkey, and his own money to house the man. Part of the beauty of the story is how uncalculated and unselfconscious the hero was.

Question 10. Ask about other spiritual disciplines that help, such as community (serving alongside someone who is selfless), confession (admitting my self-centeredness in service), simplicity (learning not to make things complicated).

Question 11. To get them started, you may want to suggest ideas such as serving without being self-conscious about what I did or how much I did, or being willing to do the thing in front of me, even if it isn't church work.

---

[7]Leo Boles, *A Commentary on the Gospel According to Luke* (Nashville: Gospel Advocate, 1972), pp. 223-24.
[8]Willard, *Divine Conspiracy*, p. 110.

Section Three

PRAYER & LISTENING

Prayer is a popular spiritual discipline. In crisis, people who don't identify themselves as Christians or who don't attend church find themselves praying. This indicates a distinct human tendency to talk to God.

While some other disciplines may seem mysterious and laborious, some folks fall into praying without thinking about it. Until we make it too complicated, that is. Over the years people have developed formulas, techniques and foolproof schemes to get God to say yes to their prayers. It's as if God has been reduced to a vending machine, and people search for the right coin to insert so that goodies will appear in the tray to be grabbed. Such frantic grasping misses the point of prayer, so well explained by Oswald Chambers: "We look upon prayer simply as a means of getting things for ourselves, but the biblical purpose of prayer is that we may get to know God Himself."

Prayer is about building a relationship with God. Knowing God teaches us to relate to God in an authentic way—not just doing the good things that good people are supposed to do. We talk and listen to this all-knowing, all-powerful Creator in ways God teaches us. We can reach out to this God who is as close as our breath. The studies in this guide outline some of those ways.

For more about prayers of praise and adoration, see session 2 of the "Worship and Celebration" section. For more about prayers of reflection and confession, see the "Reflection and Confession" section. For more about hearing God in prayer, see sessions 3, 4 and 5 of the "Solitude and Silence" section.

1

CONVERSATION WITH GOD

GENESIS 15:1-17; 17:15-22; 18:1-15

If you want a picture of what it looks like to connect with God, you might start by looking at how God interacted with someone God called a "friend." One such friend was Abraham (Isaiah 41:8; see also 2 Chronicles 20:7; James 2:23).

Abraham's friendship with God was characterized by ongoing conversations. Recorded in Genesis 12–22 (perhaps many more were not recorded), these conversations are filled with the back-and-forth elements of close communication—questions, guesses, reassertions, incredulity, calculated pauses, statements of fear and doubt, careful restatements of each other's thoughts.

Yet Christians sometimes neglect to learn the art of conversation with God. Perhaps they don't feel they are "good enough" to converse with God. But if goodness were a qualification, Abraham would have been excluded. For example, just after Abraham had a conversation with God laced with miracles and visions, he showed a lack of confidence in God. He agreed to Sarah's scheme of conceiving a child with Hagar instead of trusting that God would miraculously provide the promised child through Sarah (Genesis 15–16). But after Abraham's attempt to "adjust" God's will, God continued to converse with Abraham. Righteousness is an outgrowth of conversation with God, not a prerequisite.

Turning Toward God

What elements make for good conversation?

- being honest, asking unguarded questions

- tracking with each other's thinking

- genuine listening

- reassurances, saying, "Know for certain . . ."

- clarifying one's thoughts, perhaps saying, "Yes, but . . ."

- asking penetrating questions

- other:

Hearing God Through the Word

The three passages below record a few of the many conversations between God and Abraham. In previous conversations God gave Abram (his earlier name) vast land and promised him offspring (Genesis 13:14-17). In the conversations below Abram asks God questions about these promises.

"We are taught

by his grace in

the science of

conversing

with God!"

JEAN-NICHOLAS
GROU

Read Genesis 15:1-17.

1. What is the first question Abram asked?

   How does Abram's question fit with God's saying to him, "Do not be afraid" (v. 1)?

2. What did God do in addition to answering Abram's question (vv. 4-5)? Why?

3. What does Abram's question in verse 8, "How can I know . . . ?" tell you about Abram and his relationship with God?

---

4. If you were in a prayer conversation with God, and God said, "Know for certain that . . ." (v. 13), how might God finish the sentence? That is, what do you believe God has been trying to help you "know for certain" lately?

___ God will never abandon you or leave you helpless.

___ God wants you to change your ways about . . .

___ You don't need to be afraid of . . .

___ God would like to use you in a certain situation.

___ God loves and forgives, no matter what.

___ Other:

"Prayer is intelligent conversation about matters of mutual concern."

DALLAS WILLARD

Read Genesis 17:15-22.

---

5. What details of the covenant did Abraham question to himself and to God?

---

6. When has God answered you with "Yes, but . . ." (v. 19) or "I have heard you" (v. 20)?

Read Genesis 18:1-15.

---

7. How did God appear to Abraham this time?

---

8. When, if ever, has God confronted you with penetrating questions (perhaps ones such as, "Why did . . . ?" v. 13) or caught you denying the truth ("Yes, you did laugh," v. 15)?

9. Conversing with God means the Holy Spirit leads you and you are no longer "in charge" of your prayer. In what ways are you tempted to be "in charge" of your prayers?

___ always following a pattern: first praying X kind of prayers, then Y, then Z

___ prattling on until you run out of things to say

___ other:

10. The premier mark of Abraham was his complete confidence in God (faith). How might his conversations with God have developed such a faith?

"*We will never be*

'in charge'

in prayer if it

is real."

THELMA HALL

11. God's conversations with Abram were full of drama—starry nights, smoking firepots, mysterious visitors (Genesis 15:5, 17; 18:1-2). These were all "props" that God chose for their conversations. How open are you to letting God set terms for prayer conversations with you? Which of the following might help you increase your openness to God?

___ to ask God questions, believing that God will somehow answer them

___ to quit dictating to God how to answer your prayers

___ to quit filling your prayers with nonstop jabbering, just in case God might want to answer you

___ to be open that God might speak to you through someone else—including strangers or ordinary household objects (such as a "firepot")

Transformation Exercises

Experiment with one or more of the following.

- Take a walk and try to think of all the questions you would like to ask God.

- Pray about the self-talk that goes on in your head. Compare it with the kinds of things God often says (see question 4 above).

- Read the back-and-forth conversation in Genesis 18:20-33 and ponder why God engaged Abraham in conversation this way. Journal about whether you believe that God is really interested in your ideas.

- Read Genesis 22:1-18, in which God asks Abraham to sacrifice Isaac (the son he waited twenty-five years for). In a sense God was asking Abraham, "Am I enough?" and Abraham answered affirmatively. Take a walk and consider this question from God: "Am I enough?" Answer as honestly as you can. Consider other questions: How would you be better off if God *were* enough? Are you willing to let God ask you this question for the rest of your life?

2

PRAYING WITH AUTHENTICITY

Advice about prayer can be contradictory: "You can say anything to God because God loves you" versus "Don't be negative or despairing—remember you're talking to the God of the universe."

Authenticity in prayer is difficult. Bringing our true selves to God is tricky because God is so good and pure and we are not. Prayer is a conversation between unequals, for certain. Yet the psalms illustrate how God wants us to bring our unsanitized thoughts to prayer. We're free to state doubts, fears and questions, yet this isn't the same as blurting out self-focused rantings. We can learn to pray authentically *and* with reverence and trust.

Turning Toward God

What makes a person authentic? genuine? unrehearsed? what-you-see-is-what-you-get?

Hearing God Through the Word

Psalm 74 is the prayer of a child of God in great pain. The powerful empire of Babylon had carried away citizens of Judah into exile after devastating the capital city and destroying God's temple. Lives of individual Israelites were destroyed, and the nation of Israel was broken.

The psalmist expresses pain and despair, asking tough questions such as "Why?" and "How long?" The psalmist accuses his enemies and states their crimes in concrete terms. But the psalmist doesn't whine ad nauseam. He focuses on God as the One in charge of the universe, reminding himself of God's great deeds and mercy in history and creation. He pleads because he knows this God is the One who can make a difference.

Read Psalm 74:1-8.

1. What are the psalmist's doubts and fears? In what ways can you relate?

2. How can it be helpful to call out others' sins to God (vv. 5-8)?

"Pray as you can,

not as you can't."

DOM CHAPMAN

Read Psalm 74:9-17.

3. In what ways can a person question God without being irreverent?

4. What references to Israel's deliverance from Egypt do you recognize?

5. How does the tone of verses 9-11 differ from the tone of verses 12-17?

6. What is the significance of the word *you* occurring ten times in verses 12-17?

Practice the psalmist's technique. State a complaint about your life, but add a "you statement" about God's great mercy and justice: ". . . but you, O God . . ."

7. We're told it doesn't help to ask "Why?" when tragedies occur. So why do you think the psalmist asks "Why?" in this psalm (vv. 1, 11)?

"Prayer is the place where we can be completely ourselves."

ROBERTA BONDI

Read Psalm 74:18-23.

8. What phrases in the eight requests in these verses fit with what we know about the character of God?

9. In what ways is this prayer (vv. 1-23) as much about God as about the dreadful circumstances of the psalmist and Israel?

10. Why is this sort of authentic prayer likely to be healing to one's soul?

11. How is such prayer likely to result in greater trust in God and faithfulness to what God calls us to do?

12. If you were to pray at this moment, which of these elements from Psalm 74, if any, would you like to include in your prayer?

___ stating exactly what you think (including doubts and fears) with no bitterness or impatience

___ pleading with God

___ accusing others and naming their outrageous sins

___ asking "Why?" "How long?" and other gut-level questions

___ expressing confidence in God and retracing how God has miraculously helped you or others

___ offering requests in the form of what you think should happen in accordance with God's character and will

___ other expression of authenticity:

Transformation Exercises

Experiment with one or more of the following.

- Pray, bringing a troublesome situation before God. Include as many of the elements from this psalm as you can. (See the list in question 12.)

- Try out several postures for prayer such as kneeling, bowing before an altar, standing with arms uplifted, standing with arms outstretched to form a cross, lying prostrate and sitting in a dark, enclosed area. Which posture helps you be authentic with God?

- Journal about what it means to be "in charge" of your prayer. How do you orchestrate, organize and dominate your own prayers?

- Journal about how your prayer life would change if you did this: "Pray as you can, not as you can't."

- Pray the following prayer of Henri Nouwen several nights this week. Underline the phrases that best describe what you need to say to God.

    Why, O Lord is it so hard for me to keep my heart directed toward you? Why do the many little things I want to do, and the many people I know, keep crowding into my mind, even during the hours I am totally free to be with you and you alone? Why does

"The prayer preceding all prayers is 'May it be the real I who speaks. May it be the real Thou that I speak to.'"

C. S. Lewis

my mind wander off in so many directions, and why does my heart desire the things that lead me astray? Are you not enough for me? Do I keep doubting your love and care, your mercy and grace? Do I keep wondering, in the center of my being, whether you will give me all I need if I just keep my eyes on you?

Please accept my distractions, my fatigue, my irritations, and my faithless wanderings. You know me more deeply and fully than I know myself. You love me with a greater love than I can love myself. You even offer me more than I can desire. Look at me, see me in all my misery and inner confusion, and let me sense your presence in the midst of my turmoil. All I can do is show myself to you. Yet, I am afraid to do so. I am afraid that you will reject me. But I know—with the knowledge of faith—you desire to give me your love. The only thing you ask of me is not to hide from you, not to run away in despair, not to act as if you were a relentless despot.

Take my tired body, my confused mind, and my restless soul into your arms and give me rest, simple quiet rest. Do I ask too much too soon? I should not worry about that. You will let me know. Come, Lord Jesus, come. Amen.

3

THE PRAYER OF REQUEST

MATTHEW 6:9-13

For many years I've thought how lovely the prayers in Scripture are—the Lord's Prayer, prayers opening Paul's epistles. But I also thought they were so saintly that I'd never actually pray them. Prayer is supposed to be "intelligent conversation about matters of *mutual* concern," and scriptural prayers voice concerns I hadn't worked up much lather for. They focus on getting God's will done, while I muddled through a normal person's everyday concerns: making ends meet until the next paycheck, getting the recognition I deserved, having a stress-free life. Where is the meeting place between the mind of Christ and the mind of me? Do we pray down and dirty or high and lofty?

But as we connect with God, God's concerns slowly become ours. In the meantime prayer becomes a meeting ground of my in-the moment, immediate needs with God's enormously abundant life. This takes various forms. Sometimes we blurt out our raw needs and then examine them in prayer in the light of all the nurture God provides. Other times we ponder and paraphrase lofty prayers (such as the one we'll study in this session) and see that they contain nuggets of what our soul most desires—only we never saw it before. As we pray these prayers, we find that they form in us a God-drenched view of the world God *so loves*, pulling us out of our me-myself-and-I existence. By praying Scripture, in fact, we develop the mind of Christ. May that be your experience.

Turning Toward God

What would you say has been your most frequent prayer of request in the course of your life?

Hearing God Through the Word

Read Matthew 6:9-13.

1. What requests do you find in this prayer? Which one is most meaningful to you at this time?

"Scripture depicts a God whose heart is irrevocably set on us; prayer is the continuing work of setting our hearts on God."

JOHN MOGABGAB

2. How can addressing God first in a prayer (such as "Our Father") be helpful in connecting us with God?

3. How does the address "Our Father" remind us that prayer is not always a me-myself-and-I exercise?

4. Read the following ways of restating "Hallowed be your name" from several sources and then offer your own.

    • May your name be respected, treasured and loved.

    • May your name become our favorite word in our language.

    • "Let me never take such words on my lips that I could not pass from them to the hallowing of your Name."

    • "May that Name be hallowed in my work, keeping me in remembrance that you are the doer of all that is really done; my part is that of a humble collaborator, giving of my best."

    • "Enable us to give to Thee the unique place which Thy nature and character deserve and demand."

    • Your wording:

5. If you were to pray that God's kingdom would come (that folks would do God's will so that love and justice, mercy and truth would be the normal state of things), what specific circumstances would come to your mind to pray about?

_____

6. How would you complete the following personalization of "your will be done"? "Reign over me! Reign over my passions, my imagi-nations, my senses, my _____."

_____

7. How would being surrendered to God's will in this way make you more eager and more likely to connect with God?

_____

8. What needs to happen within people to help them move toward praying, "Your will be done," with peace and joy instead of resent-ment and bitterness?

"The point of prayer is not to get answers from God, but to have oneness with Him. If we pray only because we want answers, we will become irritated and angry with God."

OSWALD CHAMBERS

_____

9. Reread Matthew 6:11-13. Read verse 11 three times, emphasiz-ing one of these words each time: *us, today, bread*. What different thoughts are suggested in each different reading?

_____

10. Why do you think Jesus linked God's forgiveness of us to our for-giveness of others?

_____

11. How do the requests in the Lord's Prayer work toward the transfor-mation of our soul and others' souls?

12. Which phrase in the Lord's Prayer, if any, are you being impressed to pray more often?

Transformation Exercises

Experiment with one or more of the following.

- Pray the Lord's Prayer, but stop after each phrase and elaborate on it. For example, after saying "Our Father," stop and elaborate on "our" with "the Father of . . ." Then stop and elaborate on "Father" with "my tender Parent whose eyes never leave me."

- Pray one of Paul's prayers for someone (Ephesians 1:17-21; 3:14-19; Philippians 1:9-11; Colossians 1:9-12), and paraphrase the phrases as you go.

- Take a walk and sing the Lord's Prayer, using one of the many melodies it has been set to.

4

LISTENING TO GOD
IN PRAYER

1 CHRONICLES 14:8-17

As missionary Mary Geegh asked God for guidance, she would sit and wait on God. Once when she asked for help with a colleague toward whom she felt hostility, she heard God say, "Take her a fresh egg." This seemed foolish—one egg? Why not a dozen? Would the woman laugh at her? But she obeyed, giving it to the woman's child and scurrying off. Later the woman told Mary how she'd fed all her food to her ten children that day and nothing had been left for her to eat. How she had enjoyed the fresh egg Mary brought! The hostility between the two dissolved.

Many times in listening prayer God led Mary to give someone all the money in her purse (and God met her needs in other ways). One time, however, when a man came to borrow money to find his runaway daughter, Mary asked him to listen to God with her. In the silence, God revealed to this man that he needed to make peace in his chaotic home first and then his daughter would return. He did so, and she returned.

According to Douglas Steere, to listen from the heart requires

- *vulnerability:* God wants to hear my feelings, motives and thoughts.

- *expectancy:* God will meet my needs.

- *acceptance:* I can accept whatever happens in this quiet time.

- *constancy:* I can rely on God not to get fed up with me.

Mary Geegh would add that acceptance means willingness to do whatever God directs you to do.

Turning Toward God

Many people claim to have heard directly from God. What would make you believe or disbelieve such a person—circumstances? character? the person's spiritual practices?

Hearing God Through the Word

King David was a skilled military leader. Beginning with his victory over the Philistine champion Goliath, he inspired so many people that they made up songs about his military prowess. So we might be surprised that this resourceful warrior consulted with God about military moves. But David knew this from spending a long time in the wilderness tending sheep and developing a reliance on and relationship with God. Then he'd learned to rely on God even more for practical strategies when running from Saul's relentless pursuit of him. David knew how to listen to God.

"We all need

to listen

adventurously

enough to be

utterly surprised

at what we hear.

To listen with

heart and mind

opened wide

invites us to be

changed."

WENDY WRIGHT

Read 1 Chronicles 14:8-12.

1. What question(s) did David ask of God (v. 10)? What was God's answer?

2. Which of the following make "inquiring of the Lord" risky business for many people?

   ___ Your mind is too full of distractions to hear God.

   ___ You don't expect God to speak to you.

   ___ Your usual method of operation is to consult friends for guidance.

   ___ It's easy to make up God's answer so that it agrees with what you really want to do.

   ___ It's too easy to imagine God's answer to be the opposite of what you want because God never seems to want what you want.

___ God might tell you to do something you don't want to do or don't understand.

___ Other:

3. What was David's response to the victory?

Read 1 Chronicles 14:13-17.

4. David did not rely on God's previous answer (v. 10) but inquired again. When we rely on previous answers, or answers others have experienced, what assumptions do we make?

___ God has only one answer for every type of situation so if something worked once, it will work again.

___ If something worked for a friend, it will work for me.

___ God's will is always the same in every situation, regardless of inward motives or outward circumstances.

___ God isn't a personal being who examines the nuances of every situation to communicate to me a tailor-made response.

___ Other:

5. Pretend for a moment that you are a soldier in this Israelite army and you actually hear God marching in the tops of the balsam trees. How might this have affected you?

What different reactions might other soldiers have to this experience?

6. People often expect God to answer yes or no (in this situation,

"Give much time to quietness. For the most part we have to get our help directly from our God. We must each learn to walk with God alone and feed on His Words so as to be nourished. Listen and don't evade the slightest whisper of guidance that comes."

AMY CARMICHAEL

attack or don't attack). How do you respond to this demonstration that God may have a miraculous detail or even a third alternative to offer?

"Those who

have abandoned

themselves to

God always lead

mysterious lives

and receive from

him exceptional

and miraculous

gifts by means

of the most

ordinary, natural

and chance

experiences

in which there

appears to be

nothing unusual."

JEAN-PIERRE
DE CAUSSADE

7. Why is it sometimes difficult to follow through and do what God leads you to do?

____ The action God leads you to do might look silly to others.

____ You are not sure it will prove helpful in the long run.

____ Other people—wise people—don't agree or think the idea is odd.

____ Nobody believes you got this idea from God.

____ You're too embarrassed even to say you got the idea from God.

____ Other:

8. What character traits would be likely to develop in a person who listened to God in prayer as David did?

9. How does the discipline of listening to God in prayer touch on other spiritual disciplines such as solitude and silence?

    confession?

    submission?

10. If you were to ask God for guidance about a certain dilemma in your life, what would that dilemma be?

Transformation Exercises

Experiment with one or more of the following.

- Sit in a quiet place with paper and pen and ask God about a certain dilemma. Journal about what you hear. If God gives you direction, resolve to follow it, even if it seems strange or uncomfortable.

- Reread 1 Chronicles 14:8-17. Ask God to speak to you the way he spoke to David.

- Read Psalm 81 and notice the three times the word *listen* appears. What are the benefits received by the person who listens to God?

- Review questions 4 and 7 and pray about the ideas harbored in your heart that keep you from listening to God. Which quality do you need more of: vulnerability, acceptance, expectation, constancy?

5

INTERCEDING AS
JESUS DID

Luke 22:31-34

Intercessory prayer runs the gamut from the childhood prayer "God bless Mommy and Daddy and . . ." to the adult 911-emergency prayer "Stop my boss from acting like a pain in the neck." It's easy to miss the formational aspects of intercessory prayer—how it trains us to care deeply for others (especially when we'd like to criticize them) and prods us about how to truly love them. Intercessory prayer also forms us spiritually because it trains us to think about others through the lens of God's desire to transform them to into Christlikeness.

Intercession is not about "patching up" folks or getting them to do what we think they should do. This is what we're doing when we ask God to help friends and family get certain kinds of jobs, to stop taking drugs, to go back to college. Usually we've already told others to their faces what we think they ought to do, and now we offer our ideas to God. But intercessory prayer isn't about reforming people; it's about the transformation of their souls. God may have a different plan from the one you envision. In intercessory prayer we learn to let go.

Turning Toward God

Name a time when you were intensely grateful that someone was praying for you.

Hearing God Through the Word

How do you intercede for people without rescuing them? How do you pray for God's desires for them? Christ did these things when he prayed for Peter in one of his worst moments.

Read Luke 22:31-34.

1. What exactly did Jesus pray for Peter?

2. Think of someone you know who is experiencing a sifting and shaking as described by Ray Summers: "The head and stalk of wheat were beaten and trampled and placed in a sieve. By the violent shaking of the sieve, the straw was tested for any wheat content in it. As the wind blew the chaff away, the valuable wheat emerged from the violent shaking." State your fears for this person without mentioning the person's name.

"[An intercessor is like the] live wire closing the gap between the saving power of God and the sinful men who have been cut off from that power."

Hannah Hurnard

3. By what names did Jesus call Peter in this passage? Why might Jesus have done this?

4. At what moments in Peter's future (Jesus' trial, Pentecost, ministry) did it probably encourage him to remember seeing the face of Jesus saying, "I have prayed for you, Simon"?

5. Why do you think Jesus didn't pray that Peter would avoid betraying him?

"What we

must avoid in

intercession

is praying for

someone to be

simply 'patched

up.' We must

pray that person

completely

through into

contact with the

very life of God."

OSWALD CHAMBERS

6. At what points does interceding for someone cross that person's spiritual boundaries—imposing our desires to change his or her choices and relationship with God?

7. When does intercessory prayer become an attempt to "fix" someone—to manage or rescue that person?

8. Look below at Peter's responses to Jesus' warning, as recorded in the four Gospels. What unwise attitudes did Peter display? What would have been a wiser response?

Peter's Response	Attitude Displayed	Wise Response
"Peter replied, 'Even if all fall away on account of you, I never will'" (Matthew 26:33).		
"But Peter insisted emphatically, 'Even if I have to die with you, I will never disown you.' And all the others said the same" (Mark 14:31).		
"But he replied, 'Lord, I am ready to go with you to prison and to death'" (Luke 22:33).		
"Peter asked, 'Lord, why can't I follow you now? I will lay down my life for you'" (John 13:37).		

9. How are other kinds of prayer (praying Scripture, listening prayer) helpful to us in interceding appropriately?

10. How does our growth in praying the Scripture, listening prayer and intercessory prayer help us become persons after God's heart, about whom God could easily say, "Whatever she wants, she gets" or "If he's requested it, it must be okay"? (These are paraphrases of "If you believe, you will receive whatever you ask for in prayer," Matthew 21:22.)

11. How do you need to intercede for a certain person in a more fruitful way?

Transformation Exercises

Experiment with one or more of the following.

- Read John 17 and make a list of what Jesus prayed for his disciples. Intercede for someone you know, praying for these things.

- Sit with a photo of someone you know (or an object that represents this person) in front of you. Pray, asking God to show you how to intercede for him or her.

- Intercede in prayer for someone you love, praying that their faith will not fail. Tell that person what you prayed.

- Think of someone in desperate circumstances whom you'd like to fix or rescue. Pray instead that they will grow in oneness with God (John 17:21).

"If we stay with a season of prayer for long enough, the things we originally put forward in our prayer have been searched and often put aside, and a whole new layer of longings for that person or situation often emerges in their place."

DOUGLAS STEERE

6

PRACTICING
GOD'S PRESENCE

1 THESSALONIANS 5:16-18

Can you identify with this experience of preoccupation? Douglas Steere describes, "When a young man is in love with a girl, he does not think of his beloved every instant if he has important work to do. But his devotion to her permeates all that he does, and when a pause comes his mind naturally turns to the loved one."

"Praying continually" (NIV) or what has come to be called "practicing the presence of God" involves living life on two levels, as described above in the young man's devotion to a girl. It occurs naturally, and it makes life more fun because we experience what A. W. Tozer calls the "sacramental quality of everyday living." Even those people who are avid "doers" (as the apostle Paul was) learn how to also "be" in life with God.

Practicing God's presence requires an interactive life of constant companionship with the Creator of the universe, the Son who lived among us and the Holy Spirit who lives inside us. Because Jesus said, "I am with you always" (Matthew 28:20), we can say that "in him we live and move and have our being" (Acts 17:28). Enjoying God's presence then is one more way we can connect with God, making an awareness of God's presence a distinct reality in our life.

Turning Toward God

In what ordinary situations, unrelated to church or devotional life, have thoughts of God come to you?

Hearing God Through the Word

As the apostle Paul said goodbye to the Thessalonians, he poured forth short, pithy directions about how to live a life immersed in God. One of these instructions is to "pray without ceasing" (1 Thessalonians 5:17 KJV). We know this doesn't refer to a constant, uninterrupted prayer vigil, or the very active apostle Paul would never have made his missionary journeys or earned a living as a tentmaker. Instead, he took each step and sewed each stitch with a conscious awareness of God.

Read 1 Thessalonians 5:16-18.

1. What three principles for the inner life are listed in these verses? Which one strikes you as most challenging?

2. What words in this passage describe the minute-by-minute nature of our relationship with God?

"Hold on to a

constant inner

vision of Him."

3. What further insights about prayer do you find in the following passages?

AUGUSTINE

"We always thank God for all of you, mentioning you in our prayers" (1 Thessalonians 1:2).

"How can we thank God enough for you in return for all the joy we have in the presence of our God because of you? Night and day we pray most earnestly that we may see you again and supply what is lacking in your faith" (1 Thessalonians 3:9-10).

"Constantly I remember you in my prayers at all times" (Romans 1:9-10).

"For this reason, since the day we heard about you, we have not stopped praying for you and asking God to fill you with the knowledge of his will through all spiritual wisdom and understanding" (Colossians 1:9).

"And pray in the Spirit on all occasions with all kinds of prayers and requests. With this in mind, be alert and always keep on praying for all the saints" (Ephesians 6:18).

4. What do you say to someone who states that it's impossible and even inappropriate to "be joyful always" and "give thanks in all circumstances"?

5. Look at what is in front of you at this moment. How could you thank God for that thing or person or view?

6. What items in your home or workplace might serve as reminders to "hold on to a constant inner vision" of God?

7. What short, three- or four-word prayers (often called breath prayers) might help you call yourself back to an awareness of God's presence throughout the day? Use these sources if you wish or write your own:

"I put my little egg-cake into the frying-pan for the love of God. When it is done, and if I have nothing else to call me, I prostrate myself on the ground, and I adore my God who assists me in everything by His grace; after which I rise up more contented than a king. When I can do nothing else, it is enough for me to lift up a straw for the love of God."

BROTHER LAWRENCE

___ words of Jesus ("Into your hands")

___ phrases from the Lord's Prayer ("Your will be done")

___ phrases from the apostle Paul's prayers ("May love abound")

8. How then would you describe the process of praying continually while (pick one)

___ picking out items in a store?

___ mowing the lawn?

___ changing a baby?

___ listening to the person opposite you answer the question?

9. How might practicing God's presence help us become more full of love or courage or purity or humility?

10. How might practicing the presence of God make us more eager to pray for longer periods of time and even spend time in silence and solitude with God?

11. In what situations might it help you to practice the presence of God as you walk through them?

"After months and years of practicing the presence of God, one feels that God is closer; His push from behind seems to be stronger and steadier, and the pull from in front seems to grow strong."

Frank Laubach

Transformation Exercises

Experiment with one or more of the following.

- Take a walk for fifteen minutes, taking care to experience everything around you. Touch the plants. Gaze at the earth and notice all the shades of color. Take whiffs of the air and notice how it changes as you walk along. Use all five senses as much as you can.

- Journal about a certain situation that creates difficulty for you—talking with certain people, doing a certain task or making certain phone calls. Another option is to compile a photo album or video diary of that situation. Now, fashion a prayer of two or three words that you could use just prior to that situation.

- Before getting out of bed in the morning, put in your mind a biblical image of God such as God swooping down to rescue you (Psalm 18:4-19) or singing over you (Zephaniah 3:17). Before going to sleep, review your day and ask yourself, *Where did I most sense God's presence?*

- Choose three or four songs that you could hum to help you practice God's presence.

STUDY NOTES FOR
PRAYER AND LISTENING

Session 1. Conversation with God

GENESIS 15:1-17; 17:15-22; 18:1-15

FOCUS: Prayer as conversation involves a delightful rhythm of asking God questions and waiting on God for replies.

General note. Conversations with God involve hearing God too. To learn more about hearing God's side of the conversation, see "Silence & Solitude," especially sessions 3-5 about delighting in God, waiting on God, resting in God and hearing God's surprises.

Question 1. After God said, "Do not be afraid," verse 2 says, "*But* Abram said." Apparently Abram was afraid of childlessness, and he stated it clearly with God's permission. "After this" refers to Abram's rescue of Lot, Melchizedek's blessing of Abram, and Abram's standing up to the king of Sodom.

Question 2. God took Abram outside, showing him the vast number of stars to illustrate the limitless number of his future offspring. Perhaps God knew the stars would be helpful because Abram, a wealthy nomadic herdsman, would no doubt see the stars every night. Each night he would be reminded of this conversation and God's promise.

Question 3. Abram must have been unafraid to express real feelings to God. Although he "believed" God (v. 6), he also wanted assurances ("how can I know?") about taking possession of the land. Yet Abram didn't have a God-is-my-buddy attitude either; he addressed God as "O Sovereign LORD" (vv. 2, 8). Having conversation with God, then, does not mean a person demeans God's position or has license to be impertinent.

Question 4. The question is not what participants would *like* God to tell them is certain. It's about what God has been communicating to them and what God wants them to "know for certain."

Question 5. While Abraham's questions and laughter may have expressed doubt, H. C. Leupold comments that Abraham's laughter and talking to himself involved "joy and surprise" to match his falling on his face, an "act of worshipful adoration."[1] He also suggests that verse 18 is not Abraham's substitute suggestion for God's idea but an additional plea. It's difficult to know.

Question 8. These questions cannot be answered quickly. Allow sufficient time for participants to think. Prepare your own answer ahead of time so that your response can jog participants' thinking.

---

[1]H. C. Leupold, *Exposition of Genesis* (Grand Rapids: Baker, 1977), p. 527.

God usually catches us lying when we're pretending to be better than we are.

Question 9. If you have time, ask participants how

letting God lead them in prayer makes them feel. It can be scary to consider encountering the Divine in prayer and having a conversation.

Session 2. Praying with Authenticity

PSALM 74:1-23

FOCUS: Praying authentically involves expressing doubts and fears as well as truth, believing God can give strength and grace.

Question 1. He fears rejection from God yet describes his people and himself tenderly as "sheep of your pasture." If participants mention God's anger, remind them that God's anger is not about temper tantrums or slapping folks around. It's about justice and consequences given without rancor.

Question 2. (Verses 5-8 constitute an amplification of the devastation described in 2 Kings 25:8-21.) If we call them out to God, we may be able to turn them over to God rather than call them out to others (gossip).

Question 3. This is not self-focused, exaggerated railing that goes on and on. Questioning can be done *in faith*, with the belief that God will answer. The psalmist hopes to hear from God and longs for comfort from God but is still authentic. Subsequent verses (vv. 12-17) show how the psalmist does not accuse God but ponders how God normally acts (based on God's behavior in the past) and compares it with God's seeming passivity in the present crisis.

Question 4. *Leviathan* (v. 14), according to Leupold, is another name for the crocodile, which is native to Egypt. Verse 13 refers to the crossing of the Red Sea.[2] (Remember psalms are poetry, that specialize in symbols and metaphors.) Verses 15-17 refer to God's help as the Israelites journeyed

toward the Promised Land: much-needed water flowing miraculously from rocks and the Jordan River opening for them to pass (Exodus 17:6; Joshua 4:23).

Question 5. Verses 9-11 are full of despair; verses 12-17 are full of hope based on the mighty acts of God in history and creation. It appears that the psalmist is reciting the great works of God to remind himself of who God is.

Question 6. The prayer shifts from being about himself and his problems to being about God. *Your* or *yours* is used three times. In addition, God is addressed in verse 12: "O God." Compare this with the despair of verses 9-11 and the accusations of others in verses 4-8. Offer a sample statement such as "Sometimes I feel too tired to lead this study, *but you, O God*, do not hesitate to speak to me in your Word."

Question 7. Asking "why?" and other difficult questions is not futile when we do so in the context of recognizing God's greatness and goals. The psalmist here seems to be giving voice to anguish, while still trusting an all-powerful God with huge, despairing questions.

Question 8. These petitions call for mercy and justice, which reflect God's character. The psalmist makes requests that honor God's covenant and cause, rather than just advocating his own ideas.

Question 9. This isn't just about what the psalmist wants—a wish list for God. It considers the things God had a high regard for, especially God's cove-

---

[2]Ibid., p. 538

nant with Israel, which is one of the major themes of the Old Testament.

Question 10. Prayer can help us remember God's deeds and who God is.

Question 12. Read each item and ask participants who chose it to raise their hand. Then ask everyone to pick one item they checked and write a specific prayer next to it. Finally, be quiet together to allow participants time to offer that prayer.

Session 3. The Prayer of Request

MATTHEW 6:9-13

FOCUS: We learn to make requests in terms of God's concerns, not just our own.

Question 1. Answers may vary according to interpretation but the Luke 11:2-4 version of this prayer is boiled down to five requests: that God's name be hallowed; that God's kingdom come; that our needs for today be met; that our sins be forgiven; that we would be saved from the time of trial.

Question 2. Addressing God is important; this is "one of the things that distinguishes prayer from worrying out loud or silently, which many, unfortunately, have confused with prayer."[3] It helps us fix our minds on God, who is really present with us. We might also want to sing a hymn to help us fix our minds on God.

"In heaven" puts us in the reality of the kingdom. We're fooled when we assume that the steering wheel or computer keyboard in front of us is the most real thing in the world. There is an unseen world.

Question 3. It's tempting for Christianity to become an individualized practice and for Christians to regularly pray, "*My* Father," instead of "*Our* Father." We live in community with the world, and they are part of our prayer. Opening a prayer this way reminds us that the great commandment has two parts: to love God and to love others (Mark 12:30-31). Indeed, one cannot love God if he "does not love his brother" (1 John 4:20).

Question 4. Have participants choose one of these or write their own amplification. Then pause the discussion to pray these ideas.

Question 8. As we come to believe in the magnanimous love and wisdom of God, we trust that God's will is the absolute best thing we could ever experience. We no longer see it as drudgery but as fulfillment. We long for it.

Question 9. Ask three participants to read it aloud, each one emphasizing a different word. *Us* points to community. We ask for bread for the whole world. We ask that food be distributed in such a way that those who are starving and malnourished can actually get it—either by access or with money. *Today:* I need to ask only for today because I trust that when I ask again tomorrow, God will provide. *Bread* emphasizes asking only for what is necessary for life so that we live on a "need" level, not a "greed" level. (Try adding, "I'm not asking for cheesecake or steak," and see how that feels!)

Question 10. Human forgiveness is not the basis of divine forgiveness, but it is evidence that a person has accepted the grace of God and is growing in it—and is thereby empowered to forgive others. Once again, love of God and love of others are linked (see question 3).

Question 12. If no phrase impresses a group member, ask what phrase was most interesting.

---

[3]Dallas Willard, *The Divine Conspiracy* (San Francisco: HarperSanFrancisco, 1998), p. 255.

Session 4. Listening to God in Prayer

1 CHRONICLES 14:8-17

FOCUS: Prayer involves bringing our questions to God, being open to God's answers and obeying what we hear.

Question 1. You may wish to comment that the question "Shall I go and attack the Philistines?" would have been a no-brainer for most leaders. The Philistines had raided. It was wise to attack before they were attacked. But David thought God's input was important. No messenger or prophet is named. David simply asked.

And God not only gave a yes-or-no answer, but he supplied David with a battle strategy that would ensure the troops' knowing (and perhaps even the enemy troops' knowing) that something mysterious was going on: "marching in the *tops* of the balsam trees!" (v. 15).

Question 3. Besides destroying their gods, David commented on the victory (v. 11). He saw God as the doer of the action, using himself only as an instrument.

Question 4. David's behavior shows us that God is involved in the here-and-now events of ordinary life.

Question 5. No doubt these men were never the same after such an experience. Most likely they went home and described this to their families for years to come. Yet some might have doubted that God actually marched in the trees, claiming that the sound was a coincidence.

Question 6. Jesus did the same thing in instances such as being asked whether to give money to Caesar or to God. Often a third alternative is appropriate, but we will not consider it unless we "inquire of God."

Question 7. You might wish to talk about how so-called answers from God can be "checked." When in doubt, wait. Find out what wise people think and consider it carefully. See what else comes to you while reading Scripture and listening in prayer.

Question 8. Those who listen to God in prayer do not hurry. They wait because they are trusting God to answer. So they are not hasty or impatient. Their confidence in God gives them an unusual peace.

Question 9. Desiring to listen to God makes times of solitude and silence necessary. To ask God questions will in itself often involve a confession of our inadequacies and past mistakes. Listening to God in prayer is an exercise in submission when we follow through, trusting that God will work even though we don't understand why or how.

Question 10. If this is too personal, state it in vague terms: "solving a problem at work."

Session 5. Interceding as Jesus Did

LUKE 22:31-34

FOCUS: Making intercession means praying for others' oneness with God, not "patching up" folks or getting them to do what we think they should do.

Question 1. The Greek word for *fail* means "to disappear."[4] Jesus prayed that Peter's faith would not disappear or be destroyed by the sifting process. He also prayed that Peter would use his failure

---

[4]I. Howard Marshall, *Commentary on Luke,* New International Greek Testament Commentary (Grand Rapids: Eerdmans, 1978), p. 821.

and his "turning back" to strengthen the others.

Question 3. It's difficult to tell. Since Jesus seemed to use the nickname *Peter,* meaning rock, to give Peter a vision of increased stability of character,[5] perhaps he reverted to *Simon* to speak of his failure. Then he concluded with *Peter* to indicate that Peter would prevail. Or Jesus may have used both names to startle Peter into remembering the time (recorded in John 1:42) when Jesus looked at Peter and changed his name. The word used for "look" is *embelpein,* which "describes a concentrated, intent gaze . . . which does not only see the superficial things that lie on the surface, but which reads a man's heart."[6] Jesus' warning here was another heart-reading moment like the first one.

Question 4. Perhaps as he: faced the amazed and perplexed crowd at Pentecost and preached (Acts 2:12-40), healed a crippled man (Acts 3:4-7), was put in jail (Acts 4:3), or was crucified (as tradition records). If you wish, have participants shut their eyes and picture Jesus saying to them, "I have prayed for you, [your name]." Let them sit this way for a few minutes.

Question 5. Jesus had the power to stop Peter from denying him, but he didn't do this (even in prayer) because, says Dallas Willard, "it would not have advanced Peter toward being the person he needed to become. . . . How earnestly Jesus longed for Peter to come out right in his time of testing! But he left him free to succeed or fail before God and man."[7]

Question 6. When we interfere in what is not our territory: another person's choices; another person's failures through which they can learn from God. Oswald Chambers warns against having so much sympathy for people as you intercede that you lose sight of "God's interest and concern for others and step into having emotional sympathy with them. [Then] the vital connection with God is gone."[8] God's concern is not that the people we love will have a comfortable, problem-free life but that they'll grow in oneness with God.

Question 7. We often come to God with suggestions of how God should remedy a person's plight instead of "getting the *mind of Christ* regarding the person for whom we are praying."[9]

Question 8. Peter relied on his own goodness, saying, "I'd never do that!" In less than twenty-four hours, he gave in to the taunts of a maid and betrayed Jesus. Humility and a cry for help would have been more helpful.

Question 9. Praying Scripture helps us gain the mind of Christ so we can pray for others with more wisdom because we focus on what is important—not their comfortableness or convenience but their growth in Christlikeness. (See Paul's prayers listed in "Transformation Exercises," session 3.) Listening prayer helps us hear what God is saying about others instead of telling God what to do about them.

Question 10. As we learn to align ourselves with God's concerns and how God sees the universe, we acquire the mind of Christ. Then it is safe for God to say to us, "You will receive whatever you ask for."

---

[5]Leo Boles, *A Commentary on the Gospel According to Luke* (Nashville: Gospel Advocate, 1972), p. 419.
[6]William Barclay, *The Gospel of J°ohn* (Philadelphia: Westminster Press, 1956), 1:74.
[7]Dallas Willard, *The Divine Conspiracy* (San Francisco: HarperSanFrancisco, 1998), p. 240.
[8]Oswald Chambers, *My Utmost for His Highest,* updated ed. (Grand Rapids: Discovery House, 1992), May 3 entry.
[9]Ibid., March 30 entry, italics mine.

Session 6. Practicing God's Presence

1 THESSALONIANS 5:16-18

FOCUS: Prayer infuses all of life as we practice the presence of God.

Turning Toward God. One woman's strongest sense of God's presence came while watching the messy, gritty birth of her grandson. Others speak of sensing the marvelous rhythm of interacting with God as they garden, especially putting their fingers in the dirt, pulling out weeds or constructing a compost heap.

Question 1. Several commentators think verses 16-18 are about the inner life while verses 19-22 refer to principles for outward corporate spiritual life.

Question 2. Always, all, continually, every. There is not one thing in our lives that God is not interested in.

Question 4. While many horrifying circumstances are orchestrated by the "prince of this world" (John 12:31), we always have the choice to turn these circumstances over to God so that God can redeem them for good in some way. This begins with surrender and acceptance (although God may give us ideas of how to fight them), so that we become people full of thankfulness and joy.

Question 8. Encourage participants to pray *gently* for each other as they try to answer this question. This will give them a taste of practicing the presence of God.

Section Four

STUDY & MEDITATION

The techniques of Bible study are familiar to many—observing the facts of Scripture, interpreting them in light of their historical and biblical context, and thinking of ways to put them into practice. Meditation on Scripture, however, is very different. Here's a comparison:

In the Study Method, You . . .	In the Meditation Method, You . . .
dissect the text	savor the text and enter into it
ask questions about the text	let the text ask questions of you
read and compare facts and new ways of applying facts	read to let God speak to you (in light of facts already absorbed)

The Bible doesn't instruct us on how to meditate for the same reason it doesn't instruct us on how to fast. These were common spiritual disciplines of the day that folks already knew how to do, or they knew other folks who did. Through the ages, the mechanics of meditation have been kept alive mostly through monastic communities. The two most common methods of meditation are presented in sessions 5-6.

Bible study is an excellent way of setting oneself up for meditation, because through it you come to understand the main point of the Scripture. Still, study does not rule meditation. God may help you choose an obscure word in the passage to ponder or point out a sideline character for you to identify with. Each time you meditate on the passage, it's likely to be different because you will be in a different set of circumstances.

1

IMMERSING YOURSELF IN GOD'S THOUGHTS

DEUTERONOMY 6:1-9

Dead words on a page. That's how folks often approach Bible reading and study. So they long for an "exciting" teacher to make the words "come alive."

Yet the words of Scripture have been God-breathed (2 Timothy 3:16). God uses them to connect with us and communicate to us what genuine goodness is. Inhaling these carefully breathed words of life can transform us into radically different people who think as God thinks and love as God loves. Bible study, then, involves more than examination of facts. It's a communication of who God is and an immersion into God's counsel for living wisely. Each day as we read God's Word, God imparts to us a little more of what we need to know. We can look forward to hearing from God every day as we read Scripture.

Turning Toward God

If you were to read the Bible today mostly out of a sense of obligation—hoping to finish the day's reading quickly or simply to get it done—how would this help you or not help you?

Hearing God Through the Word

In today's passage, Moses reviews God's directives for the nation of Israel so they can live a life of wholeness and goodness as they enter the Promised Land.

"[The Bible] is not only a book which was once spoken, but a book which is now speaking. . . . If you would follow on to know the Lord, come at once to the open Bible expecting it to speak to you. Do not come with the notion that it is a thing which you can push around at your convenience."

A. W. TOZER

Read Deuteronomy 6:1-2.

1. If the Israelites observed the commands of Scripture, what two results would follow?

2. How do these results challenge the common idea that doing what God commands will ruin your life and make it boring (because you'll let the other guy win or you won't get to fool around sexually)?

Read Deuteronomy 6:3.

3. What does the text say would be the results of being "careful to obey" God?

4. How do these first three verses support the idea that God is *for* us, wanting to produce in us a life that is whole and good in the deepest sense?

Read Deuteronomy 6:4-6.

5. What do the statements in these verses reveal about how we relate to God (especially compared to cultural ideas of legalism and obligation)?

6. Why would love for God and trust in God's motives make us more eager to learn what God thinks about our human life and the way it works ("these commandments")?

Read Deuteronomy 6:7-9.

7. How might day-to-day conversations about God and what God wants for us (decrees, laws and commands) help parents connect with God as well as their children?

8. What do these verses tell us about letting our life with God permeate all of our ordinary, mundane activities?

9. How do the truths in verses 1-9 help us know that God is looking for more than a righteousness based only on outward behaviors?

"The Bible is the loving heart of God made visible and plain."

DALLAS WILLARD

10. Second Timothy 3:16 talks about Scripture as being "God-breathed." How would you describe what God is breathing into us through our reading of Scripture?

11. How do you think people who have thoroughly immersed themselves in the wisdom of the Scripture are likely to be different from other folks?

Transformation Exercises

Experiment with one or more of the following.

- Sit in a quiet spot and list situations and locations in your life (committee meeting rooms, relationship with a sister) where your attitude could be transformed by saying aloud or praying to God silently a passage such as one of these:

> As the deer pants for streams of water,
>   so my soul pants for you, O God.
> My soul thirsts for God, for the living God.
>   When can I go and meet with God? . . .
> Why are you downcast, O my soul?
>   Why so disturbed within me?
> Put your hope in God,
>   for I will yet praise him,
>   my Savior and my God. (Psalm 42:1-2, 5-6)

- Pretend to be a poet. List some scrumptious, nurturing, plentiful images for times of reading Scripture to finish this sentence: *Reading Scripture fills me with God the way* . . .

  a clear, majestic day of fishing/surfing does

  a lean, flavorful gourmet meal does

  a baby needing to be rocked and finding contentment in your arms does

  a late-night, close-to-the-bone conversation does

  the disciples burned with truth and wisdom on the road to Emmaus as Jesus explained things

  other:

- Journal about how much you do and don't trust God to do good things in your life. Or make a photo album or video diary showing areas in your life where you do trust God and areas where you need to trust him more. Don't be afraid to admit it if you don't trust God that way but would like to.

- Write Psalm 42:1-2, 5-6 on a small card, and memorize it as you jog or walk, letting the psalmist's words linger in your mind as you reflect on them. Careful crossing the roads!

2

READING AND RESPONDING TO SCRIPTURE

NEHEMIAH 8:1-18; 9:1-3, 38

Compartmentalized. That word describes how we often approach God's Word. We read it (physical act only); we study and interpret it (intellectual only); we sing it (worship only); we apply it (facing our will only). But the elements of processing Scripture—reading it, studying it, meditating on it, waiting in it, worshiping God, delighting in God, praying it back to God—are all of a piece. For the Israelites the reading of the Law was not a one-mode activity. They put all of themselves into it, and they responded with all of themselves. They *absorbed* it.

Turning Toward God

Picture yourself having just read some verses of Scripture. Which thoughts below characterize your most common response to it? (Circle two or three, if you wish.)

- What in the world did that mean?

- I wish I were as smart as So-and-So; then I could understand this.

- I remember a sermon about this passage—now, what did it say this meant?

- I could never do what this passage commands.

- I wish I could be like that person (or ideal) described in the passage.

- That was new!

- I already knew that!

- That's done. Now it's time to take care of the next thing on my to-do list.

- I'm so sleepy . . .

- Other:

"We are to

pray during our

reading so that

God might enable

us to properly

understand

himself and his

will and open to

us one door after

the other into

his Word."

PHILIPP JAKOB
SPENER

Hearing God Through the Word

Today's passage describes a worship service at a peak moment in Israel's history. The remnant of Judah that returned from Persia not only survived but also rebuilt Jerusalem's walls. They worked hard and trusted God well. And God gave them what they had longed for—they were once again safe in their homeland.

Now it was time to continue their conversation with God, and so the Word was read. Let's look at how they processed Scripture. They set an example for us of letting God-breathed words interrupt their lives, with the expectation that God would speak to them. They heard and responded in a variety of ways.

Read Nehemiah 8:1-4.

1. Why are the activities described in verse 1 an appropriate response after God had enabled the Jews to rebuild the walls of Jerusalem in just fifty-two days (Nehemiah 1–7)?

2. Describe the listeners and how they listened.

Read Nehemiah 8:5-9.

3. How did the Jews respond to Ezra's opening the book of the Law?

4. What does the example of Ezra and the Levites' "making [the Law] clear" tell us about what we may need to do when reading Scripture?

_____

5. As the instruction continued, how did the Jews respond (v. 9)?

_____

6. What do these responses from the Jews indicate to you about the importance of expecting to hear from God and responding in some way when Scripture is read?

_____

Read Nehemiah 8:10-18.

_____

7. What did Nehemiah and the Levites urge the people to do instead of to weep? Why was this a good idea?

_____

8. What else did the Jews do in response to the hearing of the Scripture (vv. 14-17)?

_____

Read Nehemiah 9:1-3, 38.

_____

9. In what other ways did the Jews respond to their hearing of Scripture?

_____

10. Which of the following responses to Scripture would you like to try more often? Why?
    ___ praying
    ___ worshiping

"Our modern approach to the Word is sometimes characterized by a certain sterility because it relies more on reason than on wisdom, more on speculative study than on participative knowledge, more on thinking than on praying."

ENZO BIANCHI

___   weeping

___   celebrating

___   confessing sin

11. Why is a person who connects with God through Scripture as the Jews did likely to be changed?

"When in reading

Scripture you

meet with a

passage that

seems to give

your heart a new

motion toward

God, turn it into

the form of a

petition, and give

it a place in your

prayers."

WILLIAM LAW

Transformation Exercises

Experiment with one or more of the following.

- Choose a gesture of response from this passage (such as lifting hands or bowing with your face to the ground, v. 6). As you finish this study, pray to God using that gesture.

- Read Ephesians 1:1-12 aloud slowly. Which word or phrase is most meaningful to you? Why? What does that phrase tell you about how you want to connect with God? If you were to pray phrases from Ephesians 1:1-12 back to God, what would you pray? Here are some starters:

  Open my eyes, O God, to the rich things you're blessing me with that I don't see or understand. (v. 3)

  Thank you, O God, that you loved the idea of me before I was born—even though I tend to think the idea of me is inadequate. (vv. 4-5)

- Journal about the "joy of the Lord" and its relationship to Scripture. Here's an idea to get you started: it is a "joy founded on the feeling of the communion with the Lord, on the consciousness that we have in the Lord a God long-suffering and abundant in goodness and truth."

- Give yourself permission to have a good cry about your relationship with God: how much God loves you; how you may have ignored God; how much God has helped you. Or, in lieu of a cry, go for a walk or run and talk aloud to God.

3

COMPREHENDING
GOD'S TRUTH

ISAIAH 11:1-9

I don't get it" is the phrase we use to indicate that we don't comprehend the meaning of what we read or heard. The purpose of studying the Bible is to "get it." We examine the text carefully to comprehend what the Holy Spirit is communicating through the words on the page. Although the Scripture itself says almost nothing about study, it does urge us to make the effort required to truly hear the Word and follow it, both of which involve comprehension. The goal of studying Scripture is to know God. Genuine study occurs in many ways. One common method is to ask questions about the text such as these.

1. *Gathering basic facts:* What does this passage say? Who is speaking and who is being spoken to? Based on the historical background, what did the author intend for it to say?

2. *Understanding the text:* What does this passage say about what God is like? What does it say about human nature? What does it say about how God relates to people?

3. *Applying the text:* What does the passage suggest about how I might pray? What does it suggest about how I might act?

The first set of questions helps us collect facts in order to answer the second set, which works toward comprehension (or understanding). We connect the dots between this new information and what we already know. Sometimes the new information makes ideas more clear; other times, it contradicts what we already know and challenges us to think more deeply. The third set of questions helps us reflect on the significance of the passage and ask God to show us how it applies to us.

Turning Toward God

In trying to understand the Bible, what is most helpful to you?

Hearing God Through the Word

The questions below follow the flow of the questions in the introduction. The background for this passage is that Isaiah is speaking to the southern kingdom of Judah, who keeps turning its back on God and is soon to be taken into captivity. Besides warning Judah of this, Isaiah also offers hope about the "shoot" or "Branch" (Jesus) that would come from the "stump of Jesse" (the people who would be left after Judah's captivity and return).

"Study provides a certain objective framework within which meditation can successfully function."

RICHARD FOSTER

Read Isaiah 11:1-9.

1. What time period(s) does this passage speak about?
   ___   Old Testament times
   ___   New Testament times
   ___   time yet to come

2. What does Isaiah say that Jesus will be like? (Jesus is referred to as the "shoot" and "Branch.")

3. What characteristic of Christ (vv. 2-5) is important for you today to help you trust Christ more, so he may "dwell [more fully] in your heart through faith" (Ephesians 3:17)?

4. How does Jesus relate to people in this passage, especially verses 3-4?

5. What do you learn about the Trinity in this passage—God the Father, Jesus the Son and the Holy Spirit (vv. 2-3)?

_____

6. How do the various aspects of the Holy Spirit (mentioned in verse 2 and listed below) equip Jesus to be the righteous and faithful doer of justice described in verses 3-5?

   Spirit of wisdom and understanding?

   Spirit of counsel and power?

   knowledge and fear of the Lord?

_____

7. What image (or picture) in this passage is most powerful for you and why?

   ___ a new twig (Christ) blossoms out of a nearly extinct stump (the remnant of Judah that existed in New Testament times) (v. 1)

   ___ Jesus' words are so powerful they act as weapons (v. 4)

   ___ a person (Jesus) so good and devoted that these qualities are fixed in him the way a belt and sash hold clothes on snugly (v. 5)

   ___ a wolf and a lamb (two natural, habitual foes) are perfectly reconciled (v. 6)

   ___ a baby is able to play safely with snakes that were deadly on earth (v. 8)

   ___ another image you find in the passage:

_____

8. Why do you think verses 6-9 are often subtitled "Paradise Regained"?

_____

9. What truth(s) in this passage do you need to absorb more deeply?

10. Consider the truth(s) you mentioned in the previous question. How does it suggest you might pray? How does it suggest you might act?

---

11. How do you need to study the Scripture in a more fruitful way?

Transformation Exercises

Experiment with one or more of the following.

- Before listening to a sermon or beginning a Bible study, ask God to give you openness and humility to see how it might contradict what you already believe and what needs to be corrected in your life.

- Choose a Scripture passage (Sermon on the Mount, 1 John, Psalms 145–150) and read it every day for a month. Pay attention to what you learn each day by jotting down a sentence or two about what you noticed each time.

- Examine Matthew 23:23-29 and John 5:39 to find out how the Pharisees and the teachers of the law managed to study the Scripture so well but miss out on what God was saying.

- Look up (in an encyclopedia or art book) the painting *The Peaceable Kingdom* by Edward Hicks, a Pennsylvania Quaker (1780-1849). Behind the Isaiah 11 scene, the background features William Penn and a group of Native Americans making treaties. Penn is paying them for their lands to strengthen relations with them. Ponder this painting for a while, and ask God to show you who a modern-day Edward Hicks would paint alongside you in the background. With whom do you need to reconcile?

4

MEDITATION
AND OBEDIENCE

PSALM 119:97-104

You've probably heard someone say that the longest distance in the world is from a person's head to a person's heart. What that statement usually means is that to know a fact in your mind does not mean you truly believe it in such a way that your behavior changes. The premise behind this Bible study series is that our behavior changes as we connect with God. When we do the connecting, God does the perfecting.

One of the ways we connect with God is through Scripture, but merely reading Scripture or even studying it is not enough. The connection is extended and made stronger as we meditate on Scripture.

The overlooked discipline of meditation on Scripture is mentioned many times in the Bible—fifteen times in Psalms alone. When Scripture talks about meditation, it often mentions obedience in the next breath: "Do not let this Book of the Law depart from your mouth; *meditate* on it day and night, so that you may be *careful to do everything written in it*. Then you will be prosperous and successful" (Joshua 1:8, emphasis added). The one who meditates becomes one who obeys (being careful to do).

Turning Toward God

If God were to wave a magic wand over you and cause a certain fault to disappear, which one would you like for it to be? Grouchiness? Laziness? Procrastination?

Hearing God Through the Word

Psalm 119 connects meditation and obedience. Words such as meditate, delight and heart (seeking God with all my heart or setting my heart on God's ways) occur often, as do the words statute, law, decree and obey. God does the perfecting as we meditate on Scripture and then let it resonate in our lives all day long.

"The psalmist

in Psalm 119

describes himself

as murmuring

the Scripture,

repeating the

texts interiorly,

reading the

passages of

Scripture again

and again."

ENZO BIANCHI

Read Psalm 119:97-104.

1. What does the psalmist *do* in relation to the law? How does the psalmist *feel* about the law?

2. How is loving the law different from studying the law?

   How are they related?

3. If you were to meditate on God's ideas throughout the activities of your day, what activities would lend themselves to ongoing rumination?

4. What advantages does the psalmist find that meditating on the law brings?

5. The phrases "you yourself have taught me" and "how sweet are your words to my taste" (vv. 102, 103) indicate the psalmist's personal

connectedness with God through the text. What, if any, methods of Bible study or meditation create that for you?

6. Even though the psalmist writes a lot about obedience, it isn't expressed with a cold-hearted, teeth-gritting sense of obligation but with great longing for God. How do you explain this?

7. Think back to your answer to the "Turning Toward God" question. Why would a person who loved God's law and longed for God think that the fault you mentioned is not a helpful thing to do?

8. Which style(s) of meditation fit(s) best with the way you process life?

___ soaking in and absorbing the meanings of words

___ looking for a word or phrase that speaks to you

___ picturing the ideas expressed or scenes described in the passage

___ enjoying how words are combined (such as *obedience* and *meditation*) and "connecting the dots" between these ideas

___ personalizing words of Scripture with specifics by inserting your own everyday activities ("all day long") or common sins ("every evil path") into the text

___ reading the passage aloud and waiting for a word or phrase to resonate

___ reading it aloud and simply resting or waiting

9. If you were to meditate on a passage and then "pray" it back to God during a time of prayer or even a mundane activity, what passage of Scripture would that be?

"It is not that you will think about what you have read, but you will feed upon what you have read. Out of a love for the Lord you exert your will to hold your mind quiet before him. In this peaceful state, swallow what you have tasted . . . take in what is there as nourishment."

JEANNE GUYON

10. Reread Psalm 119:97-104 aloud slowly. Which phrase stands out to you?

What do you believe God is saying to you today?

Transformation Exercises

Experiment with one or more of the following.

- Color-code Psalm 119:97-104 (or all of Psalm 119) according to the following themes. Or use symbols for each theme. You may want to do this on your computer if you can copy the text into a file first.

  heart (seeking God with all, setting the heart) = blue or heart shape

  law, statutes, decrees, commands, obeying = red or circle

  meditating, delighting = green or triangle

  Notice how the themes interrelate, especially how the psalmist doesn't just "learn" decrees and statutes but delights in them and meditates on them (vv. 16, 23).

- Take a walk, bringing along either a Bible or a printed out portion of Scripture. As you walk, put yourself completely into the text and picture yourself as part of it. For example, put yourself into a Gospel story. Imagine yourself as

  the woman with chronic bleeding who longs for a secret healing (Mark 5:25-34; add vv. 21-24 for greater drama)

  the father who only half-believes that Jesus can help his demon-possessed son, but sees Jesus heal the boy anyway (Mark 9:14-27)

5

A BIBLICAL MODEL

LUKE 1:46-55; 1 SAMUEL 2:1-10

One classic method of entering into a Scripture text is called *lectio divina,* which is Latin for "divine reading." Pronounced "lex´-eeoh di-vee´-nuh," it includes reading a Scripture passage aloud, meditating on it, praying about it and contemplating God in it. As the Bible passage is read, we wait for a word to resonate or "shimmer." Then we meditate on that word or phrase to hear what God might have to say to us. After praying about what this means, we rest in quiet contemplation before God.

The key in *lectio* is to be open to hear God afresh in Scripture. That means setting aside previous ideas of how this passage applies to us. With unfamiliar passages, it may help to do a short preliminary study to understand historical background and individual words so we can open ourselves to hear anew from God. If we are truly open, God usually communicates surprising things we could never have made up ourselves.

Turning Toward God

What is a favorite quote, saying or catch-phrase you like to use that you got from a friend or your grandma or a book? Why does it stick with you?

Hearing God Through the Word

Mary, the mother of Jesus, was a "ponderer." After Jesus' birth and the shepherds' visit she "treasured up all these things and pondered them in her heart" (Luke 2:19). After finding the boy Jesus in Jerusalem engaging in deep discussion with religious leaders, Mary "treasured all these things in her heart" (Luke 2:51). She seems to have been good at meditation.

"It is necessary to immerse ourselves in [the Bible], to let it permeate our flesh, to grow so familiar with it that we possess it in the depths of our being and hold it in our memory. A good example is the Magnificat, the Song of Mary. It flows with biblical imagery, clearly the fruit of a heart that knew the Bible."

ENZO BIANCHI

Read Luke 1:46-55.

1. What key words do you see in this passage?

2. Which phrases, if any, seem particularly wise for a teenage Jewish girl to be singing?

Read 1 Samuel 2:1-10.

3. What themes in this passage are similar to the themes in Luke 1:46-55?

4. In what do both women rejoice?

5. As each woman glorifies God in her song, what qualities of God does each woman mention?

6. People have joked that Mary must have had her Old Testament open to Hannah's song when she sang. How do you explain the similarities?

---

7. How are the two songs different?

---

8. How was it possible that Mary could "use" Hannah's song when Mary had not endured similar circumstances (infertility)?

---

9. Reread Luke 1:47-55 aloud. Which word or phrase emerges from the passage and stays with you?

---

10. What is it about that word or phrase that draws you?

---

11. What might God be calling you to *be* through this word or phrase?

---

12. Pray silently and ask God what God might be calling you to *do or refrain from doing* through your being drawn to this word or phrase. Then wait quietly, enjoying God's presence.

---

13. In what situation or frame of mind might the word or phrase from this passage be helpful to recall?

"The Great Inversion [means that] there are none in the humanly 'down' position so low that they cannot be lifted up by entering God's order, and none in the humanly 'up' position so high that they can disregard God's point of view on their lives. The barren, the widow, the orphan, the eunuch, the alien, all models of human hopelessness, are fruitful and secure in God's care."

DALLAS WILLARD

Transformation Exercises

Experiment with one or more of the following.

- In a private place, sing a song you know by heart (as Mary probably knew Hannah's song). Sing it several times, and let the words of the song deepen within you. If you know American Sign Language, sign the words as you sing.

- Pick a scriptural phrase you have studied in the past. Rest in it, wait in it and delight in it (but don't analyze it) as you do a physical activity such as mowing the lawn or vacuuming a room.

- Read Genesis 1 and Psalm 8. Compare the ideas and specific words. (Some think Psalm 8 was written as a result of meditating on Genesis 1.) Try meditating on Genesis 1 and writing your own psalm of meditation.

- Pick a passage of Scripture that speaks to you but is not so familiar that it cannot be fresh. Read it aloud to yourself and answer questions 9-13 above.

"We come to the [Bible] text with an openness to hear, to receive, to respond, to be a servant of the Word rather than a master of the text."

ROBERT
MULHOLLAND

6

ENTERING A
GOSPEL SCENE
MARK 10:17-23

Another common method of meditating on Scripture is to use the imagination and enter the biblical scene as an observer—a fly on the wall or a bystander in the crowd. This common method is explained well in *The Spiritual Exercises of St. Ignatius Loyola*, which urges participants to make use of the five senses. So we imagine what we would see, hear, smell, touch or taste if we had been present in the biblical scene. As we hear the dialogue of the text, we need to let God speak to us, asking us questions, challenging us or comforting us.

This imagination-oriented method is *word*-centered. The exact words of Scripture coach your imagination. Like *lectio divina*, certain words or phrases stand out, but in this method we imagine hearing these words said or saying them ourselves.

Are you reluctant to use your imagination for spiritual growth? C. S. Lewis said that reading George MacDonald's fantasies "converted" or "baptized" his imagination. Let meditating on Scripture baptize yours.

Turning Toward God

When, if ever, has someone confronted you in a loving, genuine way?

Hearing God Through the Word

As you read this text, picture Jesus in conversation with the rich young ruler. Close your eyes. Can you imagine the look on Jesus' face as he loved someone yet challenged him?

"Once, the Bible

was just so

many words to

us—'clouds and

darkness'—then,

suddenly, the

words become

spirit and life

because Jesus

re-speaks them

to us when our

circumstances

make the words

new."

OSWALD CHAMBERS

Read Mark 10:17-22.

1. How would you describe the manner of the rich young ruler as he approached Jesus?

2. What do you make of Jesus' answer about what a person must do to inherit eternal life?

3. Based on Jesus' behavior and words, what seems to have been in his heart when he replied to the young man (v. 21)?

4. What spiritual crisis seems to have occurred within this young man (v. 22)?

Reread Mark 10:17-23 aloud.

5. If you put yourself in the place of the young man as he approaches Jesus, how do you feel as you ask the initial question about inheriting eternal life (v. 17)?

6. Try to picture the moment when Jesus answers the young man. What expression do you see on Jesus' face?

What tone do you detect in his voice?

---

7. Imagine that you're the young man. What does it feel like inside to be invited to be a follower of this great teacher, Jesus, but to be unable to make the choice that will allow you to do so?

---

8. What is the most stunning thing to you about this passage?

___ Jesus invited the young man to be a follower.

___ Jesus' ability to be unyieldingly firm, but with great love.

___ Jesus' unwillingness to minimize or strike a deal—his insistence that discipleship involves complete reliance on God.

___ Other:

---

9. What is God saying to you today through this passage?

___ Give up this thing that blocks your reliance on me.

___ Take another small step toward giving up this thing I've asked you to give up many times before.

___ Hear the love in my voice even as I confront you.

___ I still want you as a follower, in spite of . . .

___ You won't know the treasure of heaven here on earth until you've . . .

___ Look at the people around you—they're more important than the physical things you treasure.

___ Other:

"You seek to allow the text to begin to become that intrusion of the Word of God in to your life, to address you, to encounter you at deeper levels of your being."

ROBERT MULHOLLAND

10. How might your relationship with God be affected if you practiced this sort of meditation?

Transformation Exercises

Experiment with one or more of the following.

- Retell your favorite Bible story (to yourself if no one else), but put yourself in the main character's place and tell it as if it were about you.

- Read Luke 13:10-13 and act it out. Take the role of the main character and imagine you've been crippled for eighteen years. You're sitting in the synagogue, completely bent over, listening to the teacher. Get up and walk bent over at least eighteen steps—one for every year. Walk to the front of the synagogue bent over (the length of a large room) as Jesus calls you forward. Hear Jesus' voice free you from your infirmity. Feel Jesus' hands on you, releasing it. Straighten up and praise God. What do you say? How do you feel?

"A text may have a different significance or import for me each time I turn to it . . . for the Lord will speak to me where I am."

THELMA HALL

- Journal about the idea of your imagination's being baptized. How could this save you from repeated sins? How could this change your behavior?

STUDY NOTES FOR
STUDY AND MEDITATION

Session 1. Immersing Yourself in God's Thoughts

DEUTERONOMY 6:1-9

FOCUS: We need to become thoroughly familiar with Scripture, not just for the sake of knowledge but to connect with God and be coached by God on how to live a life of wholeness. This won't happen, however, unless we trust that God genuinely loves us and that scriptural commands are the keys to the best possible life on earth.

Question 1. They would fear the Lord and enjoy long life. This helps us see that knowledge of Scripture is not a goal in itself but God's coaching for wise living. *Coaching* is an appropriate word because God comes alongside us in Scripture, offering instruction, models and encouragement.

Question 2. We struggle to believe that God offers us the best possible life, of a sort of goodness that is appealing. The enemy of our soul convinces us that God is a killjoy, when God is actually the giver of real joy. Obeying God isn't difficult: Scripture helps us connect with God, and so the "burden is light" (Matthew 11:30).

Question 3. Things would go well with them, and their lives would flow with untold benefits in the Promised Land.

Question 4. With a holy, healthy fear of God (v. 2), we look to God as the One who loves us completely and holds the keys to the transformed life. Observing God's commands wipes away the falseness we gravitate toward and leads us to live in wholeness. God's commands teach us how to build genuine relationships with others. They do not lead to a horrible life of depriving ourselves of the goodies we want.

Question 5. God was not like the false Canaaanite gods who required capricious acts of worship (such as sacrificing children). Verse 5 makes it clear that the Old Testament is not a collection of rules with no emphasis on relationship with God. Obedience is not found in constantly focusing on self and behavioral failures but in thoroughly immersing oneself in God: heart, soul and strength. Says J. A. Thompson, "Obedience was not to spring from a barren legalism based on necessity and duty. It was to arise from a relationship based on love."[1]

Question 6. To obey God in a full-hearted way requires a belief that God can be trusted to meet our needs, to care for us, not to do us harm. We

---

[1] J. A. Thompson, *Deuteronomy,* Tyndale Old Testament Commentaries (Downers Grove, Ill.: InterVarsity Press, 2008), p. 138.

need to trust that we won't have to lie or commit adultery to get our needs met. If we truly believe God has what we need and can meet our needs, we're more eager to read Scripture.

Question 7. Talking about God to a child can help adults simplify difficult concepts such as omnipotence and atonement and focus on basic but central truths (God loves you, God wants you to love and obey). This thinking process helps parents as well as children.

Question 8. Constant exposure to God's words creates an ongoing conversation between God and the reader. God becomes "the subject of conversation both inside and outside the home, from the beginning of the day to the end of the day. . . . The commandments were to permeate every sphere

of the life of man."[2] We begin to trust that God speaks to us regularly through the Word.

Question 9. Obedience flows from the central motive and activity: to love God with everything you've got. It involves having the textured heart of a deeply good person.

Question 10. God is transforming our souls, "draw[ing] men into Christ, to make them little Christs,"[3] to make people the "same kind of thing as himself."[4]

Question 11. Because they're coming to know God, they are developing a deep-down wisdom and goodness, void of pretension or religiosity.

Session 2. Reading and Responding to Scripture

NEHEMIAH 8:1-18; 9:1-3, 38

FOCUS: When Scripture is read, we respond in many ways, including praying, worshiping, weeping, celebrating and confessing sin.

Turning Toward God. Keep this lighthearted with your own answers, such as imitating how we fall asleep or try to remember what a favorite radio preacher said.

Hearing God Through the Word. If reading aloud, you may say the first letter of the names in verses 4 and 7 instead of trying to pronounce them.

Question 1. The Jews had experienced God as their helper. This made them hungry for more of God and more eager to discover how to live as God prescribed.

Question 2. This group included men, women and anyone who could understand—probably

older children. They listened attentively.

Question 3. See verse 6. They stood up. They lifted their hands. They bowed their heads and worshiped with faces on the ground. They *responded*—they seem to have been praying.

Question 4. Ezra and the Levites seem to have offered explanations of Scripture, but "making it clear" also included translating it for those who spoke only Aramaic. They set an example of diligence in Scripture reading, or "rightly dividing the word of truth" (2 Timothy 2:15 NKJV).

To help make Scripture clear to ourselves, we may need to examine the background of a passage and compare it with other passages to understand the "whole counsel of God" (Acts 20:27 NKJV). Using a commentary and reading parallel passages

---

[2]Peter C. Craigie, *The Book of Deuteronomy,* New International Commentary on the Old Testament (Grand Rapids: Eerdmans, 1976), p. 170.

[3]C. S. Lewis, *Mere Christianity* (New York: Macmillan, 1970), p. 169.

[4]Ibid., p. 162.

are helpful. Noticing the theme of the passage and how each verse relates to that are very important.

This passage will show that studying Scripture is an important preliminary activity, serving the goal of knowing God and interacting with this living God. Then I open the Bible with anticipation that God is going to impart to me today what I need to know.

Question 5. They wept. They experienced what is described in Hebrews 4:12: "For the word of God is living and active. Sharper than any double-edged sword, it penetrates even to dividing soul and spirit, joints and marrow; it judges the thoughts and attitudes of the heart."

Question 6. To read Scripture without this expectation is to neglect to let these God-breathed words interrupt our lives so that God can teach us, rebuke us, correct us and train us (2 Timothy 3:16).

Question 7. Nehemiah urged them to celebrate, but this was not mere revelry but a "joy founded on the feeling of the communion with the Lord, on the consciousness that we have in the Lord a God long-suffering and abundant in goodness and truth."[5] The Levites urged them to "be still" as in Psalm 46:10, "Be still, and know that I am God."

Any time people understand "the words . . . made known to them" in Scripture (v. 12), a dramatic response such as this celebration is appropriate. Scriptural clarity challenges our will, and we need to respond. The consequences of not doing so are described in the old saying "Impression without expression causes depression."

Question 8. These returned exiles built booths and lived in them, celebrating the Feast of Booths as it had not been celebrated since the time of Joshua. This feast was a harvest festival, commemorating the beginning of the forty years of wandering in the wilderness (Exodus 23:16). During the festival, people lived in tents or booths in Jerusalem to remind themselves of how their ancestors lived as they wandered. However, it was a joyous festival, full of games and dancing.

Question 9. They confessed their sins and worshiped God. They made written agreements with each other about how they would behave in the future. It's as if they said, "What I heard leads me to do . . . Help me." In *Praying the Word* Enzo Bianchi advises, "You should make some practical resolutions which are based on your state in life and your position in society, always allowing the Word to be the guiding force in your life."[6]

Question 10. Someone might protest that these must be spontaneous and cannot be planned. But they can be deliberate responses to Scripture. Weeping or celebration may not come automatically, but we can journal about reasons the Scripture we read might make us want to weep or celebrate.

Question 11. Back-and-forth conversation with God through Scripture reading builds a relationship that changes a person where simple efforts to obey commands will not.

---

[5]C. F. Keil, *Commentary on the Old Testament*, vol. 3, *I and II Kings, I and II Chronicles, Ezra, Nehemiah, Esther* (Grand Rapids: Eerdmans, 1973), p. 232.
[6]Enzo Bianchi, *Praying the Word* (Kalamazoo, Mich.: Cistercian Publications, 1998), p. 81.

Session 3. Comprehending God's Truth

ISAIAH 11:1-9

FOCUS: We study Scripture to comprehend what the Holy Spirit is communicating through it to give us a better knowledge of God.

Turning Toward God. Ask which methods or attitudes or settings help most. Be open to ideas other than those in the introduction. Because people have different styles of learning, different approaches work, such as analytical methods of Bible study; reading commentaries; interacting with others to stimulate thinking; simple, common-sense approaches taken by a particular speaker or a series of studies; coming up with hunches from a passage and following up with other passages to see if those hunches are true; connecting truth in Scripture to truth in art and literature.

Question 1. All three. Isaiah is speaking to Judah in Old Testament times about their upcoming captivity. His message is about Jesus' appearance in New Testament times and about time everlasting—the "peaceable kingdom" of heaven (vv. 6-9).

Question 2. The Spirit of the Lord will rest on Jesus and Jesus will delight in the fear of the Lord. Jesus will not be fooled by outward appearances but will judge with integrity based on righteousness and faithfulness.

Question 4. (This question begins the second cycle of observe, interpret and apply questions.) Jesus looks on the heart, not outward appearances (1 Samuel 16:7). The word translated "judge" in verse 4 is better understood as "do justice to."

The poor and the humble—who do not "catch a break"—will finally get the help and respect they need. (Studying the meaning of words in their original language can help us.)

The odd picture in the last phrase of verse 4 is understood better when we remember who is speaking. Prophets such as Isaiah spoke to distracted people. They were not listened to, so they often used arresting, even odd, word pictures to get listeners' attention. Isaiah referred to Jesus' words and breath, though not physical entities, as being so strong they would be capable of punishment and death.

Question 5. The Spirit rests on Jesus who then delights in but stands in awe of God the Father. You might ask participants if this enlightens or contradicts their current understanding of the Trinity. Honest study requires that we remain open to the Scriptures contradicting what we already know or think. Reconciling seeming contradictions often helps us think more clearly and understand more of God's infinite greatness.

Question 6. See ideas in the chart below.

Question 9. Here are some ideas:

• God brings redemption and reconciliation (Jesus) out of failure (the remnant of Judah)

• the community of the Trinity: the Spirit interacts with Jesus in the fear of God (v. 2)

• God judges not by outward appearance but with true rightness and justice

• in the kingdom of God, bitter enemies (includ-

What Jesus is like	This equips Jesus to be
Spirit of wisdom and understanding	guide for his people
Spirit of counsel and power	guardian for his people
knowledge and fear of the Lord	example for his people

ing those in the animal world) no longer have fierce conflicts but live together peaceably

Transformation Exercises. Encourage participants to try all of them. The second exercise is helpful for those who learn better through rep-

etition rather than asking formal questions. The third one is for those who love looking for clues and drawing conclusions. The last exercise may help those who are more visual or imaginative or who love comparisons.

Session 4. Meditation and Obedience

PSALM 119:97-104

FOCUS: Because meditation on Scripture is one more way to connect with God, it leads to obedience.

Turning Toward God. Confess a fault or two of your own to get them started. If you wish, lighten up the tone first by rewording the question to end with, "what fault would your mother or your spouse or your roommate like for it to be?"

Question 1. You may wonder what "the law" is that we love and meditate on. "The law" refers to the Ten Commandments, but "the entire law is summed up in a single command: 'Love your neighbor as yourself'" (Galatians 5:14). New Testament passages such as the Sermon on the Mount (Matthew 5–7), Colossians 3:1-17 and Romans 12:9-21 explain the nitty-gritty of the law—how to become the kind of person who obeys the law—not placing anything before God, not taking God's name in vain, not murdering people even in our thoughts.

If someone protests that Christians are not "under the law," explain that Christ's coming, death and resurrection fulfilled the law but did not abolish it. Although we are *justified* by grace (not the law), the law is now a pathway to grace through the Holy Spirit. Paul's words in Romans 7:22 resemble Psalm 119:97: "For in my inner being I delight in God's law."

What we avoid is trying to be justified by lawkeeping or being self-righteous about obeying God's commands (Galatians 5:4; Luke 11:52). If further discussion is required, set aside another

time to look at Romans 7:4-12, 8 and Galatians 3, 5.

Question 2. Having studied the law and found a treasure, one loves it by thinking about it and giving up everything else to bask in it. (Consider the parable of the man who found the treasure buried in the field and gave up everything to have it. How he must have pondered it! Imagined himself owning it! Thought about how wonderful the treasure was! Wondered that he was going to own it himself!) Loving the law is like this. It is worth the time to bask in a Scripture and taste and see that the Lord is good.

Question 3. Physical activities, especially walking, running, riding a bike or gardening, are excellent. In fact, you can train yourself to do this by doing these activities after you spend time soaking in the Word and loving it. Sometimes relatively mindless activities work well—running errands, mowing the lawn, washing dishes.

Question 5. If few participants have an answer, ask if any have experienced connecting with God through Scripture and, if so, to tell about it.

Question 6. Meditation is a very relational discipline in which you give yourself—your imagination and inner brooding—to God. God can use that part of yourself to teach you to long for all that God is.

Question 7. You might want to mention that someone who loves God's law is convinced that God's principles for goodness are not only to be cherished (v. 103) but also give exceptional wisdom.

Question 9. Encourage participants to choose passages they've recently studied and understood. Or familiar passages (the Lord's Prayer, Psalm 23) can be excellent.

Question 10. Offer to read the passage aloud at this time and let participants rest in the passage and then write their answers. Allow at least seven to ten minutes.

Session 5. A Biblical Model

LUKE 1:46-55; 1 SAMUEL 2:1-10

FOCUS: What comes out of our mouths is a result of what we meditate on. This seems to have happened to Mary in her song that flowed from Hannah's song. The *lectio divina* method helps us follow Mary's example.

Question 1. Before the passage is read, you may wish to do two things.

1. Point out that Mary sang this song when she was pregnant with Jesus. She had gone to visit her cousin Elizabeth, and after Elizabeth called her "mother of my Lord" (v. 43), she responded with this song.

2. Read this first question so that participants can listen for themes as the Scripture is read.

The question is for brainstorming purposes only. Write down the themes that are mentioned for use later. After the question is read, ask the group to hold their place in Luke 1.

Question 3. Before the passage is read, you may wish to note that this is a song sung by Hannah, a previously infertile woman who asked God for a son and later gave birth to Samuel.

Question 5. Mary sings that God's name is holy (v. 49). Hannah says no one is holy like God (v. 2). She also says that God is unique and a rock. They are both marveling at God's initiative and God's actions, which demonstrate God's power.

Question 6. Many believe Mary was singing from her heart based on what had been cultivat-
ed there through meditating on Hannah's song. (Mary also borrows phrases from several psalms, including Psalm 138:6; 71:19; 111:9; 103:17; 98:1; 107:9; 98:3; 132:11.) Noting the similarities between the women's songs, commentator Norval Geldenhuys writes, "All pious Israelites from their childhood days knew by heart songs from the Old Testament and often sang them in the home circle and at celebrations. Mary was steeped in the poetical literature of her nation, and accordingly her hymn also bears the unmistakable signs of it."[7]

Question 7. Geldenhuys points out, "While Mary sings her happiness with deep humility and holy reserve, Hannah completely surrenders herself to a feeling of personal triumph over her enemies. Where Mary borrowed expressions from the Old Testament, she gives to the consecrated words a deep meaning and higher application."[8]

Question 8. Although Mary's situation was different, she identified with many of the scriptural truths expressed in Hannah's song. When Scripture has been meditated upon and "written in the heart," it has personal meaning and can be transferred and personalized to many situations.

Question 9. Before reading the passage aloud, ask participants to shut their eyes. If you wish, read aloud the Mulholland quote on page 138. To benefit especially the men in the group, preface the reading by saying something about how this pas-

---

[7]Norval Geldenhuys, *The Gospel of Luke,* New International Commentary on the New Testament (Grand Rapids: Eerdmans, 1977), p. 85.
[8]Ibid.

sage can be a song for women *and* men who have had no reason to think God would choose to use them in any way.

Then have the passage read aloud slowly, with equal weight given to each word. Urge participants to wait quietly in the silence afterward to see what word resonates or shimmers. You may want to add this idea from Robert Mulholland: "You may find yourself in a 'holding pattern' on just one sentence [or one word]."[9] After a few minutes, ask them to share that word with the group.

Question 10. Urge participants to close their eyes again and ponder.

Question 12. Allow several minutes of quiet so that participants may pray and have a few moments of contemplation. Then ask them to open their eyes and prepare themselves to discuss the next question.

Question 13. Explain that not all participants will have an answer. We sometimes understand the importance of a word or phrase only by waiting on God for a longer period of time, maybe even a few days.

Session 6. Entering a Gospel Scene

MARK 10:17-23

FOCUS: The detailed scene of the rich young ruler is ideal for the Ignatian sort of meditation, using the imagination. We can jump into the scene and let Jesus speak directly to us.

Turning Toward God. When we're confronted, it's often in a mean-spirited tone. But a loving confrontation can have a transforming effect on us.

Question 1. He ran up to meet Jesus with enthusiasm even though Jesus was "on his way." He fell before him, which would indicate one of two things. Either he truly adored Jesus from watching him and hearing him, or he was being obsequious and fawning, making a big fuss over Jesus. Commentator Will Lane chooses the former: "The eager approach of a man while Jesus was setting out on his way, his kneeling posture, the formal address together with the weighty character of his question—all suggest deep respect for Jesus and genuine earnestness on the part of the man himself."[10] (Parallel passages tell us the man was young [Matthew 19:20] and a ruler [Luke 18:18].)

Question 2. Jesus was not at odds with the law. He saw in the Old Testament law the key components of discipleship. Jesus seems to be drawing the man forward by appealing to the law, with which the young man is quite familiar. He is putting his finger on the man's hunger. If someone comments on Jesus' refusal to accept the descriptor *good,* you might reply with this clarification by Will Lane: "In the Old Testament and subsequent Judaism only God is characteristically called 'good,' although it was possible to speak in a derived sense of 'the good man' (Prov. 12:2; 14:14, others)."[11]

Question 3. Jesus' look of love communicates that he had a tender heart of love and that he was skilled at speaking the truth in love (Ephesians 4:15). Also, Jesus must have had a high opinion of the young man, since he invited him to become a follower! Still, Jesus was tough, insisting the young man would have to do what the Twelve had done—abandon everything to follow him.

Question 4. Initially so eager to please Jesus, he was giving up the invitation to become a follower because he couldn't let go of something he loved more.

---

[9]Robert Mulholland, *Shaped by the Word* (Nashville: Upper Room, 2000), p. 55.
[10]William Lane, *The Gospel According to Mark,* New International Commentary on the New Testament (Grand Rapids: Eerdmans, 1975), p. 364.
[11]Ibid.

No wonder his face fell. Says Hugh Anderson: "Since this man is captive to what the world has offered him he is not free to receive God's offer [of discipleship], vexed though he is to say No to it."[12]

Question 5. Before reading the passage aloud (even if you're doing the study by yourself), explain that the previous three questions helped the group study the basic words and ideas of the text. Now it's time to read the text again and *enter into* it.

If you wish, ask participants to shut their eyes and imagine themselves as this young man before they answer. He seems to have been very confident: "The inquirer's idea of goodness was defined by human achievement. He regarded himself as 'good' in that he had fulfilled the commandments. . . . Now he hopes to discover from another 'good' man what he can do to assure eternal life."[13]

If you have time after answering this question, ask participants to put themselves in the place of some disciples standing by. Are they embarrassed by this boy's kneeling or his bold interruption?

Question 6. Participants will need to close their eyes to picture an expression on Jesus' face based on the words of the text. The words *loved him* "may denote either that [Jesus] openly showed affection by putting his arms around him or had the pro-

foundest sympathy for his need."[14] A certain earnestness in Jesus is appropriate too, given that he invites the young man to be one of his followers.

Question 7. Suggest that participants try letting their own faces move from expressions of eagerness to disappointment to see how that facial movement affects them inside. It must have been an episode of roller-coaster emotions: first the youth's intense enthusiasm and devotion, then his disappointment.

Question 9. Ask participants to close their eyes. Explain that you're going to read the passage aloud to them once more, then ask the question. Urge them not to jump at an easy answer or feel as if they have to make something up. When we sit quietly before God, God often has surprising things to say to us. They may want to ask themselves: *What question is God asking me through this text?*

After you've asked the question and waited a few minutes, ask participants to share their answers. If "nothing" came to them, that's fine. The quiet provided them a moment to simply enjoy the presence of God.

---

[12]Hugh Anderson, *The Gospel of Mark,* New Century Bible Commentary (Grand Rapids: Eerdmans, 1981), p. 250.
[13]Lane, *Gospel According to Mark,* p. 365.
[14]Anderson, *Gospel of Mark,* p. 249.

Section Five

COMMUNITY & SUBMISSION

The spiritual discipline of community (or fellowship) is not as warm and fuzzy as it sounds. It's about committing ourselves to people and sticking it out, no matter what. The bond is cemented by practicing other disciplines in community such as confession, prayer, service and study. Community can be practiced in various settings: a family, a friendship, a small group, a local church, a work or volunteer setting, a denomination, the church universal. However, attending a local church does not necessarily mean you practice community, although it can help you get started.

For community to occur, we need to be intentional. In fact, contemporary Western society tends to be hostile to things communal, exalting individualism and rewarding independence: "We don't know how to trust one another, how to support one another in pain, how to disagree in love, how to genuinely respect one another, how to be 'for' each other in the long haul," writes Norvene Vest.

Community is interwoven with the discipline of submission. To submit to others is to offer them community—even if you don't like them, if they don't deserve it, or if they're wrong. Community exists only with vulnerability, which is at the core of submission. Essentially, we submit ourselves to God. In the cleanness of heart God brings, we bend to submit to others as God would have us do so, not with the purpose of people-pleasing or trying to get ahead.

A word of clarification and hope: My prayer is that sessions 3, 4 and 5 of these studies will de-junk the word *submission*. In the analysis and discussion of gender roles, the general practice of submission has been eclipsed. These studies examine community and submission in the broadest sense: "Be subject to one another out of reverence for Christ" (Ephesians 5:21 NRSV). Such mutual submission is difficult for all of us; such submission is transforming for all of us.

1

INTENTIONAL
COMMUNITY

MATTHEW 26:36-45

Pretend it is before the time Jesus came to earth. You are an angel and a member of the Redemption Strategy Team. Your input is requested: how do you think the gospel should be spread? Will it work to let generations of human creatures so frequently self-centered, discouraged and confused about the gospel's meaning be strategically involved in communicating the gospel?

When you consider that Jesus had three short years to set the plan of redemption in place, it's amazing that he spent so much time hanging out with an entourage of simple men and women. By this choice, Jesus set in place the centrality of community. Through it, the disciples learned the discipline of trusting and submitting to other people, imitating the persons of the Trinity who do not haggle for authority. Dallas Willard says, "God is in himself a sweet society of love, with a first, second, and third person to complete a social matrix where not only is there love and being loved, but also shared love for another." Because of who God is, there is no such thing as private or individual Christianity.

The diversity among the disciples tells us that community is never about like thinkers patting each other on the back. (Imagine a *discussion* between Simon the Jewish political zealot and Matthew the tax-collecting puppet of the Roman government.) One of the best ways to learn to truly love others (and thus let God change our character) is to work side by side with someone who "needs to grow up!" As we continually surrender such persons to God, we allow God to speak to us through them, and we learn to treat them as we would treat Christ himself (Matthew 25:40). Is this really possible? Definitely, as we train ourselves behind the scenes by practicing community and mutual submission on a regular basis.

Turning Toward God

In what ways do other people help us connect with God?

Hearing God Through the Word

Read Matthew 26:36-38.

1. Describe what happens in this scene.

"Others can do

for us what we

cannot do for

ourselves and one

can paddle every

canoe except

one's own."

C. S. LEWIS

2. Based on what you know of the Gospels, why would Jesus have separated Peter, James and John from the group to sit closer to him while he prayed?

3. Usually we are tempted to push away those who brag and act spiritually arrogant. What does Jesus' example of love show us to do instead?

4. If you had been one of these three disciples with Jesus in the darkness of this familiar olive orchard, how might you have responded to hearing your leader admit: "My soul is overwhelmed with sorrow to the point of death" (v. 38)?

Read Matthew 26:39-41.

5. How would you put Jesus' prayer in your own words?

6. What does it tell us that, when Jesus prayed this difficult prayer, he addressed God with the affectionate, down-to-earth Aramaic term *Abba*—wording so ordinary that "to the Jewish mind the use of this familiar household term would have been considered disrespectful in prayer"?

_____

7. What reason did Jesus give the disciples for why they should stay awake (v. 41)?

Read Matthew 26:42-45.

_____

8. How did Jesus show love for his disciples in this scene? How did he show respect and submission (not imposing his will on them)?

_____

9. Where on this continuum are you in your attitude toward what the will of God is like?

_____

a horrible thing   the most positive
to be endured   possibility to pursue

_____

10. What do people desire from church that shows they hold mistaken ideas about what community involves? That church people should

___ be best buddies

___ agree on most issues

___ have interests in common

___ other:

"*Others . . .*

become agents

of grace in our

growth toward

wholeness in

Christ while we

become agents

of God's grace in

their growth."

ROBERT
MULHOLLAND

11. Think of a current situation of community for you (family, friendship, small group, local church, work or volunteer setting). Which of the following descriptions of community are helpful to you as you interact with that community?

___ Community is "the constant recognition of the Spirit of God in each other."

___ In community, we "reveal to each other the real presence of God in our midst."

___ "Celebrating together, working together, playing together—these are all ways in which the discipline of community can be practiced."

___ "But whatever its concrete shape or form, the discipline of community always points us beyond the boundaries of race, sex, nationality, character, or age, and always reveals to us who we are before God and for each other."

"God has willed that we should seek and find His living Word in the witness of a brother, in the mouth of man. . . . He needs him again and again when he becomes uncertain and discouraged."

DIETRICH
BONHOEFFER

12. Which of the transformation exercises would be most helpful for letting God work within you?

Transformation Exercises

Experiment with one or more of the following.

- Talk to someone about forming an intentional friendship where you meet weekly or biweekly. You may wish to show them some of these comments made by Friends (Quakers) involved in Spiritual Friendship groups:

  "It's very intentional. I can get to the heart of the matter. I really like having that time set aside just to compare notes and ask about, What do you pray for?"

  "Being a Spiritual Friend to someone else is a great privilege . . . to come to know about someone's personal struggle with the Spirit. It does not require great wisdom, just good listening, openness, and a willingness to hold the person in the light."

"There is always that permission to open the spiritual dimension and not have that be awkward or considered unconventional."

- Look back on opportunities for community you've previously experienced. Journal (or talk with someone) about what you did that helped build community and what you would need to do more of (or better) next time. Another option is to make a photo album or video diary depicting ways you've experienced community.

- Encourage or simply grin at someone who behaves in a spiritually arrogant way. Say nothing to them, but do pray for them.

- Study the community relationship of the Trinity in Luke 10:22-23; John 3:34-36; 6:57-63 and 14:14-17; Galatians 4:4-6; and 1 John 4:6-15; 5:5-8. Look for themes such as love and truth. What other themes do you find?

2

THE GRITTINESS
OF COMMUNITY

1 CORINTHIANS 12:12-27

Perhaps few spiritual disciplines are as misunderstood as community. We envision community as folks standing around a campfire holding hands and singing. While there may be moments of warm feelings, community as a discipline is about loving folks you prefer to ignore. It's about including people the church doesn't (seem to) need or even the disgruntled folks you secretly think the church would be better off without.

Today's passage underscores the grittiness of Christian community. Folks who have nothing in common talk and work alongside each other until some of their sharp edges are rounded off. Eventually you treasure this person who could not be more different from you.

Christ insists that we need each other. And we do—the viewpoint of the other person helps us climb out of our narrow world and learn what it means to love another person just a little bit.

When C. S. Lewis became a Christian, he initially resisted being a part of a church. For example, he disliked the hymns, which he regarded as "fifth-rate poems." Eventually, however, Lewis began to understand that the church is not a human organization but the "Body of Christ where people share the common life, complementing and helping one another precisely by their differences." That happens as we submit to God, trusting that we really do need these odd people, and —gulp—submit to them as well.

Turning Toward God

We often confuse Christian community with special friendships, which have different kinds of benefits and qualities. When have you experienced Christian community as described below?

Christian Community	Special Friendships
You disagree but still listen to each other.	You know what the other is thinking.
You're committed to listening to God's call on each other's life.	You agree on almost everything.
You're committed to praying for each other.	You say just what the other needs to hear.
Side by side with others, you give gifts of service.	You give each other special gifts.
When you're angered you walk away, process it with God and consider how God is using that person in your life.	You get upset with each other but work it out.
You have many differences with this person.	You love to do the same activities.
You're astounded at how God uses such ordinary relationships in your life.	You're astounded at what good friends you are.

Hearing God Through the Word

Read 1 Corinthians 12:12-19.

1. What do all parts of the body of Christ have in common?

2. In what ways are members of the body of Christ different?

3. How do some people complete this sentence (even if just in their minds)? "I'm not much use to the church because . . ." or "I'm not much use to God because . . ."

4. If similarities and achievements are not what pulls people together, what does?

Read 1 Corinthians 12:20-25.

5. In what ways do we often treat certain parts of the body of Christ as more valuable?

In what ways do we treat certain parts as less valuable?

6. What does it mean to consider weak folks indispensable, to honor the less honorable and to treat unpresentable folks with special modesty?

Read 1 Corinthians 12:26-27.

7. Imagine for a moment that someone is stepping hard on your toe, but you are not allowed to move a muscle in your face or utter a noise. What would you have to say mentally to your toe or to your face muscles to make this happen? When have you been that injured toe in the body of Christ?

8. How is it an act of submission to suffer with others and rejoice with those who are honored?

9. Community comes about as people act as iron sharpening iron in an atmosphere of love and submission (Proverbs 27:17). How can Christians "sharpen" each other?

10. What attitudes of love are important to express if community is to flourish when we discuss differences with each other (1 Corinthians 13:4-7)?

11. What steps do you need to take to be more resilient when community gets gritty?

___ have a more realistic view of community (see "Turning Toward God" question)

___ understand that you have value to others even though you don't feel you're very useful to others

___ value those with spiritual gifts different from yours

___ suffer with those who suffer and rejoice with those who are honored

___ show more love

___ other:

Transformation Exercises

Experiment with one or more of the following.

- Put your hand on a bruise or scar or place on your body that was formerly injured badly. Thank God for the healing that has taken place (or currently is happening). Thank God for the way this will enable your whole person to move forward in life without delay or distraction. Then pray for your church and its injuries.

- Pick someone whom you find you disagree with now and then. Intentionally engage them in conversation about something light— their new jacket, a sports team's record, the unpredictable weather. Ask God to show you that person's great value.

- When you go to church, notice the people around you and what they do. After noticing each person, pause and say a prayer of thanks that this person loves God and cares enough to do what they're doing.

- Consider who you could call to express sympathy or to congratulate. Pray for that person and then, if possible, call or talk to them, expressing sympathy or joy.

"This moment, this place, these people. I must stick with this, try to make it work, not give up, not succumb to the urge to run away."

THE RULE OF
ST. BENEDICT,
PARAPHRASED BY
ESTHER DE WAAL

"In true community we are windows constantly offering each other new views on the mystery of God's presence in our lives: a truth, a beauty, and a love which is greater, fuller, and richer than we ourselves can grasp."

HENRI NOUWEN

3

POWER AND POWERLESSNESS

MARK 10:32-45

I know many people who no longer go to church. They still love God, but they couldn't swallow the politics at their local church. Because they had tasted the sweet goodness of God, they knew instinctively that the power plays going on around them had nothing to do with a Savior who allowed himself to be executed.

Yet none of us can condemn others. If we should ever find the perfect church, we couldn't join it because then it wouldn't be perfect any longer. Most of us play power games in subtle ways. Various methods of manipulation can help *our* side win—flattery or innuendo, donation or withholding of time or money.

After a couple of years of following Jesus, the apostles James and John unashamedly asked for positions of authority and honor in Jesus' future kingdom. Perhaps they felt entitled to these because the Zebedee & Sons fishing enterprise had suffered in their absence.

When would their selfless venture pay off?

In the midst of this power-grabbing drama, Jesus explained that discipleship reverses society's expectation that we move onward and upward. Instead we submit, deny self, serve others and choose to be powerless. When we stop insisting on having our own way, we find freedom to have peace in Christ and to love others.

This link between submission to God and community with others is pictured well by Oswald Chambers, who says the key to a disciple's life is to "become broken bread and poured-out wine in the hands of Jesus Christ for the sake of others." May that be our goal today.

Turning Toward God

Why is it difficult to build community with others when we are also trying to impress people and prove ourselves?

Hearing God Through the Word

Read Mark 10:32-37.

1. How did the band of disciples' final approach to Jerusalem lead James and John to make their request (vv. 35, 37)?

2. What roles of power and honor do ordinary people dream about?

3. If Jesus were to ask you, "What do you want me to do for you?" what would be your reply?

    ___ To be known as . . .

    ___ To hold the position of . . .

    ___ To own . . .

    ___ To be friends with . . . or be part of a group of . . .

    ___ To have children who . . .

    ___ Other:

"Only by common faith in God's power to overcome our deadly love affair with self-will can genuine community be formed and sustained."

MARJORIE THOMPSON

Read Mark 10:38-41.

4. What was Jesus referring to when he said, "Can you drink the cup I drink or be baptized with the baptism I am baptized with?" (See Mark 14:36; Romans 6:3-8.)

5. What motivated Jesus' refusal to grant the brothers' request?

6. Why do you think the other ten disciples were upset?

Read Mark 10:42-45.

7. How did the rulers of the Gentiles behave? How did Jesus say his disciples should behave?

"Almost all church fights and splits occur because people do not have the freedom to give in to each other."

RICHARD FOSTER

8. Which of these methods of pushing people (lording it over others, v. 42) do you see used most often?

___ using guilt to get people to do what I want

___ having to have the last word

___ promising rewards

___ making every issue "about me"

___ other:

9. James and John made their request of Jesus out of a self-absorbed mindset (left column, next page), but the New Testament teaches us to have a community mindset (right column). To make this switch, how do beliefs and desires have to change?

10. God urges us to seek power but not position (Ephesians 3:14-21; Matthew 23:6-10). Think of examples of persons without high position that have power in God's kingdom.

Self-Absorption	Community
wanting to be admired	seeing oneself as a servant
hoping to get our way	choosing to be a slave of all
thinking we know more than others	serving others as a primary motive
pushing because we think we know what's best	giving one's self up
not looking out for others	voluntary self-sacrifice
seeking "power-up" positions	undazzled by celebrity status
using guilt and manipulation to have our way	respecting others' personhood and ideas
wishing to be loved in return for love	loving others with no strings attached
seeking power for oneself	giving away power
wanting appreciation and rewards	not recalling good deeds we've done

11. Spiritual power, given by God, usually has the marks listed below (taken from Richard Foster's *The Challenge of the Disciplined Life*). When have you seen someone demonstrate spiritual power in one of these ways? If possible, pick an instance when this person's behavior made a powerful difference in you.

    ___ love (using power for the good of others)

    ___ humility (the power of God is a gift and thankfulness is the appropriate response)

    ___ self-limitation (refraining from doing certain things out of respect for others)

    ___ joy (delight at seeing the kingdom of Christ break into darkness and depression)

    ___ vulnerability (patiently waiting instead of dominating)

    ___ submission (intimate cooperation with the Father)

    ___ freedom (bringing healing and release to others, freeing others to be themselves)

12. Which of the above marks of spiritual power would help you build community in your family, workplace, neighborhood or church?

"When God looks at our world, God weeps because the lust for power has entrapped and corrupted the human spirit. Instead of gratitude, there is resentment; instead of praise there is criticism; instead of forgiveness there is revenge; instead of healing there is wounding; instead of compassion there is competition; instead of cooperation there is violence; instead of love there is fear."

HENRI NOUWEN

Transformation Exercises

Experiment with one or more of the following.

- Study Ephesians 3:14-21, noting the power requested there (mentioned three times). What is the nature of this power? What does one ask to be empowered to do? If God were to equip the following persons with power, what would it look like: a grocery store worker who bags groceries? a senator? a physical therapist?

- Sit quietly and hold your car keys or city bus pass. Picture yourself driving your car or sitting on a bus. Imagine what you would do or think differently if you chose to practice the discipline of submission (and thus community) in your car or on the bus: let another car in front of you? scoot over to share the seat? How might you view differently the irritating person driving or sitting next to you?

- Pray about an upcoming meeting, casual lunch, family dinner or date, asking: Show me how to treat this other person with dignity. Show me how to offer a sense that this person is honored and loved. Show me how to take seriously whatever they are struggling with, even if they don't feel free to talk about it.

- Read this quotation by Oswald Chambers, and journal your response to God:

  Our Lord never insists on having authority over us. He never says, "You *will* submit to me." No, He leaves us perfectly free to choose— so free, in fact, that we can spit in His face or we can put Him to death, as others have done; and yet He will never say a word. But once His life has been created in me through His redemption, I instantly recognize His right to absolute authority over me. It is a complete and effective domination, in which I acknowledge that "You are worthy, O Lord . . ." (Revelation 4:11).

4

WHEN I THINK I'M RIGHT

PHILEMON 1-21

What a movie today's passage would make!

Imagine you're a wise old apostle stuck in prison. Somehow you meet a person who has wandered far from home into the crowded streets of the big city of Rome. Maybe he's got a job at the prison. Maybe he's a fellow prisoner. You get to know him and introduce him to God, who loves him, and to the Son Jesus Christ, who along with the Holy Spirit offer a new kind of life in which obedience is sweet and pleasant, not coerced and humiliating. After you and this stranger become devoted to each other, your friend Epaphras recognizes him as the legal slave of another mutual friend, Philemon. What are you to do?

Or perhaps the stranger recognizes Epaphras first and comes clean to you about his runaway slave past. Or perhaps the stranger has come running to you all the way in Rome for help. How long will you teach, nurture and train him before you have the inevitable conversation with him about his legal owner, Philemon?

You, of course, are imagining yourself in the shoes of the apostle Paul. You are now caught between two people you love. As you pray, you believe that the radical gospel of Jesus would persuade Philemon to free the slave, Onesimus, but since you build community with love and respect, you refuse to use your apostolic authority to insist on this. Instead you humble yourself and plead on Onesimus's behalf.

How does it feel to submit to someone you have the authority to boss around? How does it feel to be willing to give up this person you love—Onesimus—in order to do what is right and respectful? This story lets us sample some advanced character qualities to taste and see the goodness of God.

Turning Toward God

When have you seen someone in authority behave with great humility or love?

"Many people

seek fellowship

because they

are afraid to be

Hearing God Through the Word

Read Philemon 1-7.

1. What qualities of Philemon does Paul highlight?

alone. Because

they cannot stand

loneliness, they   *Read Philemon 8-14.*

are driven to seek   2. Paul could have ordered Philemon to do what he "ought to do" (v. 8). On what basis did Paul appeal to Philemon instead?

the company of

other people.

Christians who   3. Describe Paul's relationship with Onesimus: in Christ, personally, legally.

have had some

bad experiences

with themselves   4. Paul's willingness to send Onesimus back shows his trust that God would provide community for him in prison even if Onesimus had to leave. What unwise decisions do we make because we want community to cure our loneliness?

hope they will

gain some help   ____ choices in where we go to church

in association   ____ choices in friends

with others. They   ____ choices about how we treat the people around us

are generally   ____ choices about solitude with God

disappointed."

DIETRICH
BONHOEFFER

5. How was Paul an example of the love he wrote about in 1 Corinthians 13 toward Philemon? toward Onesimus?

Read Philemon 15-21.

6. What advice did Paul have for mature Christians (such as Philemon) who are in difficult relationships with new Christians (Onesimus), even ones who make a lot of mistakes? (Verse 19 hints that Onesimus had robbed his master, Philemon.)

"*[Submission] is a posture obligatory on all Christians: men as well as women, fathers as well as children, masters as well as slaves. We are commanded to live a life of submission because Jesus lived a life of submission, not because we are in a particular place or station in life.*"

RICHARD FOSTER

7. Who submitted to whom in the situation described in this passage? How?

8. Which of Paul's behaviors that promoted community do you find most intriguing and challenging?

___ He didn't come close to using his authority to get done what he thought was right (vv. 8-10).

___ He showed respect for people without imposing his wishes (vv. 13-14).

___ He welcomed back a wrongdoer (v. 17).

___ He recommended the elimination of a social barrier (v. 16).

___ He believed the best about Philemon (v. 21).

___ Other:

9. How did Paul's authority flow out of his compassion and power of character rather than his role as an apostle?

10. How did Paul behave differently from the average Christian who believes he or she is right?

11. Think of a situation in which you believe you are right or have the right to speak up. How might you show grace in that situation?

Transformation Exercises

Experiment with one or more of the following.

- Pick a quality of love from your response to question 5 and ask someone within your Christian community to pray that this quality will become part of your character. If this sounds too scary, bring the list with you to the next meeting at which people offer prayer requests. Explain the assignment and ask for prayer.

- Consider someone you know who has recently made a mistake that others know about. (This could be a non-Christian, a child or senior citizen in your church, or a disgraced public figure.) Plan an action of grace you can do to welcome that person back: offering "extra" bananas bought on sale to the non-Christian neighbor; giving a distinct wink or wave to that child or senior citizen; writing a letter of grace to that public figure.

- Take some symbol of "being right" (a petition, a set of instructions, the correct piece of clothing to wear to work) and set it on an outdoor grill or a fireplace or next to a candle. *Do not set it on fire.* Instead ask God to show you whom you need to love in the midst of that situation—perhaps in place of insisting you're right, or because you need to show more love in addition to the truth you've already spoken (Ephesians 4:15).

"Spiritual authority is God-ordained and God-sustained. Human institutions may acknowledge this authority or they may not; it makes no difference. The person with spiritual authority may have an outward position of authority or may not; again, it makes no difference. Spiritual authority is marked by both compassion and power."

RICHARD FOSTER

5

LISTENING

MARK 5:21-34

Imagine for a moment that a bunch of brainy theologians had to live together and get along. The seminary they were all attending was underground because a fascist military regime had come to power. These normally respected ministers had to live and study in inconvenient emergency-built housing, with a leader so controversial that the government had interrupted his broadcast and cut him off. How would these folks get along in this pressure-cooker atmosphere?

This actually happened. The controversial leader, Dietrich Bonhoeffer, wrote the book *Life Together* to shape the community of these twenty-five vicars who "shared a common life" in Finkenwalde, Germany, in 1935. He cautioned them, "Christians (especially ministers) so often think they must always contribute something when they are in the company of others, that this is the one service they have to render. They forget that listening can be a greater service than speaking."

Bonhoeffer kept emphasizing that having a rich life with God enables us to love others. Rich solitude builds rich community. A life with God teaches us to listen to others. He warned, "He who can no longer listen to his brother will soon be no longer listening to God either; he will be doing nothing but prattle in the presence of God too. This is the beginning of the death of the spiritual life, and in the end there is nothing left but spiritual chatter and clerical condescension arrayed in pious words."

What Bonhoeffer learned in the fiery furnace of Hitler's Germany (he was later executed) about listening and loving was something Jesus knew and demonstrated.

Turning Toward God

Bonhoeffer counseled: "Chatter does not create fellowship." What causes us to chatter?

Hearing God Through the Word

Read Mark 5:21-29.

1. Who was Jairus, and why was Jairus an important "client" for Jesus to service (in terms of networking and power structures)?

"Christians have

forgotten that

the ministry of

listening has been

committed to

them by Him who

is Himself the

great listener and

whose work they

should share."

DIETRICH
BONHOEFFER

2. How would you feel if you had had a sickness for twelve years—especially one that kept you "unclean" and therefore not touched by anyone?

3. Why do you suppose the woman touched Jesus' clothes instead of asking for healing?

Read Mark 5:30-34.

4. Why do you think Jesus stopped and looked around for the woman instead of moving on to help Jairus?

5. What facts and ideas would logically have been included in the "whole truth" that she told?

6. What reasons did Jesus have to avoid talking with her, and even more, listening to her tell the "whole truth"?

7. We can often guess well what someone has been thinking by the next thing that comes out of their mouth. Based on that guideline, what was Jesus thinking while this woman took up time by telling the "whole truth"?

"There is a kind of listening with half an ear that presumes already to know what the other person has to say. It is an impatient, inattentive listening, that despises the brother and is only waiting for a chance to speak and thus get rid of the other person."

8. Some have suggested that Jesus' little brother James wrote his New Testament letter based on how he had seen his big brother conduct the family carpentry business and lead their family in Nazareth. If this is true, what does the following verse tell us about the way Jesus did business and led the family: "My dear brothers, take note of this: Everyone should be quick to listen, slow to speak and slow to become angry" (James 1:19)?

9. How is listening an act of submission?

DIETRICH
BONHOEFFER

10. What does it mean to be truly present to someone during conversation?

11. Which of the following tips do you see yourself possibly using to be more present to others in conversation, to truly listen to them?

___ Write down someone's thoughts (or details of their illness).

___ Search the person's face, asking, *How does this person feel?*

___ Ask God to show you the person's heart.

___ Pray for people as they speak to you.

___ If you tend to interrupt, cover your mouth with your hand when someone speaks.

___ Other suggestions:

_____

12. What fears, sins or character flaws might be slowly overcome when one becomes an intentional listener and thereby practices the disciplines of community and submission?

Transformation Exercises

Experiment with one or more of the following.

- Hold a picture of someone you love. Look at their face and body posture and ask God: What do I need to know about this person? How does this person feel? How can I feel with him or her? How can I help this person connect with you?

- Prepare for an upcoming meeting, a casual lunch, a family dinner or a date by picturing yourself being totally present to the other person(s). What will be your struggles? How can you help yourself remain attentive?

- Let this inspire you: "It is said of Abbot Agatho that for three years he carried a stone in his mouth until he learned to be silent." Imagine— an abbot generally runs an abbey! Do you need to carry a stone in your pocket to help you?

- Thank God for listening to you. Express your desire to learn how to listen better to what God has to say to you—especially about how to love others.

- Try to ask more questions today than you did yesterday. To prepare yourself, read through one Gospel and note how often Jesus asked questions. What kind of questions were they: to gain information? to penetrate thoughts and motives? to get people to think?

"We pay attention only long enough to develop a counterargument; . . . people often listen with an agenda, to sell or petition or seduce. Seldom is there a deep, open-hearted, unjudging reception of the other. By contrast, if someone truly listens to me, my spirit begins to expand."

MARY ROSE
O'REILLEY

6

WELCOMING
THE STRANGER

MATTHEW 25:31-40

As I see Mr. Hubbard walking slowly from the parking lot, I could easily let my eyes pass over him as if he were simply part of the weekly furnishings. Or, I could ask myself, *How does Mr. Hubbard look today? What cues is he giving me about what his needs might be? Is his glass empty, and might I have some cool, refreshing drink to pour into it? Perhaps I could ask a question about his daughter, who lives on the other side of the country, or make an inquiry about the health of his wife. Yes, that's it; he wants to talk about her and I am available for that.*

Sometimes the Mr. Hubbards are the last folks we practice community with. We have nothing in common with them, so it takes effort. Today's passage talks about making that extra effort to create community with folks who can give nothing back to us. This is especially true of the hungry, thirsty stranger or the shabby, sick prisoner who does not inspire warm fuzzy feelings.

Welcoming odd "strangers" and serving them in respectful, loving ways is the boot camp of the discipline of community. We are so changed by this discipline that we easily welcome folks who are not strangers. We learn the essence of hospitality: welcoming people, not entertaining or impressing them.

Who are "strangers"? Jesus' extraordinary behavior toward those ordinarily excluded shows us that in "us versus them" situations, the "thems" are "strangers." A stranger is anyone who has experienced a different sort of past with different heroes and different buzzwords. You'll recognize who are strangers to you because when you meet these folks, a little "ping" goes off in your head that says, *Different. Step back.* To these strangers we offer a sense of "home," as God offers it to us (John

14:23). We pay attention to them and invite them to unfold themselves. Then we respectfully wait for them to be able to do that.

Turning Toward God

When have you experienced being a stranger in a group of people? (Think of a time when you were different for some reason or simply a newcomer.)

Hearing God Through the Word

Read Matthew 25:31-34.

1. What is happening in this scene, and who is involved?

2. If you were among "those on the right," how prepared would you feel—character-wise—to "take your inheritance" (which included ruling, reigning and serving in the kingdom of heaven according to Revelation 5:9-10; 20:6; 22:1-5)?

Read Matthew 25:35-36.

3. What preparation for ruling and reigning do "those on his right" have?

4. Most of the categories of folks helped are easy to understand. But .who qualifies as a "stranger"?

5. The issue of "strangers" was important to the Jews because they had been sojourners in Egypt.

- Strangers were protected by the same laws that governed Israel (Deuteronomy 1:16; 24:17; 27:19).

- Israelites were to go above and beyond decent behavior and love strangers (Deuteronomy 10:19 NRSV).

- Jesus said to go an extra mile with a Roman soldier—clearly an uncomfortable stranger for the Jews (Matthew 5:41).

- Jesus, Mary and Joseph had been political refugees (or immigrants or "strangers") in Egypt until Herod died (Matthew 2:13-23). What do you imagine would have been particularly hard for Mary and Joseph as they tried to survive in Egypt?

6. Add your ideas of contemporary "strangers" to this list:

- someone outside the common economic class (an apartment dweller in a church of homeowners or a rich person among middle-class people)

- people of a different age (an elderly person in a church of younger folks)

- those with different capabilities (a disabled person in the midst of fitness buffs, a nonreader among well-read folks)

- someone from a different place (immigrants or refugees, military or missionary kids, a parolee or drug rehab graduate)

- someone whose theological persuasion is different from yours

- other:

"To merely welcome another, to provide for them, to make a place, is one of the most life-giving and life-receiving things a human being can do."

DALLAS WILLARD

Read Matthew 25:37-40.

7. What do we learn from the fact that "those on the right" don't even realize how they have served and loved others?

8. Such unselfconscious service is typical of those who serve with a sense of community rather than self-consciously "helping those needy folks." What are the marks of unselfconscious service? Here are a few ideas to get you started.

____ reciprocity (welcoming help from the people you help)

____ humor and lightness (not thinking too highly of yourself)

____ respect (valuing others and listening to them)

____ other:

____ other:

____ other:

"The spiritual discipline of hospitality is a continual process of transforming sojourners into kinfolk and strangers into friends."

MICHAEL E. WILLIAMS

9. How might Jesus' words that we are really serving him when we serve people quite different from us help us if we are shy or afraid or intimidated?

10. What does it mean to take the role of host in a conversation (the one who reaches out to help others feel comfortable)? in a relationship?

11. What fears or sins might be slowly overcome as we practice this discipline of hospitality?

12. Who are the strangers in your life (see question 6) God might be asking you to welcome? What would that look like?

Transformation Exercises

Experiment with one or more of the following.

- Choose someone who is a stranger to you in some way. (See question 6 for ideas.) Pray for that person and then ask God to show you how to engage him or her in a conversation, beginning with a warm greeting and a question.

- Look through your newspaper for stories about any sort of stranger to you, especially the immigrant, the disabled or the person in trouble with the law. Read the article with an effort to understand their world. Pray for these persons' wholeness in Christ, and pray for your increased capacity to welcome them in your life.

- Look into the eyes of the next homeless person or two you pass, and smile at them. (Most folks don't look into their eyes, even if they give them money.)

- Ask a friend to help you identify who the strangers are in your life. Don't balk at odd ideas your friend may bring up. Pray that God will then show you who are the strangers you are to welcome.

"Someone knocks at my door. If I am anxious or resentful, I may 'put on a good face,' offer a cup of tea, but offer no real hospitality. The person I really am at the center of my being is unavailable, blocked by worry or the wish to control. . . . My business, whether as host or guest, is to be as open and real as possible in any situation."

SUSAN MANGRAM

STUDY NOTES FOR
COMMUNITY AND SUBMISSION

Session 1. Intentional Community

MATTHEW 26:36-45

FOCUS: Jesus built community with people on earth just as he lives in community with the Father and the Holy Spirit in an atmosphere of submission.

Question 1. Besides the events in verses 36-38, clarify that this scene occurred in the garden of Gethsemane after the Last Supper in the Upper Room and immediately before Jesus' arrest.

Question 2. While it is usually assumed that Jesus did this because they were his core team (also witnessing the transfiguration in Matthew 17:1-13), perhaps he wanted them nearby to overhear his prayer on accepting the cup of suffering (Matthew 26:39) and learn from it. These three had just bragged on themselves. James and John had declared that they could drink the cup Jesus drank (Mark 10:38-40), and Peter had proclaimed: "Even if all fall away, I will not" (Mark 14:29). Will Lane explains that "their glib self-confidence exposes them to grave peril of failure in the struggle they confront, and for that reason they are commanded to be vigilant."[1] Though groggy with sleep, they may have been in a "stunned stupor, which per-

mitted them to hear, but not to register, the words of Jesus' prayer until afterwards."[2]

Question 3. Jesus pulled them in instead of pushing them away. He asked them to sit near him to hear his prayer and witness his struggle. We can embrace the erring and wounded and bring them into our spiritual life as Jesus did.

Question 4. It may have shocked these disciples to see Jesus so transparent, but this is essential for community.

Question 5. "Cup" often referred to a necessary suffering (Psalm 60:3; Isaiah 51:17, 22).

Question 6. Jesus did not view God as a terrible tyrant imposing death on him, but still as his intimate companion. Discussions among the Trinity are respectful and full of love. If this idea of community among the Trinity intrigues any of the participants, direct their attention to the last transformation exercise.

Question 7. Jesus was concerned for them, not for himself. He wanted them to be alert to temptation. To "watch" means to "be spiritually awake so as to face the severe sifting of loyalties which was to

---

[1]William Lane, *The Gospel According to Mark*, New International Commmentary on the New Testament (Grand Rapids: Eerdmans, 1975), pp. 515-16.
[2]Ibid., p. 519.

come in the arrest and death of Jesus."[3]

Question 8. First, he warned them about their susceptibility to temptation (v. 41). He didn't bring up their prior arrogance (see question 2). When they were unwilling to watch and pray, he didn't nag them or interfere (v. 44).

Question 10. People complain about not having any friends at church or they complain about people at church who have "weird ideas." People distance themselves from others who have different ideas. If you wish, you might ask participants how these mistaken ideas are different from community (mentioned in the introduction).

Question 12. At the end of each session encourage each member of the group to choose an activity to use during the week. Talk about what you experienced at some point in the following sessions.

Session 2. The Grittiness of Community

1 CORINTHIANS 12:12-27

FOCUS: Community is not sentimental feelings but an agreement to let iron sharpen iron in a stable environment of love and submission.

Question 1. They are part of one unit (v. 12), part of the body of Christ (vv. 12-14), baptized by the same Spirit and continually nourished by that Spirit (v. 13). All parts need each other (v. 19).

Question 2. They may have different ethnic backgrounds and different socioeconomic status (v. 13). They will perform different functions for the body (vv. 14-17).

Question 3. If you wish, ask participants how each of them completes the sentence about herself or himself.

Question 5. Doers (especially high achievers) are often valued more than those with limited resources, talents and time. Gifts of money, prestige and knowledge are valued more than gifts of service and mercy. Folks on the platform are often valued more than behind-the-scenes folks.

Question 6. To honor means to value, and so you're not giving out prizes but valuing the "less honorable" by the way you treat them. To be mod-

est about a person's unpresentableness means that you are not appointed to reveal their unpresentableness.[4]

Paul never identified who fit in what categories but kept the categories of folks nonspecific so I can never be sure that it is not *I* who am weaker, less honorable or unpresentable. Thus we seek God, asking, "How do you wish me to honor this person who I think is dishonorable?" Such is the grittiness of Christian community.

Question 7. To help participants have fun with this question, you might start off with "Shut up, toe!" or "Eyeballs, you have nothing in common with a toe. Get over it!" Martin Luther pointed out, "See what the whole body does when a foot is trodden on, or a finger is pinched: how the eye looks dour [gloomy], the nose draws up, the mouth cries out, and all the members are ready to rescue and to help."[5]

Listen to participants' answers to the follow-up question and, if you wish, ask, "How did the body of Christ feel your pain with you?"

Question 8. Paul is clear about having "equal

---

[3]Ibid., p. 520.

[4]F. W. Grosheide, *The First Epistle to the Corinthians,* New International Commentary on the New Testament (Grand Rapids: Eerdmans, 1979), p. 296.

[5]R. C. H. Lenski, *The Interpretation of St. Paul's First and Second Epistles to the Corinthians* (Minneapolis: Augsburg, 1963), p. 533.

concern for each other." So we empathize and rejoice—relinquish our rights to our own selfish impulses—no matter what.

Question 9. Because we have different spiritual gifts, we can discuss different insights to help each other do tasks in a more Christlike way. This will "sharpen" our service. Being around "sharp" people who are faithful and work hard

spurs us on to do the same.

Question 10. Qualities found here include being patient, being kind, not envying, not boasting, not being proud, not being rude, not being self-seeking, not being easily angered, keeping no record of wrongs, not delighting in evil but rejoicing with the truth, always protecting, always trusting, always hoping and always persevering.

Session 3. Power and Powerlessness

MARK 10:32-45

FOCUS: God challenges us to give up power plays and become servants, which creates true community.

Question 1. James and John apparently understood that important events were imminent. Feeling desperate, they requested positions of honor and power before it was too late.

To sit on the right and left of Jesus in glory would signify power and honor. If you had these seats, folks would look up to you. It would be like being a rock star. Your talent and glamour would finally be recognized. You would not only finally belong but be sought after.

Question 2. After participants offer a few answers, rephrase the question this way: What roles of power and honor do ordinary church members aspire to?

Question 4. The cup of suffering in martyrdom and the baptism of death into Christ. "To share someone's cup was a recognized expression for sharing his fate."[6]

Question 5. Submission to the Father (Mark 13:32; Acts 1:7).

Question 9. Community-oriented people have to believe that God truly loves them, is for them and invites them to participate in an eternal community, beginning now and continuing forever. Such folks delight in God and receive the desires of their hearts because those desires are for the person of God.

Question 10. Seeking power is usually destructive because it often involves seeking position too. But people with relatively little power (earthly speaking) can have an enormous effect of good on others. You may need to give an example or two to get them thinking. A school janitor may have an enormous effect on a child by freely loving that child (without regard to achievement) as few other adults can. A student in a classroom may ask insightful questions that make the class a true learning situation.

Question 11. Think beforehand of an answer to use to get the group started. Do not give it immediately, however. Let them think for a few minutes.

---

[6]Lane, *Gospel According to Mark*, pp. 379-80.

Session 4. When I Think I'm Right

PHILEMON 1-21

FOCUS: Building community involves trust in God so we do what is right and good, showing respect and grace instead of making authoritative demands or selfish decisions.

Question 1. Paul emphasized Philemon's *love* and his *faith* (each word appears twice, vv. 5-7).

Question 2. Paul had the right to order him, given Paul's apostolic authority, but he doesn't mention his apostleship in the greeting or in verse 8.

Paul appealed to Philemon on the basis of love. Because of Philemon's mature character of love and faith (vv. 1-7), Paul can appeal to him as he could not have appealed to an immature person.

Question 3. Paul was a spiritual father to Onesimus as he was to the Corinthians and to Timothy (1 Corinthians 4:15; 1 Timothy 1:2). Personally, Onesimus had been helping Paul so much that Paul did not want to let go of him. There seems to have been deep affection: Paul refers to Onesimus as "my very heart" (v. 12). Legally Onesimus was a runaway slave, and Paul was breaking the law by harboring him.

Paul may have been asking to keep Onesimus with him. The verb for "sending" can be understood as "referring back," meaning that "Paul is not intending Philemon to retain Onesimus but is referring the matter to him for a decision in the hope that he will be allowed to return to Paul."[7] Verse 13 seems to support that as well.

Question 5. Paul demonstrates love that is kind, not manipulative; patient instead of pushy; respectful, not self-seeking; not keeping a record of wrongs; rejoicing in truth and right rather than in getting what he wants.

Question 6. Receive the person as you would receive the apostle Paul. "The Christian must always welcome back the man who has made a mistake. Too often we regard the man who has made a mistake and who has taken the wrong turning with suspicion; too often we show that we are never prepared to trust him again . . . and in [our] self-righteousness and lack of sympathy, make it harder [for the mistaken person]."[8]

Question 7. Paul submitted to Philemon as the legal slaveowner. Paul submitted to Onesimus by keeping him for a while and teaching him without turning him in. Onesimus submitted to Paul by allowing him to write to Philemon. He stood ready to submit to Philemon. The question was whether Philemon would submit to both Paul and Onesimus.

Question 11. Not everyone will be transparent. Pray for group participants as they ponder.

Session 5. Listening

MARK 5:21-34

FOCUS: Jesus listened to people and gave them his full-hearted attention even when he could have been distracted.

Question 3. As a woman, she could not speak to Jesus (a well-known teacher-rabbi) in public. As an unclean woman, she had to stay away from oth-

---

[7]Donald Guthrie, "Philemon," in *The New Bible Commentary*, ed. Donald Guthrie and J. A. Motyer, 3rd ed. (Grand Rapids: Eerdmans, 1991), p. 1189.

[8]William Barclay, *The Letters to Timothy, Titus and Philemon* (Philadelphia: Westminster Press, 1960), p. 322.

ers. By touching his garment she might "sneak" a healing.

Question 4. Doing good deeds is never enough. We need to connect with people and give them attention.

Question 6. Her interruption was inconvenient because Jairus was standing by with a dying daughter. Couldn't her healing wait? The daughter's couldn't, it would have seemed. This interruption was also not appropriate because she was a woman to whom Jesus should not have been speaking in public, and especially because she was unclean.

Question 7. Jesus didn't seem to wish she'd be quiet so he could move on. He didn't hush her. We may wonder about the disciples, though. If they weren't

mesmerized by Jesus' exchange with her, they may have been thinking, *Can we move along now?*

The first word out of his mouth, *daughter,* was a word of endearment. He went on to commend her saying that her faith had healed her. Perhaps he'd seen the suffering leave her face and body (v. 29), for he projected that freedom as her future.

Question 11. After the discussion, ask participants to try practicing being truly present to other group members as they answer the next question.

Question 12. Some possibilities: being changed from pride to humility; from having a conniving heart to having a clean heart; from apathy to charity; from deceitfulness to honesty; from laziness to diligence of faith; from self-centeredness to God-centeredness.

Session 6. Welcoming the Stranger

MATTHEW 25:31-40

FOCUS: Community becomes intentional as we welcome strangers and submit to the interruptions of life.

Question 2. Preparation is important as Jesus has just emphasized in the parable of the ten virgins (Matthew 25:1-13) and the parable of the talents (25:14-30). "As we learn through increasing trust to govern our tiny affairs with him, the kingdom he had all along planned for us will be turned over to us, at the appropriate time. Come you who are under my Father's blessing and take over the government assigned to you from the beginning."[9]

Question 3. Their preparation came with all that feeding and welcoming they did on earth.

Question 4. The text uses the Greek word *xenos* (from which we get the word *xenophobia,* fear of foreigners) and refers to foreigners.[10]

Question 6. Urge those stirred by this question to

investigate the first transformation exercise.

Question 7. First, they haven't served in a self-congratulatory way. Second, they somehow do not even realize how magnanimous their deeds were. This is typical of those who serve others as equals instead of looking down on them.

Question 8. For such unselfconscious servers, the homeless person on the street is not "the homeless person on the street" but Mary or Ed or Bill. Their friend on parole is not an ex-convict but Jay or Gary or Denise. The service is relational. They offer friendship as well as food and clothing, conversation as well as soup.

Question 9. To keep picturing Jesus' face in those we serve is incredibly helpful. Welcoming the needy stranger especially retrains us. That's why it's the boot camp (strenuous, exhausting and stretching experience) of the discipline of community.

---

[9]Dallas Willard, *The Divine Conspiracy* (San Francisco: HarperSanFrancisco, 1998), p. 25.
[10]W. E. Vine, Merrill F. Unger and William White Jr., *Vine's Expository Dictionary of Biblical Words* (Nashville: Thomas Nelson, 1985), p. 603 of NT section.

Question 10. As host, you think about the others' welfare and do what you can to make them feel welcome. Those well practiced in this discipline often take the role of host even when they're the stranger and you would assume they would hold back and be the guest (receiving the welcome). They also recognize when an unlikely person is choosing to step forward and be the host, and they honor him or her by responding warmly.

Question 12. If it is scary for some in the group to move so far out of their comfort zone, assume a playful attitude and say something like, "We're just pondering here." Pray especially for those participants.

Section Six

REFLECTION & CONFESSION

The practices of reflection and confession don't sound as upbeat as worship and celebration or as intimate as prayer and listening. Yet when they are rightly understood, learned and practiced, these disciplines become a valuable part of our conversation with God that enlivens our days and brightens our soul.

Yet many people find that the idea of reflecting on mistakes and owning up to them is discouraging. For today's performance-driven Christians, self-examination might as well be self-annihilation. But such thinking is part of the murky distortion that God is upset with you unless you do everything right and that your spirituality is really about you. Quite the contrary: we realize that as disciples of Jesus we are "dust" and that God delights in shaping us into new creations. Faith is centered not on our performance but the constant choice of God to love us, accept us and transform us into creatures who know how to love. Reflection and confession are some of the many ways God shows us the way forward—if we're willing to look.

Scripture is clear that confessing sins and praying with others is a positive move in the healing process (James 5:16). The never-giving-up love of God, who doesn't keep a record of wrongs, far outweighs our sins. Our brutal honesty is met by God's gritty acceptance and the result is that we are bonded to the heart of God.

Because God's goodness and love are foundational to reflection and confession, this series begins with a session on the compassionate nature of God, who is not shocked by our sin. Instead of getting mad, God wants to forgive and heal. After this foundational study, we move into reflection, confessing to God and confessing to others. Then we look at the practical methods of the classic prayer of examen (examining both our conscience and our daily consciousness of God) and journaling.

1

BELIEVING IN A GOD WHO HEALS

PSALM 103

How skilled are you at admitting you're wrong? When I was wrong in my newly-wed years, I choked in my attempts to admit it. So I would say to my spouse in a cartoonish voice, "Yes, you are right, and I am wrong." It took years before I could admit mistakes in a normal tone of voice.

Why are we so reluctant to admit our errors—even to God? It probably has to do with our view of God. Belief in a forgiving, healing God provides a safe atmosphere in which to admit our sins. Our objections to admitting sin fade away.

Objection 1: *Admitting sins makes us feel like failures.*

Truth: Unlike us, God is not shocked that we sin.

Objection 2: *Admitting sins makes us feel as if God is mad at us.*

Truth: The scope of God's grace is nothing short of astonishing. God is so compassionate we cannot imagine it.

Turning Toward God

How would you verbalize our objections to confessing sin?

Hearing God Through the Word

Psalm 103 is ordinarily thought of as a cheery psalm about blessing God. But if you track the references to sins, iniquities, transgressions and healing (vv. 9-12), you see that it also has confessional aspects. To this psalmist, however, confession was not about beating himself up but about recounting God's goodness. God is not shocked that we are fragile, sinful creatures. God is eager to forgive and heal.

"To confess your

sins to God is

not to tell him

anything he

doesn't already

know. Until you

confess them,

however, they are

the abyss between

you. When you

confess them,

they become the

Golden Gate

bridge."

FREDERICK
BUECHNER

Read Psalm 103:1-5.

1. What "benefits" of God does the psalmist long to remember?

2. What does the psalmist tell himself not to do regarding God's benefits? Why might those examining their soul and "inmost being" be prone to do this?

Read Psalm 103:6-13.

3. Verse 6 has been dubbed a definition of God's anger, indicating that God shows anger not in meanness or intimidation but with straightforward consequences for wrongs done. What other clues to the character of God's anger does this passage offer?

4. What good news do these verses have for people conscious of their sins and willing to confess them?

5. Find the three illustrations of how vast God's love is in verses 11-13.

Read Psalm 103:14-18.

6. What images are used to describe the frailty of humans?

7. Why is it helpful for people confessing sin to be mindful of the frailty of humans, even those who love God passionately?

8. How does remembering that I am like dust or a blown-away flower help me be more compassionate to others?

9. Fearing God is mentioned three times ("those who fear him," vv. 11, 13, 17), but look at the words around this phrase. What does appropriate fear of God involve?

"Humility allows us to be real. We no longer have to put on a good face or false front. There is no need to impress or to hide. We are not trying to protect or advance ourselves in God's eyes."

MARJORIE THOMPSON

Read Psalm 103:19-22.

10. What does the psalmist say is the proper response to such a compassionate, benevolent God?

11. What does it teach us about confession of sin to see how this confessional psalm stays focused on God and the goodness of God?

12. How would a regular habit of reflection and confession build your trust in God's love for you?

Transformation Exercises

Experiment with one or more of the following.

- Pick a word or phrase from this passage (perhaps, "heals all your diseases" or "as far as the east is from the west, so far has he removed our transgressions from us"). For several minutes, sit or stand in that phrase. Don't think about anything much, except the grandness of God who loves you. Respond with a gesture, movement or facial expression.

- Imagine God's face of disappointment and tears as God forgives your sin and heals you. Based on what you know of God in Scripture, what might God say to you?

- Hold an object in your hand that symbolizes a wrong you've done—a wooden spoon you used to spank your child in anger, the key to a car you drove as you treated another driver with contempt, an article of clothing you wore to attract someone inappropriately. As you hold it, read Psalm 103:8-10, and try to confess aloud to God what you did. Then toss the object aside and read aloud verses 11-13.

"God becomes

the constant

examiner of your

soul, but His

exams are not

shameful, painful

events. You're

eager to follow

God's ways, so

the 'repentance

is sweet,' and

confession of sin

brings love and

tranquillity."

JEANNE GUYON

2

LETTING GOD
SEARCH MY HEART

1 Corinthians 13:1–7

For many years I confessed my sins to God by scanning a long checklist of possible sins. If nothing else popped out at me, I could count on having to confess laziness and grouchiness. I'd leave my confession time hoping I'd felt guilty enough to shape up.

But shaming myself did not help me grow in God. It just made me a guilt-drenched, navel-gazing Christian. I was spiritually self-absorbed—a condition that contradicts everything in Christianity. I see now that I was taking the wrong thing seriously: my supposed righteousness. What I needed to take seriously was God's grace and desire to live in me. God would change me as we interacted, not as I shamed myself.

In interaction with God, we hear God's voice of gentle correction especially when we're serving others (what attitudes I have!) and when we're reading and meditating on Scripture. In such moments God probes our hearts, helping us see what causes us to offer hurtful innuendo, to ignore people, to pretend to be better than we are.

In the last session we saw that the foundation of confession is a belief in God's radical love for us. This frees us to examine feelings, questions, observations, suspicions, beliefs and commitments in the safety of this interactive life. The Holy Spirit helps us: "The lamp of the LORD searches the spirit of a man; it searches out his inmost being" (Proverbs 20:27). In this we find the liberty to stop beating ourselves up.

Turning Toward God

God often seems to ask us to look at our behavior and see how we fall short. What do we do instead?

Hearing God Through the Word

Read 1 Corinthians 13:1-3.

1. What remarkable gifts, qualities or actions are named in this passage that people can do but still have no love in them?

"*Lay your entire soul open before God. You can be sure the Lord will not fail to enlighten you concerning your sin. Your Lord will shine as a light in you; and through His shining, He will allow you to see the nature of all your faults.*"

JEANNE GUYON

How is it possible to do such admired, heroic actions without love?

Read 1 Corinthians 13:4-7.

2. Read 1 Corinthians 13:4-7 a second time, replacing the words *love* and *it* with *God.*

Which of the qualities of God below do you admire most, desiring to incorporate them into your life?

God is patient.	God is kind.	God does not envy.
God does not boast.	God is not proud.	God is not rude.
God is not self-seeking.	God is not easily angered.	God keeps no record of wrongs.
God always hopes.	God always protects.	God always trusts.
God does not delight in evil.	God always perseveres.	God never fails.

3. Close your eyes, and ask God to show you whatever you need to know about yourself in light of this passage. Don't beat yourself up. Stay out of the way, and see what comes to you.

_____

4. What are some common statements about God that make it sound as if God is rude, self-seeking or easily angered?

_____

5. Notice the other activity of love (and of God) listed in verse 5. How could we imitate God in this way and treat ourselves more graciously?

"Self-examination is not an invitation to psychoanalysis, problem solving, self-lecturing, or ego-absorption.

_____

6. What do these verses tell us about the process of self-reflection?

   • "Let us examine our ways and test them, and let us return to the LORD " (Lamentations 3:40).

   • "If we claim to be without sin, we deceive ourselves and the truth is not in us. If we confess our sins, he is faithful and just and will forgive us our sins and purify us from all unrighteousness" (1 John 1:8-9).

   • "Examine yourselves to see whether you are in the faith; test yourselves" (2 Corinthians 13:5).

   • "So then, each of us will give an account of himself to God" (Romans 14:12).

The whole point of self-examination is to become more God-centered by observing the moments when we are or are not so."

MARJORIE THOMPSON

_____

7. Reflection is about posing questions to oneself. What are some helpful questions to ask when examining yourself?

8. Where does the process of reflection most often break down for you?

___ I don't ask myself reflective questions because it's too scary.

___ I don't ask myself reflective questions because it's too much work.

___ I don't ask myself reflective questions because I believe in thinking positively.

___ I don't ask myself reflective questions because I don't want to know my real motives and my real self.

___ Other:

---

9. What do you need to believe deeply about God in order to examine your real self and your real motives without beating yourself up?

---

10. What traps do you fall into during reflection?

___ being blind to my character flaws

___ making excuses for wrong behavior

___ berating myself, hoping that feelings of shame will force me to improve

___ letting self-examination be a onetime event

___ evaluating myself on my own power and not relying on the Spirit to search me

___ being surprised (and even horrified) that I've failed again

___ keeping the focus on me and how I'm not good enough

___ other:

---

11. How does a clear-eyed recognition of our faults help us choose which spiritual disciplines can help us most?

> "Real damage comes when we indict ourselves for misdeeds far more vindictively than any of our friends—or God—ever would. [Healthy] guilt feels like a simple recognition of a truth in the presence of someone lovingly forgiving us."
>
> TAD DUNNE

Transformation Exercises

Experiment with one or more of the following.

- When you catch yourself in a moment of lust, pride, greed or envy, ask God to reveal to you the neediness in your heart that causes this sin.

- Before going to sleep, review your day and confess thoughts and deeds that were not motivated by love. Don't drift off to sleep until you have rested in God's love.

- Sit in a swing or bath, or perch somewhere with a pleasant view. Review the events of your past week. Look at specific events and ask yourself, *Was I motivated by God's love, or was there something else I was loving and pursuing instead?*

- Journal about how safe or unsafe you feel in giving the Holy Spirit official permission to probe you and show you what needs to be revealed to you.

- Read Colossians 3:1-12, and notice how people who had been "raised with Christ" are encouraged to put off certain qualities and put on others. Then read the how-to instructions in verses 13-17. What phrase in this passage speaks to you?

3

CONFESSING TO GOD

PSALM 51

For years I attended a support group in which we reflected on our behavior in light of what we were learning about more healthy ways to respond to life. During the first few sessions I hung my head as I confessed, looking at the floor and covering my face with my hands. I dreaded looking up. But I soon learned that when I looked up, I would see nodding, smiling faces of people who accepted me. Thus I found the group to be a safe place to confess my latest mistakes and even my deeper character flaws. This experience provided me with a powerful picture of how God receives our confessions with unfailing love.

If we have a clear-eyed view of God's full-hearted compassion, admitting our wrongs to God can be one of our great moments of connection with God. This session's passage shows us a confessing sinner who did not run away from God but ran to safety in the refuge of God's arms.

This image of running to safety can help convince us that the purpose of confession is not to feel beaten up and overwhelmed. The purpose is always to love God more and be more enthralled with the great God who loves us. Confessing is not about destructive introspection or morbid brooding on failures. It brings freedom and all sorts of benefits, including transparency with God and with others. Coming clean this way helps us accept our weaknesses as well as strengths, our brokenness as well as giftedness.

Turning Toward God

If you were to imagine God in the form of a person, what gesture or facial expression would indicate God's willingness to forgive and restore?

Hearing God Through the Word

The confessing sinner in Psalm 51 is Israel's greatest king, David. His misdeeds began with adultery with Bathsheba, after which he murdered her husband Uriah to cover up the deed. His sin affected the entire nation and stained the name of God with scandal. This "man after [God's] own heart" (Acts 13:22) lived in self-delusion for almost a year. After being confronted, he confessed.

"We are inviting the Lord to search our hearts to the depths. Far from being dreadful, this is a scrutiny of love."

RICHARD FOSTER

Read Psalm 51:1, as well as the introductory sentence to the psalm.

1. On what truth does David base his plea for pardon?

2. What does this verse say to people who have sinned so grievously that they feel God can't forgive them?

Read Psalm 51:2-5.

3. What phrases indicate David's frankness about his sin?

4. How does such transparency train us to be authentic people?

5. Why do you think David emphasizes that his sin was against God, even saying, "Against you, you only, have I sinned" (v. 4)?

"Once you have establ"

Read Psalm 51:6-15.

"Once you have

established a

relationship with

your Lord, you

will soon discover

that no fault in

you escapes the

reproof of God.

As soon as you

commit a sin, you

are immediately

rebuked by an

inward sense.

It will be a kind

of deep, inward

burning . . . a

tender confusion.

He will not

allow any sin

to be hidden or

concealed."

JEANNE GUYON

6. What phrases describe the way forward into restoration?

7. What sorts of things does David pray for in his prayer of renewal (vv. 12-15)?

Read Psalm 51:16-19.

8. What prevents us from having a broken and contrite heart?

9. What are the chief benefits of admitting our sins to God?

10. What negative character qualities might be slowly overcome as we practice this discipline of confessing to God?

11. How might confession build humility?

How might it build courage?

Transformation Exercises

Experiment with one or more of the following.

- Reread Psalm 51 aloud slowly. Which word or phrase is most meaningful to you? Why? What does that phrase tell you about how you want to connect with God?

- Picture or draw an image to represent how God receives our confessions (such as my mental image of the nodding face of another support group member).

- Go for a walk and pause. Pick up a rock and hold it gently in your hand. Name it after a sin you've committed. Lift it up and offer it to God. Sit in silence for several minutes. Then respond however God leads you to respond.

- Figure out something you could say to a friend or acquaintance that would allow you to be more transparent than you've ever been before. Pray and ask God if you should say it.

- Find a song that expresses your sorrow for your sin ("Dear Lord and Father of Mankind," "Create in Me a Clean Heart, O God," "There Is a Balm in Gilead"). Sing it to God after acknowledging a sin.

"Confession

unlocks a process

of spiritual

healing, opening

us to forgiveness,

cleansing,

reconciliation and

renewal."

MARJORIE THOMPSON

4

COMING CLEAN TO OTHERS

2 SAMUEL 11:22—12:14

To many people, admitting one's sins to another person seems unnecessary. As long as you confess to God, the issue is taken care of, right? Yet Scripture provides examples and instructions for acknowledging sins to a spiritual adviser or to others. The crowds confessed to John the Baptist in the wilderness (Matthew 3:6). The new Ephesian believers confessed their evil deeds to Paul (Acts 19:18).

The assumption that confessing only to God is always enough is a reflection of the individualistic mindset inherent in Western culture. Since the beginning of the church, confession to others has been practiced widely. When early-twentieth-century Canadian missionary Jonathan Goforth preached throughout China, it was not unusual for Christians to confess their sins publicly for several hours. The result was that the townspeople saw a tremendous change in these Christians, came to the meetings and became Christians themselves.*

Many advantages come to those who unburden themselves to another person. "He who conceals his sins does not prosper, but whoever confesses and renounces them finds mercy" (Proverbs 28:13). Confession, followed by prayer, facilitates healing: "Therefore confess your sins to each other and pray for each other so that you may be healed. The prayer of a righteous man is powerful and effective" (James 5:16). We are all a "chosen race, a royal priesthood" with a ministry of reconciliation, equipping us to receive each other's confessions (1 Peter 2:9; 2 Corinthians 5:18-20).

---

*Illustrations abound in every chapter of Jonathan Goforth, *By My Spirit* (Minneapolis: Bethany Fellowship, 1964).

Being open and honest about our mistakes facilitates true community, which isn't just about people agreeing and affirming each other. It's also about people who have reason to hate each other choosing to love instead.

Turning Toward God

What is (or would be) the most difficult aspect of admitting your sin to another person?

- embarrassment

- finding the right words

- finding someone I could trust enough to confess to

- other:

Hearing God Through the Word

King David, whom we encountered in the last session, confessed not only to God but to his spiritual adviser, Nathan. After Nathan confronted him, David could have made excuses or railed or even had Nathan executed. Instead he said words many of us find difficult to say: "Yes, I am wrong. You are right."

Read 2 Samuel 11:22-27.

1. Describe David's mindset upon hearing of the death of his brave warrior Uriah (whom he had murdered).

Read 2 Samuel 12:1-6.

2. What method did Nathan use to confront David?

3. When, if ever, has God used one of these methods or approaches to help you see yourself?

- you observe a situation parallel to one you're experiencing

- you observe someone whose attitude is as bad as yours

- a story told by a wise person

- the words of a person who has been a positive influence in your life

- you see that you're like a person you hotly condemned

- other (perhaps not used in 2 Samuel 12):

"The more

isolated a person

is, the more

destructive will

be the power of

sin over him."

DIETRICH
BONHOEFFER

Read 2 Samuel 12:7-14.

4. What phrases in verses 7-9, spoken by Nathan from the viewpoint of God, communicate the heartbreak of God over David's sin?

5. Why were such severe consequences in order for this esteemed man (vv. 10-12)?

6. What difference does it make that David made a distinct confession: "I have sinned against the LORD" (v. 13)?

7. How do you explain that even though God forgave David, David still had to experience consequences?

8. In this case, God provided Nathan's story to help David face his hidden sin. What sorts of people are open to letting God use the Holy Spirit to help them face their unrecognized or hidden sin?

9. If someone were to confess a sin to you, how—ideally—could you respond with grace and gravity?

_____

10. When is it helpful to confess to a person you sinned against?

_____

11. How might admitting sin to others—whenever you become conscious of it—change your character?

___ moving from pride to humility

___ moving from fear to courage

___ moving from apathy to charity

___ moving from deceitfulness to honesty

___ moving from turmoil to peace

___ other:

_____

12. What is the next step for you?

___ asking God's forgiveness for sin

___ finding someone to confess to because you have something to confess

___ confessing simply: There is a sin that I cannot bring myself to confess. Pray for me.

___ confessing to the person you have sinned against

___ asking God to show you the next step because you have no idea

___ other:

"In the confession of concrete sins the old man dies a painful, shameful death before the eyes of the brother. . . . In confession the break-through to new life occurs."

DIETRICH BONHOEFFER

Transformation Exercises

Experiment with one or more of the following.

- Reread Psalm 51 and note how far David had moved from his hardened heart evident in 2 Samuel 11:27.

- Try writing out a confession of a sin you have committed. Ask God to show you who might be a wise, trustworthy person to whom you could reveal it. Be patient in waiting to hear. (You also have the option of tearing it up as a sign of God's forgiveness.)

- Make a list of situations that have annoyed you recently. Then take a walk and ask God to "connect the dots" between those situations and the sinful behaviors you do habitually. Don't try too hard. Just walk.

- Look at someone you love and say, "You are right, and I am wrong." How does it feel? In what matter is it usually true that you are wrong and this person is right?

5

RECOGNIZING GOD'S PRESENCE IN MY LIFE

PSALM 65:1-13

In movies, country folk often say, "Well, I recollect . . ." and they tell you what they remember. Many sentences in Scripture begin with "Remember," because we need to recollect how we have experienced God. Not all of these experiences happen at church. We can be drawn to God while reading a letter, holding a memento or glancing at the sky before getting into a car in a parking lot. Recollecting these moments is another facet of reflection and confession. We take time to acknowledge how God is speaking to us in our lives.

This process of recollection is part of what has been called the "prayer of examen," a prayer pattern used for centuries by Christians. It has two parts—the examination of *conscience* and the examination of *consciousness*. In the former we search for wrongs done and admit them (sessions 2-4). In the latter we gently search our lives for divine moments. We ask ourselves questions such as these:

- Did I meet God in the joy or pain of others?

- Did I bring Christ into my world in some way?

- Did anyone bring God to me?

- Did I reach out to someone in trouble or sorrow?

- Did I fail or refuse to do so?

- Did something that happened to me today give me a keener sense of being loved, or being angry or tired, or needing God in some special way?

- Is there any concrete event of the day that revealed some part of my life that I am withholding from God?

Prayers of examen change our way of seeing and become a rhythm of life. In fact, many use such prayers every evening, while others use them once a week or month or year. They enlighten us to the brilliant hues of our connection with God.

Turning Toward God

What is the best thing that has happened to you recently?

Hearing God Through the Word

The writer of Psalm 65 seems to have had many moments of experiencing God. In this thanksgiving psalm, he speaks directly to God, recalling, reflecting and recollecting how God has forgiven, worked in power and provided.

Read Psalm 65:1-4.

1. Even though the psalmist was at one time overwhelmed by sin (v. 3), what is his state now?

2. In prayers of reflection and confession, why is it important to include expressions of what we intend to do to change our ways (such as the psalmist's vows mentioned in v. 1)?

3. Think of something you've done recently that you're not proud of. What is the way forward from that behavior? As you answer, don't mention the wrong deed, but begin your answer by saying, "Learning to . . ."

Read Psalm 65:5-8.

4. How did God answer the psalmist's prayer?

5. What are some ways you have recently experienced "answers" from God?

    ___ something good or right happened ("deeds of righteousness," v. 5)

    ___ God's power created a new outward circumstance or inner condition in you or someone else ("armed yourself with strength," v. 6)

    ___ God's power stilled a troublesome circumstance or inner condition in you or someone else or even in a nation ("stilled the roaring," v. 7)

    ___ those living far away saw God at work (v. 8)

    ___ other:

"God invites us to discern the footprints of the Holy, to rehearse the mighty deeds of God."

RICHARD FOSTER

6. What are some simple ways we can recollect with "songs of joy" when "morning dawns and evening fades?"

7. When do you regularly reflect on what God has done in your life? (If you don't, when might you like to?)

Read Psalm 65:9-13.

8. How did the psalmist experience God's intervening in his life and providing?

9. What are the "grasslands" and "meadows" in your life that have sprouted in the past year? in the past week?

"If we pray

the Examen

regularly,

10. What categories of things did the psalmist recollect about (see vv. 1-13)?

generously, and

courageously, . . .

we will begin to

11. Think about yesterday and recollect by considering one of these

see ourselves and

questions and then reflecting on what that tells you about God and

understand our

yourself:

actions in a whole

• What surprised me?

new way. We will

• What touched or moved me?

begin to recognize

• What encounters nurtured me?

God in all things,

to rejoice in the

12. How might a discipline of recollection lead to development of disci-

invitational,

plines of practicing the presence of God and worshiping throughout

relational love of

the day?

God."

DEBORAH
SMITH DOUGLAS

Transformation Exercises

Experiment with one or more of the following.

- At the end of a day, consider two or three of the questions in question 11.

- Compare the elements of the prayer of examen of conscience developed by Ignatius Loyola (below) with the elements in Psalm 65. How many are similar?

    give thanks to God for benefits received

    ask grace to know my sins and rid myself of them

    account for my soul from the hour of rising to the present moment

    ask God's pardon for faults

    resolve with God's grace to amend them (How can I change? What is the way forward?)

- Pray, asking God to help you notice the "answers" from God listed in question 5 for the next three days.

6

JOURNALING

JEREMIAH 15:10-21; 17:5-8

A help to me in working things out has been to keep an honest . . . unpublishable journal. . . . Not long ago someone I love said something which wounded me grievously. So, in great pain, I crawled to my journal and wrote it all out in a great burst of self-pity. And when I had set it down, I saw that something I myself had said had called forth the words which had hurt me so. It had, in fact, been my own fault. But I would never have seen it if I had not written it out.

In the quote above, Madeleine L'Engle describes the revelatory nature of a journal written with God as the audience. As we put experiences and feelings into concrete words, we create an opportunity for God to speak to us. The point of journaling is to reveal the inner workings of our hearts with complete honesty so we see ourselves and our behavior more clearly. That's why a journal is an ideal place to admit our sins or sort out what we need to say to God.

A journal also invites us to explore issues of neediness behind our sin: *why am I so angry?* Journaling must not, however, degenerate into spiritual navel gazing; it's merely another way to connect with God. If writing words seems too tedious for you, you can jog or ride a bike or do stitchery and release thoughts to God in a similar way. We focus our bodies on an activity while pondering before God in a less formal way.

Turning Toward God

Which of these concerns might keep you from journaling?

- worry that someone will read the journal

- feeling that it's too painful to go over a conflict

- disliking to write things down (a friend of mine is so intimidated by the idea of journaling that she insists she merely "scribbles" now and then)

- feeling obligated to write in it every day (actually you can journal once a week, once a month or whenever you need to)

- thinking you need to have a special sort of book (really a spiral notebook or a computer will do)

- other:

Hearing God Through the Word

In a journal-like fashion, the prophet Jeremiah recorded confessions, laments, monologues, dialogues and disputes with God. Called as a boy to preach doom and destruction, Jeremiah was asked to remain celibate (Jeremiah 16:1-3). He was shunned by friends, plotted against by residents of his hometown (11:18-19) and put in a cistern by government officials (38:1-6). You can see why he processed so much grief before God!

Read Jeremiah 15:10-14.

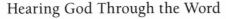

1. What was Jeremiah's complaint?

2. Jeremiah's despair stemmed from his interactions with God, recorded in chapters 14–15.

"I have been keeping these notebooks of thoughts and questions and sometimes just garbage (which needs to be dumped somewhere) since I was about nine, and they are, I think, my free psychiatrist's couch."

MADELEINE L'ENGLE

Jeremiah's Request	God's Reply
asked for relief from the drought (14:1-9)	did not agree to send rain (14:10-12)
interceded for Judah by saying that their prophets had misled them (14:13)	agreed with Jeremiah, but continued to condemn the people of Judah (14:14-18)
acknowledged Judah's guilt but asked for mercy (14:19-22)	did not relent about sending Judah into captivity (15:1-9)

When have you gotten "no" answers from God and felt discouraged as Jeremiah did?

Read Jeremiah 15:15-18.

3. What truths about the character of God does Jeremiah state (vv. 15-18)?

"In journaling, we

know ourselves

as we really

are and feel

4. What does Jeremiah state of his personal experiences?

the acceptance

of the one who

5. What does Jeremiah state of his feelings?

loves us without

reservation."

6. What questions does Jeremiah ask?

ANNE BROYLES

7. If you were to write in a journal, which of the following elements of Jeremiah's lament would you probably include?

___ complaints

___ reminding yourself about the character of God

___ personal experiences

___ feelings

___ questions you want to ask God

___ other:

Read Jeremiah 15:19-21.

8. What did God want of Jeremiah?

9. What did God promise Jeremiah?

10. How do you think God "answers" people as they journal?

Read Jeremiah 17:5-8.

11. How did God later describe the person who is cursed and the one who is blessed?

12. Why would it be easier to confess to God in a journal than aloud to God or to another person? Why would it be more difficult?

"I confess, O God—that often I let my mind wander down unclean and forbidden ways; . . . that often, by concealing my real motives, I pretend to be better than I am; that often my affection for my friends is only a refined form of caring for myself; that often I do good deeds only that they may be seen of men, and shun evil ones only because I fear they may be found out. O holy One, let the fire of Thy love enter my heart, and burn up all this coil of meanness and hypocrisy, and make my heart as the heart of a little child."

JOHN BAILLIE

Transformation Exercises

Experiment with one or more of the following.

- Journal or draw or record your thoughts on a tape or CD about a complaint, a personal experience or a feeling. Be alert to anything you need to confess, questions you need to ask or characteristics of God you need to remind yourself of. (Any time you journal, feel free to tear it up when you're finished, if you need to do so.)

- Think of a resentment you feel and work through the following questions in a journal.

    Examine the cause—how did this resentment occur?

    What have been the effects of this resentment on you (withdrawal, defensiveness, fear of rejection, need to prove self, isolation, repressed anger, approval seeking, control, caretaking, fear of abandonment, fear of authority figures, frozen feelings, over- or underdeveloped sense of responsibility)?

    What was your part, if any, in bringing this resentment or its effects upon you?

    If you would like freedom from this resentment, confess it to God and ask God to help you be delivered from it.

- Draw something or play an instrument, and notice how such activities can resemble journaling. What do you learn from the songs you choose to sing or the objects you choose to draw? What could you sing or draw that would serve as a confession for you?

STUDY NOTES FOR
REFLECTION AND CONFESSION

Session 1. Believing in a God Who Heals

PSALMS 103

FOCUS: Even when confessing sin, we bask in the love and compassion of our almighty God.

Turning Toward God. Bring up images of people sitting under bare lightbulbs in military prisons and in back rooms of organized crime. More benignly, confessing reminds us of our failures.

Question 1. "Healing" diseases (v. 3) is more than "merely bodily diseases, but all kinds of inward and outward sufferings."[1] Also, the parallelism of Hebrew poetry, as in verse 3 (two parallel lines offering the same meaning with different words), shows that to be forgiven is to find healing.

Question 3. The word for *accuse* (v. 9) was used in a legal sense and does not refer to harping or nagging or being mean. God also does not "harbor anger," indulging it or brooding. God's anger is "not carried to the full extent" of what it could be, considering God's power.[2] God's justice or anger is not measured out according to what we have done but according to what God believes is right. God is not about "payback" (v. 10).

Question 5. As vast as the distance from heaven to earth, as vast as the distance from east to west, as immense as a father's love for his child.

Question 6. Dust and "grass, which in the dry Orient is often of such short duration. It takes no more than the passing of the hot wind of the desert over it on certain hot days, and the grass is gone."[3]

Question 7. Humility comes from a realistic understanding of who we are in relation to God. Otherwise it's easy for Christians to view themselves as superior to others or "better" than they were before their life in Christ. Humility helps us understand that everything depends on Christ. Awareness of our fragility leads to an uninflated, realistic view of ourselves.

Question 8. Says Marjorie Thompson, "As we perceive the realities of sin in ourselves, we can identify with the brokenness of others. Instead of condemning someone whose behavior is irritating or unacceptable, we may recall similar behavior in our own lives."[4]

Question 9. The words for fear in Hebrew and Greek are sometimes translated as *dread* or *terror*.

---

[1]Franz Delitzsch, *Commentary on the Old Testament,* vol. 5, *Commentary on the Psalms* (Grand Rapids: Eerdmans, 1973), p. 120

[2]Ibid., p. 122.

[3]H. C. Leupold, *Exposition of the Psalms* (Grand Rapids: Baker, 1972), 1:719-20.

[4]Marjorie Thompson, *Soul Feast* (Louisville, Ky.: Westminster John Knox, 1995), p. 98.

Other times they're translated to imply a healthy fear, even reverence. The translators seem to rely on the context, and so should we. The context in the psalm points to a compassionate, merciful God. This makes it clear that the fear mentioned here is not dread or terror but a holy, wholesome fear of disappointing or grieving the great God we love and are devoted to. God does not delight in terrifying folks but in finding a contrite, willing heart within them.

Question 11. The purpose of confession is not to feel beaten up and overwhelmed. The purpose is always to love God more and be more enthralled with the great God who loves us. We are limited, finite followers of God, being slowly transformed into Christlikeness.

Session 2. Letting God Search My Heart

1 CORINTHIANS 13:1-7

FOCUS: We can experiment with the process of asking God to show us where our hearts lack love, confessing that lack and reestablishing ourselves in God's love.

Question 1. An eloquent speaker, a person with prophetic power, an especially wise person, someone whose faith everyone trusts, a donor who gives up the rest of his fortune, a martyr. The heart is so deceitful that people can do good (even devout) deeds without a heart of love. "The heart is deceitful above all things and beyond cure. Who can understand it?" (Jeremiah 17:9). Think of it—Paul was worried about martyrs dying with hearts of self-righteousness. We'd figure, "Gee, they're martyrs! They must be pure no matter what's in their heart!"

Question 2. After reading the passage the second time, explain that reading this convicting passage this way will help us avoid the sin of emphasizing human flaws rather than being enthralled with the great God who loves us. Confession is to be grounded in the self-giving love of God.

Question 3. Read the Marjorie Thompson quotation on page 195 before reading question 3. Allow three to five minutes of silence for this. Gently end the silence with a quiet prayer, thanking God that God speaks to us, and asking God to keep speaking and prodding us about whatever we need to know about ourselves.

Question 5. Because God "keeps no record of wrongs," we need to do the same for ourselves (after we've confessed and asked for forgiveness). By focusing on our mistakes and faults, we are focusing on or "delighting in evil," instead of rejoicing in the truth that God's power is transforming us (v. 6).

God's love moves us forward instead of beating us back.

Question 7. You may wish to suggest this question about any situation: Was I motivated by God's love, or was there something else I was loving and pursuing instead?

Question 10. *Berating myself, hoping . . .* You may wish to have group participants look up these verses: "The Spirit searches all things, even the deep things of God" (1 Corinthians 2:10). "I the LORD search the heart and examine the mind, to reward a man according to his conduct, according to what his deeds deserve" (Jeremiah 17:10).

If you try to be the one who does the examining, there is a very good chance that you will deceive yourself. You will never really allow yourself to see your true state. This is the simple fact about the nature of your own self-love. "We call the evil good, and the good evil"[5] (Isaiah 5:20).

---

[5]Jeanne Guyon, *Experiencing the Depths of Jesus Christ* (Beaumont, Tex.: SeedSowers, 1975), p. 74.

Letting self-examination be . . . Colossians 3:1-10 shows that even as we've been "raised with Christ," we need to continually "put to death . . . whatever belongs to [our] earthly nature" and "put on the new self, which is being renewed in knowledge in the image of its Creator."

Question 11. As you see your faults, you can ask God to show you which spiritual disciplines would be helpful. For example, if you discern that you are lazy, you might ask God for a spiritual discipline of service. If you see that you are angry, you might ask for a spiritual discipline of meditation (brooding on God instead of self) or fasting (not getting what I want and learning to live with that).

Session 3. Confessing to God

PSALM 51

FOCUS: David's confession helps us explore the subtleties and benefits of confessing to God.

Question 1. God's unfailing love, not any mitigating factors or minimizing of David's sin.

Question 2. This verse shows that forgiveness is never based on how bad or not so bad the sin was, but always on God's forgiveness. To say "God can't forgive me," then, is to say that God's love is not encompassing enough. It suggests a failure on God's part.

Question 3. He speaks of his iniquity (v. 2, using a Hebrew word meaning "perversion and twisting of moral standards"), sin (v. 2, "divinely appointed goal has been missed") and transgressions (v. 3, "rebellion").[6] David does not minimize his sin, make excuses, speak defensively or rehearse how wrong the other people were. He doesn't say, "I'm such a successful soldier and king—I deserve some pleasure," or "I had no choice but to . . ." When he speaks of being "sinful at birth, sinful from the time my mother conceived me," he isn't making excuses but stating the fact that all sin and fall short of the mark. As exalted as he was in Israelite society, he didn't see himself as superhuman but as flesh born of flesh.

Question 4. We freely admit who we are, not pretending to be better than we are. Like David, we keep our sins before us (v. 3). We don't try to make our confession sound light or casual even though we're sure of God's forgiveness. What we say is who we really are.

Question 5. While David did also sin against Bathsheba and Uriah, he lived as the Puritans lived—as if standing before an audience of One, that is, living to God alone.[7] All sin is then against the Holy One. This is not a reason for terror but a mark of intimacy with God. It's as if we say, "Only you, O God, know who I am truly."

Question 6. We need renewal not just in behavior but in the "inner parts." Even though we've been "crushed," God leads us into rejoicing. God's creativity includes purifying our hearts and giving us a steadfast spirit.

Question 7. A restored person naturally becomes a teacher of transgressors and one who sings of God's righteousness. Formerly crushed but newly healed bones shout of the efficacy of a great God who makes diamonds out of crushed coal.

Question 9. We shortchange ourselves by rushing to God to ask for forgiveness without fully confessing our sins. Being silent about sin can immobilize us (Psalm 32:3-4), but confessing sin is

---

[6]Leupold, *Exposition of the Psalms,* 1:401.
[7]Dallas Willard, *The Divine Conspiracy* (San Francisco: HarperSanFrancisco, 1998), p. 190.

a constructive way to deal with guilt. Instead of languishing in shame, we can (with the help of the Spirit) determine which of our character flaws was involved and ask God to show us how to fur-

ther address that flaw. Confessing sin allows us to move forward (vv. 13-15) instead of being haunted by past mistakes. It also teaches us the skill of surrendering to God who is holy yet loves us.

Session 4. Coming Clean to Others

2 SAMUEL 11:22—12:14

FOCUS: The importance, power and process of confessing our sins to others.

Question 1. David covered up well. He pretended to be unconcerned and feigned encouragement to Joab (2 Samuel 11:25). Wanting to continue the cover-up, he waited until a respectable time of mourning was over before marrying Uriah's widow, Bathsheba. Overall, he was "flippant and insensitive. While he grieved deeply for Saul and Abner, his rivals (2 Sam. 1; 3:31-39), he showed no grief for Uriah, a good man with strong spiritual character. Why? . . . Deliberate, repeated sinning had dulled David's sensitivity to God's laws and others' rights. The more you try to cover up a sin, the more insensitive you become toward it."[8]

Question 2. Nathan used a story, which drew David in rather than causing him to be defensive. The story was about sheep owning, and David's first occupation had been to herd sheep. Nathan's details are keen: The poor man has not inherited or been given this lamb but has gone out of his way to purchase it. This creates a huge contrast between the poor man and the wealthy rancher.

Question 4. "I anointed . . . I delivered . . . I gave . . . I gave . . . I would have given": God communicated all he had done for David. (Verse 8 is the only mention in Scripture that David had received all of Saul's household and wives. This seems to mitigate any reason for adultery.)

"Despise the word of the LORD by doing what is

evil in his eyes" tells us that in a relationship with God, disobedience is not impersonal. It's an affront to the God we have devoted ourselves to.

Question 5. David was a public figure with God's hand on him. For God to have overlooked this sin or to let him off lightly would have encouraged all kinds of sin in others. Often the sin of a public figure gives permission to people (even that person's children) to stop persevering against sin. The fallout is enormous. "David's children shared his weakness, but few demonstrated his redeeming characteristic of contriteness. In his frequent departures, David remained open to correction. Not so his sons."[9] To help group participants understand verses 10-12, mention that the results were the deaths of David's sons Amnon (2 Samuel 13:28-29), Absalom (2 Samuel 18:5, 9-15) and Adonijah (1 Kings 1:5-53, 2:13-25). Second Samuel 12:11 refers to Absalom's public seizure of the royal concubines (2 Samuel 16:22).

Question 6. It showed immediate and contrite repentance. He could have lashed out against Nathan. King Ahab, for example, called Elijah his "enemy" when Elijah confronted him about murdering Naboth for his vineyard (1 Kings 21:20).

Question 7. God offers *pardon* but, like a good parent, may still employ *consequences*. These are two different issues. Christians sometimes choose to sin because they know God will forgive

---

[8]*Life Application Bible* (Wheaton, Ill.: Tyndale House, 1991), p. 511.
[9]Lawrence O. Richards, *The Teacher's Commentary* (Wheaton, Ill.: Victor, 1987), p. 237.

them. And God does. But consequences remain: we "set into motion events with irreversible consequences."[10] It was important that the child not survive because David needed to receive no reward for his sin.

Question 8. Those well versed in listening to God in Scripture, solitude and all of life (including the "Nathans") will hear the Holy Spirit confront them.

Question 9. You would: take their confession seriously; not brush it off by saying everyone has these problems; not be shocked and judge those who confess; not try to fix them with self-help books and Scripture quoting; not give advice; pray for them and encourage them without bringing up past sin; ask them if they wish to be accountable,

meaning that they will check in to report progress and perhaps make contact when tempted. Even when people check in with failures, they need words of grace and empowerment.

Often it helps to say distinctly to confessing people that their sin is forgiven by God. You are reminding them of what they already know intellectually but are struggling to believe in their deepest selves.

Question 10. Confessing to the person you sinned against can bring healing and reconciliation. Do not confess when it will cause harm to the other person. When in doubt, ask God for direction and then follow it. You may want to back up and ask, "When is it not helpful?" and then move on to this question.

Session 5. Recognizing God's Presence in My Life

PSALM 65:1-13

FOCUS: Recalling moments of the day when God's touch was noticed or needed.

Question 1. He is well off, being "filled with the good things of your house." ("Your house" could be the temple or the "invisible courts of God's spiritual presence.")[11] He has even made vows, which are voluntary promises to do certain things or abstain from them.

Question 2. In all of the Christian life, it's important to be asking God, What is the next step? But this is especially true when we confess sin. Many confessions in Scripture identify what the way forward is and how the confessing person intends to follow it (see Psalm 51:13-19, a third of the psalm). When we are unsure of what the next step is, we need to ask God to show us what it is and perhaps talk with a wise friend.

Question 4. Although the exact prayer is not stat-

ed (v. 2), God's answer is clear: "awesome deeds of righteousness." Then the psalmist seems to say, "Why am I so surprised by this? After all . . ." and describes creation and how it exhibits God's qualities: hope through creation's vastness (v. 5), power and strength through forces of creation (vv. 6-7), and glory through the way those far away recognize God's greatness (v. 8).

Question 5. We do a lot of asking in our prayers. We need to watch for God's responses and acknowledge them.

Question 6: Some suggestions: Making it a point to enjoy each sunrise and sunset, even with a special prayer or song; using a prayer of recollection or thanksgiving each day.

Question 7. If participants feel blank, ask about such moments as at the Thanksgiving dinner table or in Communion.

---

[10]*Life Application Bible*, p. 512.
[11]Leupold, *Exposition of the Psalms*, 1:474.

Question 10. The psalmist recollected how God heard prayers (v. 2), forgave (v. 3), filled them with good things (v. 4), did actions of goodness (v. 5), gave hope (v. 5), exhibited qualities of power and strength (vv. 6-8) and exhibited constant care for creation (vv. 9-13).

Session 6. Journaling

JEREMIAH 15:10-21; 17:5-8

FOCUS: Journaling can help us face and confess thoughts and feelings.

Question 1. Jeremiah was in anguish, wishing he had not been born because his job of foretelling misery and ruin upon Judah was so unpopular and discouraging. Scholars generally interpret verse 10 to mean that Jeremiah cursed the day he was born. "His call dated from his mother's womb (1:5), and to curse the day of his birth was tantamount to a rejection of his very mission."[12] The second portion shows that he had not brought others' curses upon himself through fraudulent dealings.

Many commentators agree that Jeremiah 15:11-14 are difficult verses to interpret because the Hebrew words can be translated in various ways. C. F. Keil's sense of it is as follows: Those who cursed Jeremiah would eventually see Jeremiah was right. They would not be able to oppose Babylon, just as men can't break iron. Every word Jeremiah prophesied would come true—even the taking of Judah's treasures.[13]

Read Jeremiah 15:15-18. Ask that as the Scripture is read aloud the group count the personal pronouns—*you, your, me, my, I.* One person can read aloud (emphasizing the pronouns) while another participant counts. This is better than counting silently. Save this information for question 5.

Question 3. God understands us (v. 15); God is long-suffering (v. 15); God's words can be our "heart's delight" (v. 16). Jeremiah was acknowledging these truths before God, but he may have also reviewed them to remind himself since he was so discouraged.

Question 5. Suffering (v. 15), delight (v. 16), indignation (v. 17), unending pain (v. 18). Ask about the number of personal pronouns in the text. Their abundance (twenty-four in NIV) indicates how deeply personal Jeremiah's prophetic book was (as well as his relationship with God). Some have compared his book to a journal.

Question 6. Note especially the question, "Will you be to me like a deceptive brook, like a spring that fails?" (v. 18). A brook was deceptive "when it went dry in summer and couldn't be depended on for water."[14]

Question 8. God wanted Jeremiah to repent of his hopelessness in cursing the day he was born. If group participants respond by saying that Jeremiah had a right to feel sorry for himself (see details in the paragraph before "Hearing God Through the Word"), state that God's response reflects the personal nature of a journal. The person journaling can often hear very difficult things from God that would sound too harsh if God used another person as a messenger.

Question 10. Reminding them of the truths of God; revealing truths about themselves as they

---

[12]J. A. Thompson, *The Book of Jeremiah,* New International Commentary on the Old Testament (Grand Rapids: Eerdmans, 1980), p. 392.

[13]C. F. Keil, *Commentary on the Old Testament: Jeremiah, Lamentations* (Grand Rapids: Eerdmans, 1973), pp. 259-62.

[14]Thompson, *Book of Jeremiah,* p. 397.

reread what they've already written, as described by Madeleine L'Engle (quotation in this session's introduction).

Question 11. Note also that Jeremiah's new view (Jeremiah 17:8) answers his earlier questions about pain and wounds and doubts about God (15:18). He now has confidence instead of fear and worry: "Blessed is the man who trusts in the LORD, whose confidence is in him. He will be like a tree planted by the water that sends out its roots by the stream."

Section Seven

SIMPLICITY & FASTING

Simplicity and fasting are both disciplines of abstinence. In simplicity, we abstain from participating in activities and owning possessions that are extraneous and do not further the purposes God has given us. To fast means we don't get to eat what we want or don't get to engage in some activity that we prefer (watching television or listening to music). Both disciplines train us in self-denial, which is a key mark of a Christian. They help us empty ourselves so we become hungry for the things that really matter. We find a new focus on God. As we die to self, we are free to reorient ourselves to life lived fully in God.

But that death to self is difficult! Both simplicity and fasting train us to relinquish what we want. But when done as God leads, they do not need to make us miserable. Indeed, simplicity is richness and fasting is feasting in the truest sense. They both teach us to truly enjoy each blessing of creation as it comes—enjoying one simple luscious grape at a time, being grateful for a car that runs well and gets us from one place to the next.

These two disciplines, as with all disciplines of abstinence, teach us a way to be in the world but not of the world. We learn to love the world God so loves without running on the fuel it runs on—unlimited amounts and varieties of foods, media, and words. We take a break from the sicknesses of our culture—information anxiety, obsessing over just the right food, endless competition with whomever I'm standing next to. We learn to be immersed in the concerns of our world but completely different from it. Our responses are different, enabling us to be salt and light.

1

THE SINGLE-HEARTED
PERSON

MATTHEW 6:19-24, 33

When we say we're "going in twenty directions" or "feeling scattered," that's usually not a good sign. It means we feel torn and frustrated, as if we never get anything done or never do anything well. It leads to a life of regret. Yet we also talk as if we think it's good or even saintly to be busy.

As we practice simplicity, the Holy Spirit trains us to cut busyness and hurry out of our lives by remaining focused on God and God's kingdom. We refrain from participating in activities and owning possessions that are superfluous and do not further our union with God. The result is singleness of heart, so that we are deliberate and purposeful in everything we do and say and think.

But simplicity may look different for each person and for each culture. For many of us, it means not caring about owning the kinds of things that a self-respecting thief would break in and steal. But it also means not being "holier than thou" about what we don't own or don't do. In and of themselves, simplicity choices mean nothing. We discard certain objects and activities because they take us away from what God created us to do: to have union with God, to hear what God is calling us to do in the kingdom and to take the next step in doing that.

Turning Toward God

Describe the last time you remember feeling hurried, torn and pulled in different directions.

Hearing God Through the Word

Simplicity is the alternative for those who heard Matthew 6:19-24 as part of the Sermon on the Mount. In this section, Jesus urged people to stop trying to secure themselves through reputation and wealth. Instead, they should seek God and God's kingdom and everything else would take care of itself.

Read Matthew 6:19-21.

1. What reasons does Jesus give for not storing up treasures?

"Were our lives

simpler, we

would be more

vulnerable to the

subtle workings of

the soul."

MARY CONROW
COELHO

2. What objects or goals often become "treasures on earth" that we "store up"?

    How do they complicate our lives (v. 19)?

3. How do these treasures get destroyed or stolen, much to our despair?

4. What would it look like to live with God as one's "treasure"?

Read Matthew 6:22-24.

5. Verse 22 in the King James Version reads "if therefore thine eye be *single*." How are you full of light instead of darkness when the eye of your soul has a "single" focus?

6. Richard Foster notes that "when Jesus said that 'no one can serve two masters,' he did not mean that it was unwise to serve two masters, but that it was impossible." When we try to do this anyway, what miserable results do we experience?

7. What inner motives drive us to serve so-called earthly treasures while we are trying to serve God?

Read Matthew 6:33.

8. What does "all these things" seem to refer to?

9. How do we get distracted from primary characteristics of Christians: seeking God, being conduits of God's grace?

10. Simplicity can be defined as "being clear and uncomplicated." How is God calling you to be clear and uncomplicated in one of the areas listed?

___ your life with God

___ your relationships with others

___ what God has called you to do

> *"[The Puritans]
> lived as if they
> stood before an
> audience of One,
> carrying on their
> lives as if the only
> one whose opinion
> mattered were
> God."*
> Os Guinness

11. What do you believe God is calling you to do in relation to one of these patterns of thought or action?

___ have clear and uncomplicated purposes

___ be deliberate about focusing on God

___ minimize the things that distract you from seeking God

12. Which of the transformation exercises would be most helpful in letting God work within you?

Transformation Exercises

Experiment with one or more of the following.

- Walk around your house or apartment and pick up or gaze at items you truly treasure. Kneel next to them (or hold them) and ask God,

   What is it within me that causes me to treasure this?

   What would have to happen within me to help me be willing to give it away?

- Visit the places where you do your "treasuring" of God (perhaps the bed where you read your Bible, the paths where you walk and talk to God, even the driver's seat of your car where you've pondered what God is saying to you). Say a prayer of thanks for the moments you've known of treasuring God. Ask God to help you live a God-centered life.

- Find the hymn "Be Thou My Vision" and read the words of the stanza that begins, "Riches I heed not" and ends with "my treasure thou art" (speaking to God). Take these words with you on a walk and sing this song, especially this stanza, to God. Or use another song that speaks of God as one's treasure.

"There is a prevailing philosophy today that has dominated culture, including religious culture, that it's a positive virtue to satisfy absolutely every human passion. Whole churches have been created around these tin gods of good feelings and affluence."

RICHARD FOSTER

2

LESS IS MORE

MATTHEW 6:24-34

Wen Jean-Nicholas Grou, a highly touted, well-established priest, was forced to flee to England to escape the bloodshed of the French Revolution, his friends were horrified. He lived his final eleven years in a cell the size of a big cupboard, but he didn't mind. He said, "There is no reason for me to be rich, no reason why I should not suffer a loss of temporal goods which, while reducing my luxuries and depriving me of certain comforts, will still leave me a decent livelihood." This was where he wrote the classic work *How to Pray*.

The adage "less is more" is about simplicity. Often, the less that is said, the better. The less that is spent, the better. The less fuss on clothes, the better. Simplicity is an expression of frugality, which means we refrain from spending or using resources to add to our status, glamour or sense of luxury.

Simplicity's opposite is indulgence. Perhaps you've caught yourself grabbing for more at a sale, a buffet or a networking meeting. The frenzy to save money, eat scrumptious food or make influential contacts takes over. We gotta do, gotta be, gotta have, until we're exhausted. Disciplines of simplicity train us away from those cravings and teach us to trust God, to let our character speak for itself.

Yet God may speak to each of us differently about what disciplines of simplicity we need. Different values pull at us, and thus we begin in different places.

Turning Toward God

Which of these actions would be most difficult for you if you had to do it for a week?

- eating food that is bland and poorly prepared

- wearing mismatched clothes in public places

- wearing clothes that aren't stylish in public places

- drinking only water for a week

- going without coffee or _____

- other (related to choices in eating, drinking or clothing):

Hearing God Through the Word

Read Matthew 6:24-30.

1. What reasons did Jesus give for not worrying about food, drink or clothes?

2. Jesus' jokes were usually statements of absurdity. For example, it's absurd to believe that for every hour you sat and worried about when you were going to die, God would automatically credit you with another hour of life (v. 27). What other issues do we routinely worry about even though worrying doesn't do any good?

   ___ what others think of us

   ___ losing weight

   ___ generating more income

   ___ other:

3. What choices of clothing or ways of dressing are least likely to distract you from seeking God and following God in the building of the kingdom (primarily through loving others)?

Read Matthew 6:31-34.

4. Why does Jesus say that worry is an issue for "pagans" but not for Christians?

5. How are worry and anxiety natural results of lack of simplicity or singleness of purpose?

6. Jesus used the examples of food, water and clothing to talk about not being preoccupied with certain things. If Jesus were speaking to our culture, what other examples might he have used?

7. If you were to let go of the things you're preoccupied with (the passage cites food, drink and clothing), what worthwhile activities might you have more time for?

8. Verse 33 has been paraphrased by Dallas Willard as follows: "Direct your actions toward making a difference in the realm of spiritual substance sustained and governed by God. Invest your life in what God is doing, which cannot be lost." What spiritual practices or down-to-earth influences have helped you to invest in "what God is doing"?

9. How is living one day at a time (v. 34) a sign of simplicity?

"The fallen human now lives as if there were no legitimate limits. It is considered a God-given right to use every resource and creature on earth for personal enjoyment or gain. The goal of human life is to acquire more, to experience more, to stimulate every sense to capacity and beyond."

MARJORIE THOMPSON

10. What sort of relationship with God does a person need to have in order to do what this passage says (vv. 24-34) and let go of worry and preoccupation with simple earthly matters?

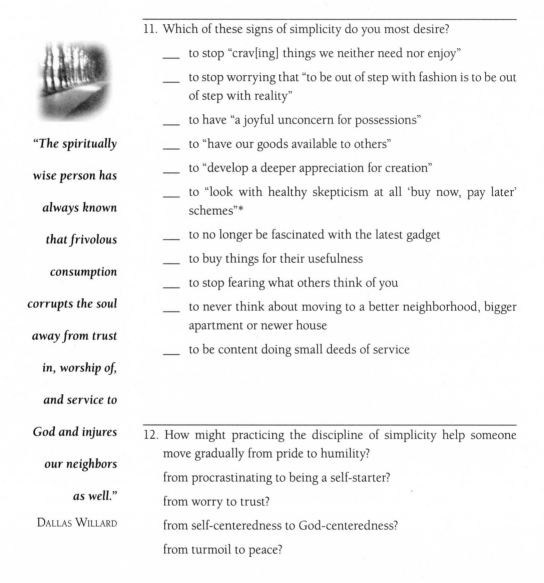

"The spiritually wise person has always known that frivolous consumption corrupts the soul away from trust in, worship of, and service to God and injures our neighbors as well."

DALLAS WILLARD

11. Which of these signs of simplicity do you most desire?

___ to stop "crav[ing] things we neither need nor enjoy"

___ to stop worrying that "to be out of step with fashion is to be out of step with reality"

___ to have "a joyful unconcern for possessions"

___ to "have our goods available to others"

___ to "develop a deeper appreciation for creation"

___ to "look with healthy skepticism at all 'buy now, pay later' schemes"*

___ to no longer be fascinated with the latest gadget

___ to buy things for their usefulness

___ to stop fearing what others think of you

___ to never think about moving to a better neighborhood, bigger apartment or newer house

___ to be content doing small deeds of service

12. How might practicing the discipline of simplicity help someone move gradually from pride to humility?

from procrastinating to being a self-starter?

from worry to trust?

from self-centeredness to God-centeredness?

from turmoil to peace?

*The quotations are from Richard Foster, *Celebration of Discipline* (San Francisco: Harper & Row, 1988), pp. 80, 87, 89, 93.

Transformation Exercises

Experiment with one or more of the following.

- Reread Matthew 6:24-34 aloud slowly. Which word or phrase is most meaningful to you? Why? What does that phrase tell you about how you need to connect with God?

- Ask God to show you how to let go of the possessions you serve. For example, you might give away an object that needs frequent maintenance and repairs and replace it with something more sturdy and less luxurious.

- Talk with a friend about one of the items that stood out to you in question 11. Discuss these questions: What would it look like for you to be that way? How would you be different? Ask your friend to pray that God's abiding love would be so apparent to you that doing something like this would be easy.

- Look at your checkbook or bank statement and take note of how you spend your money. Ask God to show you what to let go of.

3

SIMPLE TALK

MATTHEW 5:33-37

Have you ever tried to talk out a problem with someone, only to discover that the more you talked, the worse things got? While learning communication skills is helpful, talking has its limits. Discussing a problem can help people see each other's heart, but something more than an exchange of words is required to solve problems. We may need to reflect more on the other person's needs or on our own shortcomings.

Talking too much is often about pressuring people. With elaborate facial expressions and hand gestures, we make sure coworkers or children know "we mean what we say." Dallas Willard puts it like this: "When we're with those we feel less than secure with, we use words to 'adjust' our appearance and elicit their approval. Otherwise, we fear our virtues might not receive adequate appreciation and our shortcomings might not be properly 'understood.' In not speaking, we resign how we appear to God. And that is hard."

Simplicity of language teaches us to be who we are and leave it at that.

Turning Toward God

In what situations do you think talking is overrated: disciplining children? doing well in a job interview? Resolving conflicts?

Hearing God Through the Word

In this session's passage, Jesus addresses the problem of manipulative language in the common Jewish practice of "evasive swearing." So a person could swear by something other than God and have no intention of following through. Their thinking seemed to be, *As long as we avoid God's name, anything goes.*

Read Matthew 5:33-36.

1. What was the goal of the command given to "people long ago"?

"The man whose heart is true to God utters every statement he makes as though it were made in the very presence of God before whom even his heart with its inmost thought lies bare."

R. C. H. Lenski

2. What seems to have been the goal of those who swore carelessly as long as the oath didn't include God's name?

3. Why, according to Jesus, was it ridiculous to think that swearing by your head did not involve God?

4. What are the negative effects of leading a life in which we are conscious of God's presence only part of the time?

Read Matthew 5:37.

5. What makes us think it's necessary to say more than a simple yes or no in response to a question or request?

   ___ believing we're obliged to verbalize every thought that pops into our head

   ___ trying to impress people

___ worrying about what others think of us

___ trying to win folks over to our side to sell them a product or idea

___ being pushy

___ trying to prove we're sincere

___ attempting to be forceful so people will believe what we believe or do what we tell them to do

___ other:

"Develop a habit of plain honest speech. Strike 'I am starved' from your speaking vocabulary. It's not true and obscures the fact that many indeed are starving. When you are hungry say that you are hungry and reserve the word 'starvation' for the real thing."

RICHARD FOSTER

6. How are each of the reasons listed in question 5 actually temptations that come "from the evil one"?

7. What sort of heart is required for someone to state an idea briefly and allow the other person full freedom to make their response?

8. In what situations are people most likely to talk too much?

___ when afraid of being overlooked

___ when nervous and worried about what others think of them

___ when defending themselves

___ when they think they know the answers

___ when they want to feel important by showing their knowledge of details of others' lives

___ other:

9. In conversations where we're likely to talk too much, what prayers might we pray under our breath for the other person or ourselves?

10. Penn used the words *fewness* and *fullness* to describe Fox's speech (see sidebar quote). What two words would you like for others to use to describe your speech?

---

11. What changes in your speech would need to take place to make that happen? (Check out the "Transformation Exercises.")

Transformation Exercises

Experiment with one or more of the following.

- As you begin each day, ask God to help you love and respect those who speak to you by engaging only in simple speech. You could make this your prayer every morning in the shower or as you tie your shoes.

- At least three times this week, try to answer a question with a simple yes or no. Then smile to let the other person know you're finished talking and ready to be attentive.

- Arrange a day where you can be silent. (Perhaps you will want to check with retreat centers in your area about personal or group silent retreats.) Enjoy the communion with God (and even with others in quietness) that occurs without the burden of making small talk. Look at how you often use small talk to try to adjust others' opinions of you.

- Talk to a friend and ask to be held accountable for speech habits that are not filled with simplicity: using elaborate words or gestures to get your point across, interrupting others, thinking of what you're going to say while others are talking.

- Journal about moments when talking is distracting rather than helpful, or compile a photo album or video diary depicting these moments.

"The fewness and fullness of his words have often struck even strangers with admiration."

WILLIAM PENN, WRITING ABOUT QUAKER LEADER GEORGE FOX

4

WHEN FASTING
BECOMES FEASTING

MATTHEW 4:1-11; JOHN 6:48-51

J esus not only feasted but also fasted from food—not even missing it at times! He also spoke of having access to a mysterious source of nonfood nourishment (John 4:32). Later, he presented himself as that nourishment:

> I am the bread of life. Your forefathers ate the manna in the desert, yet they died. But here is the bread that comes down from heaven, which a man may eat and not die. I am the living bread that came down from heaven. If anyone eats of this bread, he will live forever. This bread is my flesh, which I will give for the life of the world. (John 6:48-51)

While feasting on Christ may intrigue you, fasting may put you off. But you don't have to be Olympic-skilled. You might begin by fasting from people (solitude), conversation (silence), spending (frugality), media or using the telephone. Perhaps you'd like to experiment with abstaining from overpackaged, highly processed foods, from lack of exercise (or fitness mania), or from living with an overpacked schedule.* Or you may attempt a partial fast of eating no rich food, meat or wine (Daniel 10:3).

Do such ideas seem like "cheating" to you—as if you wouldn't be *really* fasting? The purpose of spiritual disciplines is not to get high scores on spiritual SAT tests or to get yourself suggested for sainthood. They are simple ways to connect with God, to feast on the One who loves you.

---

*These three items are listed in Marjorie Thompson, *Soul Feast* (Louisville, Ky.: Westminster John Knox, 1995), p. 77.

Turning Toward God

When have you seen God provide for you in surprising ways?

Hearing God Through the Word

Read Matthew 4:1-4.

1. Describe Jesus' predicament.

2. How did Jesus' refusal to turn the stones into bread demonstrate his complete trust in God?

"One of the main purposes of fasting is to wean us from our dependence upon God's gifts and enable us to become dependent upon God alone."

3. When Jesus answered the devil (v. 4), he quoted a Scripture passage that describes how God provided for the Israelites while they wandered in the wilderness (Deuteronomy 8:3). What good things did God do to provide for Israel (see Deuteronomy 8:2-6), which Jesus described as "word[s] that come from the mouth of God"?

Robert
Mulholland

4. In John 6:48-51 (printed in the introduction), underline all the words that have to do with life and living. Then circle all the food-related words. What is Jesus saying about himself as food?

What is Jesus saying about himself as life?

5. How does fasting, then, create a situation in which your faith is likely to grow?

6. If you were to fast from food or another item or activity, what character qualities would be most likely to grow in you?

__ humility

__ courage

__ purity

__ charity

__ other:

"When we fast,

we are invited to

feast on Jesus, the

bread of life. . . .

Fasting unto our

Lord is therefore

feasting—

feasting on him

and on doing his

will."

DALLAS WILLARD

Read Matthew 4:5-11.

7. The temptations in this passage have been cataloged in many ways. Three of these ways are charted below. Imagine for a moment that you had been without food for many days. Which of these temptations would have presented itself to you most boldly? Why?

8. How does refusing temptation invite you to feast on God?

9. How do you respond to the idea of fasting from something other than food: conversation, television, radio, spending, telephone, eating chocolate?

	TURN STONES INTO BREAD (vv. 3-4)	JUMP FROM TEMPLE (vv. 5-7)	WORSHIP SATAN (vv. 8-10)
DOUBTS	Will God provide?	Will God protect?	Will God "win"?
WEAKNESSES	Hunger, impatience, need to prove self	Pride, insecurity, need to test God	Craving quick power and easy solutions
DESIRES	Desire to be relevant	Desire to be spectacular	Desire to be powerful

10. Fasting is a discipline people sometimes tenaciously force themselves to do because it seems important or because their entire church is fasting. How are our attitudes different when we force ourselves to try hard versus when we rely on Jesus minute by minute?

---

11. If you were to fast from something this week, how would you keep yourself focused on feasting on God?

Transformation Exercises

Experiment with one or more of the following.

- Pick a word or phrase from John 6:48-51 (perhaps "living bread" or "came down from heaven" or "live forever"). For several minutes, sit or stand in that phrase. If you wish, focus on the grandness of God who loves you. Respond with a gesture, movement or facial expression.

- Try eating one grape at a time (or another small food you enjoy, such as kernels of popcorn or M&M candies). Sink your teeth into it and taste its richness. Thank God for this truly pleasant feast of only one grape.

- Sit in a park or in your backyard with some stones in front of you. Consider all the reasons you do not (wish to) fast. For each reason, pile one stone on your left. Consider the reasons to fast presented in this session (and any other reasons that come to mind). For each reason, pile one stone on your right. (Or if you wish, do the same using Yes and No columns in a journal.) Pray quietly, asking God what you need to know about these reasons. Wait for answers throughout the following week.

- Talk to one or two people who fast. Ask them what they do to ensure that it helps them connect with God instead of being a sign of an advanced spiritual life.

"Our physical desires are not just needs to be met, but opportunities to encounter God's goodness."

ROBERT MORRIS

5

HEARTS LAID BARE

1 Samuel 7:3-13

While fasting teaches us to feast on God, it also may take us to the edge. Just as our worst side is revealed when we're hungry, lonely and tired (as on a long, hot, dusty backpacking trip), fasting reveals the things that control us, the parts of ourselves we'd hoped would go away. Our fears and faults stare us in the face.

That's why fasting often leads to repentance and confession of sin. Without our usual comforts (food, television, shopping), we turn to God with more honesty and intensity. There we connect with the richness of God, who truly meets our needs. As a result, we experience new levels of humility, simplicity and peace.

When practicing fasting regularly (or other disciplines of abstinence), we find we don't feel so thwarted when we don't get what we want in the everyday events of life. We have more patience. We repent and confess more easily. Our character grows, and we become the kind of people God can easily use as a servant in the kingdom.

Turning Toward God

How can not getting what you want turn your heart to God?

Hearing God Through the Word

In this session's passage, Israel had been mourning after failing for twenty years to bring home the ark of the covenant, a symbol of God's presence. They had fallen into idol worship and needed to repent. As they fasted and confessed their sin, their hearts were laid bare.

Read 1 Samuel 7:3-6.

1. What did the Israelites need deliverance from? What did Samuel tell them was the way forward?

2. What are some of the sins that many of us need deliverance from?

"Fasting reveals our excessive attachments and the assumptions that lie behind them."

MARJORIE THOMPSON

3. What did the Israelites do after putting away their idols?

Read 1 Samuel 7:7-9.

4. Someone might say that the Israelites' trouble with the Philistines began *after* Israel gathered, fasted, confessed and repented. How do you think Israel's fasting and repentance prepared them for this trouble?

Read 1 Samuel 7:10-13.

5. Put yourself in the place of one of the Israelites in this scene of fasting, confessing and offering a sacrifice. What aspects of your whole person would have been affected by these acts of devotion to God? (Start by listing which of the five senses are involved.)

6. How did God respond to their prayers for rescue from the Philistines?

7. Think of a situation in which you need to trust God more and relinquish your focus on self. How might regular times of fasting and repenting help you rely on God alone to meet your needs and build your inner character to meet these situations?

8. How would your life be different if you were more patient and humble because you've practiced not getting what you want when you want it (perhaps by fasting regularly)?

"Fasting teaches

us to be sweet

and strong when

we don't get what

we want."

DALLAS WILLARD

9. How do the humility, patience and peace that result from fasting make it easier to practice simplicity (staying focused on God and God's kingdom)?

10. How might those who fast regularly make better servants?

11. If for one day you fasted from people or conversation or spending or media or using the telephone (pick one), how would you need to arrange your life differently that day to help it happen?

Transformation Exercises

Experiment with one or more of the following.

- Sit in a chair, shut your eyes, and pretend for a moment that you don't get to do what you want to do (and have planned to do) this evening or this weekend. How does this feel? Now lay your hands in your lap and turn the palms upward. If you were to relinquish this pleasant activity to God, how would that feel?

- Make a list of the feelings that come up when you are thwarted—anger? despair? hopelessness? loneliness? What qualities would grow in you if you found contentment even when you were thwarted?

- Think of a habitual sin of which you've repented over and over. If you were feeling needy (maybe hungry or standing in the cold without a coat and gloves), how would you speak or feel more intensely about that sin? Try speaking to God about that sin out of your neediness. Then—with heart laid bare—fall on your knees and worship God.

- Study Ezra 8:21-32 to see how fasting also humbles us, teaches us to trust God in urgent circumstances and prepares us with strength and grace for service.

"The ancient Christian literature on repentance is beautiful—full of simplicity, humility, and spreading peace. . . . [It is] not some masochistic self-humiliation, but a re-evaluation leading to action. . . . Repentance is insight, not emotion."

FREDERICA MATHEWES-GREEN

6

WHAT'S BEHIND
THE FAST?

MATTHEW 6:16-18; ISAIAH 58:1-11

When a certain friend began fasting, I knew he meant business. His runaway daughter had not called home for days. He later realized that, at first, he had fasted to earn his daughter's return by showing God how serious and spiritual he was. But gradually the practice of fasting led him to weep and mourn for the agony his prodigal daughter felt. His shame at having a runaway child melted. God gave him a heart for her, so that when she did return their reconciliation was genuine.

Motives in fasting are so crucial that the first mention of fasting in the New Testament is a warning about motivation. It's easy to fast for wrong reasons. Fasting can become a spiritual trophy, an instant ticket to supposed spiritual superiority as others look up to us. Even if we keep our fasting a secret, it can become a source of self-congratulation as we compete with ourselves to "improve" our fasting record.

So what is the proper motive? According to Richard Foster, the only reason to fast is "an urging or call to it, a prompting, a sense of rightness." We hear that call of God because we have been connecting with God and we long to connect even more.

Turning Toward God

When have you been unduly proud that you went without something and others would not or could not do so? (Perhaps sleep, food, sitting down, coffee breaks.)

Hearing God Through the Word

Not only did Jesus talk about motives and attitudes in fasting (as the first passage shows), but God also chided the nation of Judah about motives. In our second passage, God speaks to the prophet Isaiah about how Judah has behaved during fasts and what God sees a true fast consisting of.

Read Matthew 6:16-18.

1. What do Jesus' words "when you fast" tell us about fasting?

2. What reward did the hypocrites receive when they looked somber and disfigured their faces?

3. If we fast, how can we ensure that our fasting does not, as Arthur Wallis put it, "become devoid of spirit and life"?

4. Let's say you feel miserable (somber, v. 16) during a fast. Should you make yourself look happy to obey Jesus' directive here? Why or why not?

5. Why isn't it deceitful to keep a spiritual discipline a secret?

"God is not merely concerned with what we do but why we do it. A right act may be robbed of all its value in the sight of God if it is done with a wrong motive."

ARTHUR WALLIS

Read Isaiah 58:1-4.

6. What were the results of Judah's fasting?

7. What do these people's selfish behaviors reveal about what went on inwardly when they fasted?

Read Isaiah 58:5-11.

8. How is God's description of a true fast different from Judah's fasts?

"The question

we need to ask

ourselves with

any spiritual

9. In what ways could a person's fast involve acts of charity, justice, liberation or generosity (vv. 6-7)?

discipline is,

What does

God want to

10. Which, if any, of the following questions about spiritual disciplines (adapted from Arthur Wallis in *God's Chosen Fast*) speak to you about your motives?

accomplish in

___ Am I confident that this desire to fast is God-given?

me through this

___ Are my motives right? Is there any hidden desire to impress others?

practice?"

MARJORIE
THOMPSON

___ What are my spiritual objectives in this fast? Personal sanctification or consecration? Intercession—what special burdens? Divine intervention, guidance, blessing? Spirit's fullness for self or others? To loose the captives? To stay the divine wrath, to bring revival?

___ Do my objectives tend to be self-centered? Is my desire for personal blessing balanced by genuine concern for others?

___ Am I determined above all else to minister to the Lord?

11. Both the hypocrites and the people of Judah used fasting as a spiri- .
    tual trophy (Matthew 6; Isaiah 58). How do we tend to use other
    spiritual disciplines as trophies—proving to ourselves, to God and
    to others that we're spiritually better off or getting better?

---

12. If you were to fast, which sort of fast would you be ready to try
    (knowing that only God can miraculously free us from hunger)?

    Duration of fast:
    ___ fasting one meal a week

    ___ fasting one day a week

    Item(s) to abstain from:
    ___ abstaining from _____ (an activity)

    ___ absolute fast from food: no food, minimal water

    ___ partial fasting: eating no rich food, no meat or wine (Daniel
        10:3)

    ___ partial fasting from food you normally crave (bread, sugared
        foods)

> "Fasting, then, is
> a divine corrective
> to the pride of the
> human heart."
> Arthur Wallis

Transformation Exercises

Experiment with one or more of the following.

- Pick a word or phrase from Isaiah 58:6-11 (perhaps "loose the
  chains of injustice" or "your light will break forth" or "he will satisfy your needs in a sun-scorched land"). Rest in that phrase for
  several minutes. Consider what it would be like to be satisfied in
  God and do the work of God's kingdom while fasting from food or
  an activity.

- Pick two of the questions in 10 and journal about the answers. Keep
  this private so you can be as honest as possible.

- Rephrase a question from 10 to refer to another spiritual discipline in
  your life. (This will help you sift your motives in outward activities.)
  For example:

Am I confident this desire to serve the youth group is God-given? (the discipline of service)

Why do I sing? (worship)

Do I interact with others for personal blessing or out of genuine concern for others? (community)

- Compose an honest prayer that confesses self-serving motives in fasting or some other discipline. Allow yourself to receive God's grace in your admission. Finish by asking God to change your heart so that pure desires motivate you.

- Consider how you could fast from something that would involve an act of charity, justice, liberation or generosity. Make at least one phone call to investigate this possibility.

STUDY NOTES FOR
SIMPLICITY AND FASTING

Session 1. The Single-Hearted Person

MATTHEW 6:19-24, 33

FOCUS: Simplicity involves arranging our lives so we are devoted to the clear, uncomplicated purposes of seeking God and God's kingdom, minimizing any distractions from that.

Question 1. "In Palestine the walls of many of the houses were made of nothing stronger than baked clay; and burglars did effect an entry by literally digging through the wall. The reference here is to the man who had hoarded up in his house a little store of gold, only to find, when he comes home one day, that the burglars have dug through his flimsy walls and that his treasure is gone."[1]

Question 2. In the next question you'll refer to this list of treasures, so make note of them if you need to.

Question 4. If participants question the source of the idea of treasuring God, point out that to love God with all one's heart, mind, soul and strength (Mark 12:28-34) is to treasure God.

Question 5. The KJV uses the word *single* (NIV uses *good*) because the literal meaning of the italicized word in Greek is "single."[2] Says *Vine's Dictionary of New Testament Words:* "'Singleness' of purpose keeps us from the snare of having a double treasure and consequently a divided heart." This also helps us "seek first God's kingdom" because we don't get sidetracked.

Question 7. Feelings of inner neediness and inadequacy drive us to strive for reputation and wealth.

Question 8. Some say it refers to earthly treasures, but the context seems to indicate the simple needs mentioned in intervening verses: food, drink, clothing and a place to sleep (vv. 25-32).

Question 12. This question only appears in this session as a follow-up to question 11. However, at the end of each session encourage group members to choose an activity from the "Transformation Exercises" that they want to use during the week.

---

[1]William Barclay, *The Gospel of Matthew* (Philadelphia: Westminster Press, 1958), 1:241-42.

[2]W. E. Vine, Merrill F. Unger and William White Jr., *Vine's Expository Dictionary of Biblical Words* (Nashville: Thomas Nelson, 1985), p. 578 of NT section.

Session 2. Less Is More

MATTHEW 6:24-34

FOCUS: Living in simplicity involves arranging our lives so that we live purposefully without being distracted by possessions and worry.

Question 1. Life is more important than these things (v. 25); we are more valuable than birds and field grass and God takes care of them (v. 26, 30); worrying is not constructive (v. 27-29). In verses 32-33, Jesus tells his listeners that only pagans worry about these things, but we seek God's kingdom instead.

Yet Jesus wasn't saying that we do nothing or refuse to take responsibility. We work hard and stay away from idleness (2 Thessalonians 3:6-13). We take responsibility for caring for the folks given to us (1 Timothy 5:3-4), but we don't worry about it.

Question 3. It can be helpful to ask ourselves these questions: Do I enjoy pulling together an outfit as a creative venture? Or do I use clothing to impress (perhaps manipulate) others so they think I know more than I know and I can be trusted? Is my clothing appropriate and honoring to God and others?

If you wish, consider modifying the question to, "What choices of cars/sports equipment/household gadgets are least likely to distract you . . . ?"

Question 5. If you love money (v. 24) and your treasure in life is something other than God, you will be worried and anxious.

Question 6. In our culture, it's easy to *devote* our spare time to entertainment (watching movies and television), overwork (on the job, keeping a perfectly clean house or perfectly manicured lawn), staying fit, keeping a flashy car looking great. None of these activities are wrong unless we become *fully preoccupied* with them. They distract us from our life with God.

Question 7. Spending more time listening to people, studying the Word, reading books that connect you to God, making things for people, calling people you haven't talked to in a long time, visiting old friends.

Question 8. You may not, however, have time for these things. Part of the purpose of simplicity is to clear out your life so you do have time for them.

Question 9. We learn to do the simple thing in front of us, not concerning ourselves with "great matters" (Psalm 131:1).

Question 10. Move group participants beyond obvious answers by probing with one or more of these questions: What do you have to believe about God? What sort of trust do you need to have in God? What kind of ongoing interaction with God do you need to have in your life? What do you need to do to "set your mind" and "set your heart" on things above? (This means to have your mind and heart *fully preoccupied with* God and what God is doing, Colossians 3:1-2.)

Question 11. If anyone seems particularly struck by this question, recommend the third transformation exercise on page 235.

Session 3. Simple Talk

MATTHEW 5:33-37

FOCUS: Simplicity in speech means not trying to manipulate or convince others with a lot of words, but speaking simply and having confidence that God will move and work.

Question 1. To keep promises to God and to each other; to always mean what you say.

A little more background on "evasive swearing": People divided "oaths into two classes, those which were absolutely binding and those which were not. Any oath which contained the name of God was absolutely binding; any oath which succeeded in evading the name of God was held not to be binding."[3]

Question 2. To be able to make a statement using forceful oaths, but not really meaning what they said. Jesus decried the quibbling, hair-splitting rationalization that swearing by the altar didn't count but swearing by the gold of the altar did count (Matthew 23:16-22).

Question 3. It's ridiculous to imply that God has nothing to do with one's head when God is Creator of all things. Everything we do involves God, who is omnipresent even if God's name is not used. Yet these Jews believed that only when God's name was used in an oath did "God [become] a partner in the transaction."[4] The people Jesus described were living their lives partially in the presence of God (when they used oaths that included God's name) and partially out of God's presence (when they used oaths void of God's name). Go over this before the next question.

Question 4. Life becomes divided into compartments of "sacred" and "secular." In the so-called secular parts of our life, we can behave any way we like. So our heart is divided (Psalm 86:11), and our witness is destroyed.

Question 7. A heart that trusts God to manage things instead of trusting words to manage things. A heart that respects other people, which is one of the aspects of loving others. This leaves others with their freedom of choice intact. Jesus respected others' needs to "make their judgments and decisions solely from what they have concluded is best."[5]

Question 8. If you wish, ask participants to tell which situation is most difficult for them.

Question 9. Some prayers might be, *Help me to be present to this person*, or *Help me hear this person's heart.* If you have a lot of quiet folks in your group, ask this same question again but begin it this way: "In conversations where we're likely to withdraw and say little . . . "

Session 4. When Fasting Becomes Feasting

MATTHEW 4:1-11; JOHN 6:48-51

FOCUS: Fasting can teach us to nourish ourselves on Christ himself.

Question 2. He refused to work out situations for himself without relying on God. He also seemed to refuse to use power for selfish reasons and instead performed miracles to serve others. Alfred Plummer says of Jesus: "He leaves all in God's hands"[6] (including whether he starved or ate).

Question 3. God provided clothes and sandals that stayed sturdy and stitched together through

forty years of travel. God provided manna and later quail for them to eat.

Question 4. Jesus said he himself is nourishment that is as rich and filling as food.

Question 5. Fasting stretches us and forces us to rely on God in new areas. We learn to wait for God to help us. Fasting expands our ideas of "feasting" on Christ. We also grow in character, as discussed in the next question.

Question 8. By refusing a temptation, you're stat-

[3]Barclay, *Gospel of Matthew,* 1:157.
[4]Ibid.
[5]Dallas Willard, *The Divine Conspiracy* (San Francisco: HarperSanFrancisco, 1998), p. 175.
[6]Alfred Plummer, *An Exegetical Commentary on the Gospel According to St. Matthew* (Grand Rapids: Baker, 1982), p. 40.

ing that you trust in God to provide. God becomes the rich source of nourishment in your life.

Question 9. Let group participants talk about whether this feels like they're cheating. (If your group has used the study *Prayer and Listening,* they may remember the quote "Pray as you can, not as you can't"[7] from session 2. This is a guiding principle in the use of all spiritual disciplines.) Let participants know also that among the desert fathers of the third to fifth centuries—ardent fasters—"moderation was the rule, and someone who went totally without food might be showing off."[8]

Question 10. Steeling ourselves and trying to be strong makes whatever spirituality we have about ourselves. Relying on God is a vulnerable, unguarded way to let our spirituality be about God.

Question 11. Praying or doing another activity that connects you with God during the time you normally do what you're abstaining from—mealtime if fasting from food, normal times of watching television if fasting from TV. When you have the desire to do what you're abstaining from, use it as a reminder to pray for a certain person or issue. Bathe the entire time of fasting in prayer.

Session 5. Hearts Laid Bare

1 SAMUEL 7:3-13

FOCUS: Fasting helps us hear our true selves, leading us to repent of sin and confess more readily. As a result, we relinquish sinful behavior, especially having to have what we want when we want it. We learn patience, humility and peace.

Question 2. Get participants started with common faults such as these: greed, self-pity, grouchiness, laziness.

Question 3. In repentance they fasted, confessed their sins and probably prayed, even though the text says only that Samuel interceded (v. 5). They showed outward signs of repentance as they "drew water and poured it out before the Lord." Commentators agree that "with fasting, it was no doubt a symbol of repentance."[9]

Question 4. They had connected with God sufficiently so that they relied on God. They asked Samuel to keep crying out to God for rescue when otherwise they could have quaked in fear.

They continued connecting with God by offering the sacrifice of the lamb, a token of "loyalty and devotion."[10] (Offering sacrifices was a customary spiritual discipline for the Israelites.) In troubled times, we trust God and stay connected to God.

Question 5. A relationship with God is not something that happens only in our mind. It involves our total self, which is why disciplines such as fasting retrain our bodies.

Notice how the Israelites' discipline of sacrifice involved their body. Some *saw* the sacrifice; they and those farther back *saw* and *smelled* the smoke—and the *taste* of roasted lamb! Those who poured the water *touched* it with their hands. They all *heard* with their ears the cries of Samuel (and probably of others). Many confessed their sins with their *lips*. Possibly they fell on their knees and worshiped God.

---

[7]Quoted in Thelma Hall, *Too Deep for Words: Rediscovering Lectio Divina* (New York: Paulist, 1988), p. 40.

[8]Frederica Mathewes-Green, *The Illumined Heart* (Brewster, Mass.: Paraclete, 2001), p. 53.

[9]D. F. Payne, "1 and 2 Samuel," in *The New Bible Commentary,* 3rd ed., ed. Donald Guthrie and J. A. Motyer (Grand Rapids: Eerdmans, 1991), p. 290.

[10]John Mauchline, *1 and 2 Samuel,* New Century Bible (London: Oliphants Marshall, Morgan & Scott, 1971), p. 85.

Question 7. Fasting clears the mind and puts us in a posture of relinquishment. We give in to God better. "Fasting is one of the more important ways of practicing that self-denial required of everyone who would follow Christ (Matt. 16:24). In fasting, we learn how to suffer happily as we feast on God."[11]

Question 8. Fasting often reveals to us that we have anger, a controlling spirit or a manipulative heart. In fasting, we find the opportunity to repent and confess to God. One person reported, "Surprisingly, after the fast is when I began to realize something from the fast. I came back from the fast with a clearer sense of purpose and a renewed sense of power in my ministry. The anger which I unleashed at my wife and children was less frequent and the materialism that was squeezing the life out of my spirituality had loosened its grip."[12]

Question 10. They are less likely to insist on having their way in disagreements. They're likely to be less needy for small comforts in life in order to serve contentedly. Fasting prepares us for important tasks by helping us humble ourselves and trust God through urgent circumstances. Servants of God often find fasting helps them know the mind of God about circumstances and people.

Session 6. What's Behind the Fast?

MATTHEW 6:16-18; ISAIAH 58:1-11

FOCUS: Examining our motives in fasting enriches our life in God.

Turning Toward God. Start the discussion with your own story. If appropriate, laugh at how proud you were that you deprived yourself.

Question 1. Jesus assumed that his followers would indeed fast. Fasting itself is not wrong, but fasting to impress people is.

Question 2. Their looks told people they were fasting, and those people admired them for it. The Jewish fasting days, Monday and Thursday, were also market days when people came to town. "The result was that those who were ostentatiously fasting would on those days have a bigger audience to see and admire their piety. There were many who took deliberate steps to see that others could not miss the fact that they were fasting. They walked through the streets with hair deliberately unkempt and disheveled, with clothes deliberately soiled and disarrayed. It was a deliberate act of spiritual pride and ostentation."[13]

Question 3. Don't simply abstain from something, but spend time focusing on God and activities that connect you with God. Rely on God's provision and be delighted at how God becomes your feast. Before, during and after a fast we must continually check motives. It's important to "guard our heart," to pause in the exercise when we discover wrong motives and can't change them (Proverbs 4:23).

Question 4. Hypocrisy is wrong, even in fasting. Misery may indicate one of two things: you have something to repent of and you should pay attention to what God is saying to you; or fasting is not the right discipline for you at this time. Says Dallas Willard: "When we have learned well to fast, we will not suffer from it. It will bring strength and joy."[14]

Question 5. Spiritual exercises are sometimes

---

[11]Dallas Willard, *The Spirit of the Disciplines* (San Francisco: Harper & Row, 1988), p. 167.
[12]Dallas Willard, "The Key to the Keys of the Kingdom," <www.dwillard.org/articles/artview.asp?artID=40>.
[13]Barclay, *Gospel of Matthew*, 1:237.
[14]Willard, "Key to the Keys."

private between God and yourself. You're doing something to enhance that special connection with God. Just as you and a best friend may have had secrets when you were young, you and God have business that counts only with each other.

Besides, secrecy is also a discipline (see "Service & Secrecy"), used often with serving and giving.

To keep from being deceitful, be honest but gracious. Turn down a lunch invitation with a warm, polite smile. Or participate in a lunch out without eating but being a part of the conversation. When asked why you're not eating, say you're not hungry. But if you are miserably hungry, you need to interact with God about finding a different version of fasting or different spiritual discipline more appropriate for you.

Question 6. Exploiting workers, quarreling and strife, fighting.

Question 7. They were apparently not connecting with God as they fasted. Based on their pretense ("seem eager to know my ways"), we can deduce they were trying to fool God and perhaps themselves. Verse 3 tells how they wanted God to notice what they were doing, which may indicate they were fasting to get God's approval rather than in repentance. They demanded that God notice how humble they were. None of this speaks of repentance.

Question 8. Judah's fasts included humbling themselves for a day, bowing their heads and wearing sackcloth and ashes (v. 5). The true fast involves doing good deeds toward other people, especially deeds of justice, liberation and generosity (vv. 6-7). Writes Derek Kidner: "True fasting is more than what we don't eat; it is pleasing God by

applying his Word to our society."[15]

Concerning results, a true fast would result in their healing; God's glory would be revealed; conversation between God and them would take place; their needs would be met (vv. 8-11).

Question 9. Our fasts can serve: the wounded creation (a fast from using plastic shopping bags, thus alleviating potential waste cluttering the earth); the hungry (fast from a meal and send that money to an organization that feeds the hungry, forego a holiday dinner and spend the day serving a meal at a street mission); those "yoked" in prison or the oppressed (fast from leisure during a weekend or vacation moments to spend time visiting an imprisoned person, investigating issues of oppression in another country and what can be done, or doing a short-term service project).

Prayer, repentance and confession usually accompany fasting. These "fasting" efforts also help us remember to pray for these concerns. They help us look at our motives and habits and to repent and confess as needed.

Question 10. Ask participants who seem willing to speak to tell why they picked the questions they did. Point out that these questions not only help us adjust our motives but also create a conversation with God that helps us develop a habit of sifting motives. Suggest that those particularly intrigued with these questions try the second and third transformation exercises.

Question 11. You may wish to ask first about how we use Bible study or service as spiritual trophies.

[15]Derek Kidner, "Isaiah," in *The New Bible Commentary*, 3rd ed., ed. Donald Guthrie and J. A. Motyer (Grand Rapids: Eerdmans, 1991), p. 620.

Section Eight

WORSHIP & CELEBRATION

Worship is, more than anything else, a response to God. God created us in love and nurtures us in love; one of the ways we respond to that love is worship. A vivid sense of God's love creates in us a deep longing for God, which fuels our desire to worship. Celebration is also a response to God, an expression of joy about who God is and what God does:

- God's character, such as God's love, joy, peace. These qualities grow in us through the Holy Spirit because God overflows with them.

- God's attributes such as transcendence and immanence (closeness), wisdom, power and majesty.

- God's actions, such as creation, careful attention to us, keeping us "under his wings."

Worship and celebration flow from and feed into other spiritual disciplines, especially study. Study without worship breeds arrogance but study with worship can result in more substantive worship. "The study of God in his Word and works opens the way for the disciplines of worship and celebration. In worship we engage ourselves with, dwell upon, and express the greatness, beauty, and goodness of God through thought and the use of words, rituals and symbols."[1] Worship is also helped by the disciplines of solitude and silence because they teach us to be still before God and wait expectantly for God. Other disciplines such as Scripture meditation, prayer and confession are forms of worship. Worship enhances our sense of community and permeates our service.

1

LONGING FOR GOD

PSALM 63

How can we explain the difference between worship in which "something happens" within us and worship in which this "something" doesn't happen?

The "something" that happens is our response to God in some way—awe, joy, speaking back to God. Worship is about responding to God more than anything else. As we make it a habit to respond to God every time we worship, a longing for God permeates our lives. If you've sensed that longing, even for a moment, you know what follows: a sense that God will never leave you, a deep confidence that God meets your needs, an alert expectancy that God will "show up" in your life and speak to you.

This anticipation changes all our worship experiences. Distractions—a baby crying, a person sniffling, the sun's glare through a stained-glass window—don't matter anymore. Even an ordinary sunset becomes an occasion of personal worship. And in our worst moments, we still want to rise up and worship.

Turning Toward God

What sorts of things (if anything) make you more eager to attend a worship service or to worship God personally?

Hearing God Through the Word

King David was practiced at connecting with God, even in crises. When his son Absalom orchestrated a government takeover, David was run out of Jerusalem into the "desert waste that extends along the western shore of the Dead Sea" wilderness of Judah. In this dry, hot land with its "uniform ash-colored tint," he penned a psalm of deep longing for God. Psalm 63 reveals how David sought close fellowship with God, found satisfaction in it and felt secure in his expectation that God would bring about justice.

Read Psalm 63:1-2.

1. What is David's state of mind as he comes to God?

2. How does this psalm contradict the idea that we can sense God's presence only when we feel comfortable, secure or emotionally "up"?

3. What does this psalm tell us about our attitude when we think we can't worship because the music or speaker or atmosphere is not "right"?

   What can we do when we're having a difficult time worshiping because these things do not seem right?

Psalm 63:3-8.

4. Look at how the psalmist responds to the truth that God's love is better than life. List all the verbs (actions, words of doing) David uses in verses 3-8.

5. How do you know that worship isn't something that just goes on inside David's head?

_____

6. What metaphor for the satisfaction of your soul might you use in place of enjoying "the richest of foods" (v. 5)?

_____

7. What did David do about his sleeplessness?

_____

8. Picture yourself in the shadow of God's wings. How are you positioned?
   __ standing with arms lifted
   __ seated and rocking in contentment
   __ squatting close to the body under the wing joint
   __ variation of above:
   __ other:

"Thou art hidden behind the curtain of sense, incomprehensible in Thy greatness, mysterious in thine almighty power; yet here I speak with Thee familiarly as child to parent, as friend to friend."

JOHN BAILLIE

_____

9. When things go wrong, some people become bitter at God while others turn to God, as David did. What do you think makes the difference?

Read Psalm 63:9-11.

_____

10. How could David possibly speak of praising God in the midst of the death and destruction of his son Absalom and his buddies?

11. How would a person's life be different if he or she worshiped as David did in this psalm?

12. Reread Psalm 63:1-11 aloud slowly. Which word or phrase is most meaningful to you? What does that phrase tell you about how you want to connect with God?

Transformation Exercises

Experiment with one or more of the following.

- Try to picture the phrase "your right hand upholds me." How exactly is God's right hand holding or upholding you? What other details are apparent in this scene? How do you need to respond to being held or upheld in such a way?

- Read Psalm 61 or 62 in the next few days, asking yourself these two questions: What picture of God is presented here? How should I respond to God?

- While lying in bed (before falling asleep, after waking up or during sleeplessness), whisper aloud, "I remember you, O God" (v. 6).

- Journal or make a photo album or video diary about what it's like for you to worship in times of stress.

2

RESPONDING IN WORSHIP

PSALM 104:31—105:5

Empty-headed worship. We say worshipful words, go through the motions and greet a few folks. Then we're glad to go home. If we responded to God, it was a quick wave and "hello."

To respond to God (which is what worship is about), it helps to focus on the great worth of God—especially God's character, attributes and actions. The verb *worship* developed from the ancient noun *worthship* and means "to attribute worth" to an object.

But even then, cultural tendencies interfere. Without meaning to, we find ourselves wanting to be entertained, as if we were spectators at a performance put on by musicians and pastors. Instead of responding to God, we take on a detached attitude, hoping God's representatives (a worship leader, a devotional book) will pique our intellect, lift our spirits or even tickle our funny bone. When we assume this "entertain me" posture, we drain the essence of worship—which is responding to God, who is downright crazy about us.

As we form the habit of responding to God, an expectant longing for God is cultivated in our personal moments of worship. To "seek [God's] face always" in all of life becomes a goal (Psalm 105:4).

Turning Toward God

What do you think causes us to want to be entertained instead of "entering into" worship?

Hearing God Through the Word

The book of Psalms, which has been called our book of worship, mentions many forms of response to God, such as singing, rejoicing, dancing, clapping, meditating and telling God's great deeds. The focus of worship and the practices of worship are presented in Psalms 104 and 105. The first is about the wonders of God's creation, and the second is about praising God for divine involvement in Israel's history.

"I trust your

unknown

wisdom—you are

utterly beyond

me, beyond the

sweep of my

imagination,

beyond the

comprehension

of my mind, Thy

judgments being

unsearchable and

Thy ways past

finding out."

JOHN BAILLIE

Read Psalm 104:31—105:5.

1. What positive qualities stand out to you about God's character (love, joy, peace and so on) as it is described here?

2. What information does the passage give about what God is like (such as being powerful or wise)?

3. What actions or activities of God does this passage mention?

4. What specific responses of worship to God does the psalmist describe?

5. Reread Psalm 104:31-35. How do you respond to the idea that God rejoices (v. 31)?

6. How do you reconcile the negative quality of verse 35 with the other verses?

7. Reread Psalm 105:1-5. What does it mean to "glory" in God's name (v. 3)?

8. If a person were going to "seek his face always," what do you think that would mean (v. 4)?

9. Name three deeds God has accomplished in your life, in the life of your small group or church, or in the life of the world.

10. How is worship linked to the spiritual discipline of Bible study?

11. How does worshiping help us in other spiritual exercises—such as solitude, prayer, confession, service?

12. Character grows out of worship. In what ways do you think the practice of personal worship could change you?

"We normally think of perceiving beauty with our eyes, but the beauty of God is in His complete goodness. . . . These high truths—love, holiness, faithfulness and the like—we may look upon only in the depths of our soul."

AUGUSTINE

Transformation Exercises

Experiment with one or more of the following.

- Study passages about seeking God's face and come up with a description of what it means to be the kind of person who seeks God's face. (See 1 Chronicles 16:11; 2 Chronicles 7:14; Psalm 24:6; 27:8; Hosea 5:15.)

- Reread Psalm 104:31—105:5 aloud in a quiet place. What phrase stands out to you? Why are you drawn to that phrase?

- Come up with a gesture, or find a song, sculpture or picture (or draw your own), that exemplifies Psalm 104:31—105:5 or a phrase from it, such as "glory in his holy name" or "seek his face always."

- Kneel before God, and sing a song or hymn of praise that fits with Psalm 104–105, such as "How Great Thou Art," "For the Beauty of the Earth" or "Shout to the Lord."

"All enjoyment

spontaneously

overflows into

praise. . . . We

delight to praise

what we enjoy

because the

praise not merely

expresses but

completes the

enjoyment;

. . . the delight is

incomplete till it

is expressed."

C. S. LEWIS

3

ENTERING INTO
CORPORATE WORSHIP

1 Chronicles 16:1-36

T*hat pastor can leave an audience spellbound* or *can really get a group going* or *never leaves a dry eye*. When we have thoughts like these, we're revealing that our theology of worship goes something like this: the people up front are actors putting on a show, and the folks sitting in the pews are the audience. In truth, says K. C. Ptomey, the "worship leaders are like prompters (and stage hands) who stay behind the scenes. The worshipers are the actors. God is the audience." What are we acting out? Our response to God in worship.

But even when I remember that I'm an "actor," I can be sabotaged by another cultural force that works against my participation—sophistication, or more familiarly, "being cool." I worry about how I look. Can I throw myself into spontaneous praise in an informal contemporary worship service? Can I enter into a delightfully high liturgical service without caring if I don't sit and stand as promptly as others? Am I put off by any worship service that asks me to respond with energy and effort, immersing myself in God?

Worship is something I enter into fully, whether quietly or noisily. It invites the full participation of my soul—mind, feelings, body, will.

Turning Toward God

People often say that you don't get anything out of corporate worship unless you put something into it. What can we "put into it"?

Hearing God Through the Word

As David transported the ark of the covenant to Jerusalem, Michal watched from her window, and "when she saw King David dancing and celebrating, she despised him in her heart" (1 Chronicles 15:29). It seems she was worried about what people would think and was unable to be drawn into worship.

The ark was being brought home. Years earlier it had been captured by the Philistines, who then decided it was destructive to them so they sent it back (1 Samuel 5–6). It went first to Beth Shemesh, then to Kiriath-Jearim (1 Samuel 6:18, 21). After Saul died and David was made king, the ark was finally brought back to its people. The passage below tells about the worship service that followed the ark's homecoming. It's full of gritty responses requiring so much energy that worshipers were bound to get their hands dirty.

"Worship has become something that someone does for us. Ministers lecture at us, move us into decisions and entertain us. But the Bible understands worship as God-centered. Through the telling and acting out of the Christ-story we respond to God in prayer, praise, confession, and thanksgiving. Our purpose is to give, not to get."

ROBERT WEBBER

Read 1 Chronicles 16:1-6.

1. How did the Israelites participate in the worship as the ark was brought into its tent?

2. Imagine yourself participating in such a sacrifice. What part would be most dramatic to you? most meaningful to you in your relationship with God?

3. If you were to bring to the next session an object that symbolized your total dedication to God or friendship between you and God, what would that object be?

4. Let's say you were a member of the planning committee that helped David provide "a loaf of bread, a cake of dates and a cake of raisins to each Israelite man and woman." What would have been neces-

sary to make all this preparation an act of worship for you?

5. Describe the jobs of the "worship team" for this service (vv. 4-6).

6. How would you describe the physical energy that went into everyone's involvement in this worship service?

Read 1 Chronicles 16:7-12.

7. How would the words of this psalm—similar to Psalm 105:1-5, studied in the last session—take on a special tone when used for worship by this group of Israelites at this important moment in their history?

8. If your neighborhood or your church went through an experience in which all of you felt a renewed sense to follow God's call, what old favorite song would you want to sing?

Read 1 Chronicles 16:13-22.

9. How has God been faithful to your family or your neighborhood or your church?

"Worship is the practice of regularly seeking to bring the complete focus of our being upon God. It is the discipline of returning to the true center of our individual and corporate existence as God's people."

ROBERT MULHOLLAND

Read 1 Chronicles 16:23-36.

10. What action verbs do you find in this passage to give us clues to what happened in this worship event?

11. Which of the actions in verses 23-36 do you need to put more energy into during corporate worship?

"The perspective

of praise is none

other than the

throne room

of the universe

where we see

God sitting on

a throne. God

reigns! . . . When

we see God as he

is, we will praise

God as we ought."

JACK TAYLOR

Transformation Exercises

Experiment with one or more of the following.

- Look through a hymnal or songbook and find songs that speak of God's greatness. Memorize a stanza or two of one of these songs.

- Try a different tradition or experience of corporate worship this week.

- Reread the episode of Michal's despising David's worship (1 Chronicles 13–15). Put yourself in her place, and see if you can detect any of her feelings in you. Journal about them, and be open to what God is saying to you.

- Attend a worship service, planning beforehand that when your mind wanders or you feel annoyed by something, you will pray for someone near you or up front.

4

CELEBRATING
THE LIFE OF GOD

LUKE 15:1-32

What makes you want to have a party? Seeing someone you love experience a milestone? Coming into a special time of year? Wanting to share your joy with others?

Get-togethers, parties and holidays—outward signs of the spiritual discipline of celebration—teach us to recollect God's goodness to us. They allow us to make a big deal out of what God has given us: opportunities to make a living, companions along the way who love us and make us laugh, scenery and foods and cultures unknown to us before, stories and art that inspire our souls.

Special circumstances—overcoming a hardship, achieving a goal—call for overt, festive celebrations to recognize God's interaction in our lives. The intentional celebrations described in Scripture (especially in the last passage studied, 1 Chronicles 16:1-36) tell us that saying "That was nice" is not enough. We need to throw ourselves into it—perhaps even as the Israelites did. Dallas Willard observed that they used their tithe "in a feast before the Lord on a vacation trip to the big city of Jerusalem." Elaborate outward expressions of celebration are not inappropriate or superfluous but important responses (therefore worship) to honor the greatness of God.

Without such recollecting, we become despairing people who forget God's work in our lives. So we arrange our lives in order to remember God in every pleasure.

Turning Toward God

If we assume for a moment that God laughs, what do you think would make God laugh? (Keep in mind that God is never rude or self-seeking—1 Corinthians 13:5.)

Hearing God Through the Word

In this session we'll be exploring the three "lost and found" parables Jesus told to describe life in the kingdom. In particular, we'll examine the similar ending of each one: a party (vv. 5-7, 9-10, 22-30). Partying does fit into the invisible kingdom of God.

"In commanding

us to glorify Him,

God is inviting us

to enjoy Him."

C. S. LEWIS

Read Luke 15:1-10.

1. What behavior of Jesus were the Pharisees complaining about (vv. 1-2)?

2. Note the unusual actions of the shepherd in this parable: (1) Shepherds didn't usually leave their sheep out in the open country. This poor economic decision would have risked the life of ninety-nine for one sheep. (2) It would not have been unthinkable for the shepherd to scold the straying sheep for getting itself lost.

   What does the shepherd's odd behavior say to you about God and God's kingdom?

3. Based on the circumstances described and what you conjecture about biblical times, what do you think the parties ("rejoice with me") in verses 6 and 9 would have looked like?

4. Put yourself in the woman's place for a minute by describing something you've lost and are still looking for, or by describing how you felt after searching carefully and finding something you valued. How does it feel to find something this important?

5. We can imagine the woman recollecting at the party how she discovered the coin was missing and then dramatically telling how she found it—the dark corner, the misplaced item under which it had rolled. If you were to recollect what God has done or "found" for you, which of these categories from Psalm 103 might it fall under?

    ___ forgiving your sins and healing your diseases (v. 3)

    ___ pulling you back from some sort of pit in your life (v. 4)

    ___ crowning you with love and compassion (v. 4)

    ___ satisfying a desire of yours, making you feel young and strong again (v. 5)

    ___ other:

Read Luke 15:11-25.

6. What details of the celebration (including clothing) did storyteller Jesus provide about what's involved in a celebration (vv. 22-25)?

7. Which of the following examples of celebration in Scripture is most interesting to you? Why?

    ___ Lifting hands, symbolizing surrender, blessing, authority, supplication: "I will praise you as long as I live, and in your name I will lift up my hands" (Psalm 63:4).

    ___ Kneeling and bowing, symbolizing humility, reverence, submission: "Come, let us bow down in worship, let us kneel before the LORD our maker" (Psalm 95:6).

    ___ Leaping and jumping for joy (the Greek word used here for "rejoiced" also means "jumping for joy"): "Jesus rejoiced in the Holy Spirit and said, 'I thank you, Father, Lord of heaven and

"When outward business diverted him a little from the thought of God, a fresh remembrance coming from God invested his soul, and so inflamed and transported him that it was difficult for him to contain himself."

BROTHER LAWRENCE

earth, because you have hidden these things from the wise and the intelligent and have revealed them to infants" (Luke 10:21 NRSV).

___ Dancing (see Luke 15:25).

___ Using banners, signs, standards and flags: "Pass through, pass through the gates! Prepare the way for the people. Build up, build up the highway! Remove the stones. Raise a banner for the nations" (Isaiah 62:10).

"We shall not be able to adore God on the highest occasions if we have learned no habit of doing so on the lowest. . . . Joy is the serious business of heaven."

C. S. LEWIS

Read Luke 15:25-32.

8. Why is it difficult for the older son to celebrate? Why is it important for him to celebrate?

9. What is it you most enjoy, that most lifts your heart? (For example, watching children play or walking on the beach or listening to music?)

How might you do that in celebration of God?

10. How might you experience the church service you usually participate in more as a time of celebration?

11. In what other ways can you develop a habit of celebrating, especially with bodily action?

12. What sins may fade from our lives as we practice the discipline of celebration?

Transformation Exercises

Experiment with one or more of the following.

- Choose a favorite hymn or worship song. Sit by yourself and sing it (or listen to it on CD). Embellish the parts that are most meaningful to you. Put your whole self—your body and all your senses—into it. Don't be afraid to use a "big voice," opera style. Try stopping at the end of each line, lingering thoughtfully in the phrase and celebrating in your heart.

- Listen deeply to a favorite hymn or worship song. Then experiment with dancing to it, using gestures that correspond to the words in some way—bowing, lifting hands and so on. Open your soul and your body to it.

- Glance back through a journal or a daily event calendar and recollect the things that God has done for you. Respond in some celebratory way.

- Look in a concordance, searching for passages with these two words: *celebrate* (or *celebration*), *Lord*. Based on this, journal and try to get a sense of how God celebrates.

5

COMING TO THE TABLE

JOHN 6:47-58

Why do small children in worship services long to take Communion? The mystery and pageantry of the sacred feast intrigues them (and us) because it is a full-bodied, five-sense worship response; we see the bread and wine, touch them, taste them, smell them. We hear the invitation spoken and the music sung. The drama of the ceremony invites us to participate and respond, which is what worship is about. There's no such thing as sitting back and being entertained by Communion.

When we enter into Communion this way, we allow Christ to invite us into an everlasting life that is a new, fuller life of love, joy and peace. Participating in Communion this way becomes a way of saying, "I am willing to participate in You, Lord, to be changed forever by this meal." We can thank God that Christ invites us, sitting side by side with one another, to form an intimate relationship with him by taking him in and experiencing him on a regular basis, as pictured by Communion.

Turning Toward God

What memorable Communion experience has spoken to you in some way?

Hearing God Through the Word

In Jesus' sermon recorded in John 6, he prepared the disciples and all those listening to participate in the Lord's Supper. Later they would watch Jesus take bread, give thanks, break it and give it to them, saying, "Take and eat; this is my body." (See Matthew 26:26; Mark 14:22.) Let's look at how our partaking of Christ invites Christ to transform our souls.

Read John 6:47-58.

1. What information does the passage give about those who have everlasting life (vv. 47, 51, 54, 58)?

2. Focus on John 6:47-51. What does bread do for our physical life that Christ (the "bread of life") does for our spiritual life (and thus our whole life)?

3. To "eat" or "partake" of Christ means to participate in Christ, to sample Christ or to take in Christ. What ways are most easy for you to take in Christ or experience Christ in your life? (Think broadly. These can be solitary or communal experiences in outdoor or academic settings.)

"All who are made one with Christ by faith are joined to him and are made full partakers of his life . . . [and of] what he himself is."

R. C. H. LENSKI

4. How is taking Communion an outward picture of the way you take in Christ or experience Christ?

5. Jesus compared himself to the manna the Hebrews ate in the desert after their exodus from Egypt and throughout their wandering

years. Which of these qualities of manna did Jesus resemble in some way?

___ Manna descended from heaven to earth.

___ Manna may have been made in heaven, but it was something people could see with their eyes and touch with their hands.

___ Manna lasted for a day and then spoiled.

___ Manna puzzled the Israelites, which is why they called it manna, which means, "What is it?"

___ Manna sustained physical life for the wandering Israelites.

___ Other:

How was Jesus so much more than manna?

6. Now reread John 6:52-58. Jesus used many word pictures to describe himself and his roles, such as being the Good Shepherd, the Door, the Way. This word picture of being the Bread of Life and of our eating his flesh and drinking his blood adds the idea of Christ coming inside us. Why is that an important truth for Christians?

7. Communion is an invitation to let Christ come inside us continually throughout our lives. Which of these specific invitations from Jesus do you need to incorporate into your Communion experiences?

___ Have (real) life in me (v. 53).

___ Let me give you eternal life (v. 54).

___ Let me change you (v. 56—remain in me so you may bear fruit: love, patience, kindness, self-control—John 15:4-5, Galatians 5:22-23).

___ Keep feeding on me (v. 57).

___ Other:

8. The popular phrase "You are what you eat" reflects a truth from this passage: you "eat" Christ and so become (like) Christ. Complete this sentence: "I would like to be what I eat (Christ), because I need to be more . . ."

How would your being more like Christ change your relationships with the people around you, perhaps even those who sit near you during Communion?

9. Another word for Communion is *Eucharist*, which means thanksgiving. In what way is Communion a time of thanksgiving?

10. Knowing that Communion is Christ's invitation to partake of him and let him transform our souls, why do you think it's important to do it on a regular basis?

Since Communion involves the transformation of our souls, why is it appropriate to take it sitting in a community of people, some of whom may confuse or even annoy you?

11. How do you need to approach Communion differently?

"The veil between the worlds, [is] nowhere else (for me) so opaque to the intellect, is nowhere else so thin and permeable to divine operation [as communion]. Here a hand from a hidden country touches not only my soul, but my body."

C. S. LEWIS

Transformation Exercises

Experiment with one or more of the following.

- Pick a word or phrase from John 6:47-58 (perhaps "I am the living bread that came down," or "If anyone eats of this bread, he will live forever," or "The one who feeds on me will live because of me"). For several minutes, sit or stand in that phrase. Don't think about anything much, except the grandness of God who loves you. Respond with a gesture, movement or facial expression.

- In your journal, draw a sketch of a nourished soul and a withered soul. Then write about how Christ nourishes your soul within himself.

- While taking Communion at your church, picture Christ offering you his inner life, his personality, his entire self. Then take the Communion elements, and enjoy what it means to abide in God.

- Hold your hands in front of you at the waist level, palms upward. Then lay one on top of the other so they form a small X. Stretch out your fingers toward God and say something like:

  I want you to be the bread of my life.

  I will feed on you and live because of you.

  Because of you, I will live forever.

  "Lord, I am not worthy to receive you, but only say the word and I shall be healed" (a common phrase in liturgical church services).

  Be still for several minutes.

6

LIVING IN
TRANSFORMATION

PHILIPPIANS 4:4-13

Ever wonder how folks can look so saintly during a worship service but behave so badly in private conversation? Ever choke on your own pious devotion when you feel like turning around and strangling the kid who's kicking your chair or pew during worship services? What good is the discipline of worship if we remain the same crabby people as before?

In and of themselves, spiritual disciplines are worth little. If we merely go through the motions of doing them, they don't affect us. If we notice how much we do or don't do them and evaluate our spirituality accordingly, we turn our relationship with God into a bunch of rules. But if we use them to connect with God, we let Christ disciple us. Certain character qualities are more likely to emerge. For example, responding to God in worship and celebration usually makes a person more joyful, thankful, generous and dependent on God.

Philippians 4:4-13 describes how rejoicing people (which means worshiping, celebrating people) change inside and out. They may even develop what the world describes as "an optimistic outlook." Faith-based optimism is never empty-headed. Worship that is grounded in Bible study and meditation keeps our feet planted firmly on the ground, able to see the need for justice and courage in life. Yet we draw from the resources of an alternate reality—the invisible kingdom of God. Responding to God in worship trains us to anticipate that God is at work around the next corner.

Turning Toward God

Come up with a list of typical moments when the worship bubble is burst by humdrum difficulties of life. For example:

- After a delightful worship service, you get in your car to drive home and rudely cut off another driver.

- After gaining a sense of trust in God during a worship service, you worry about finances on the way home.

- After enjoying moments of private prayer and worship, you lapse into a petty argument with your kids.

"Worship is the

means by which

we recover our

focus and return

to our center."

ROBERT
MULHOLLAND

Hearing God Through the Word

Read Philippians 4:4-9.

1. What does rejoicing look like when it's part of worship and celebration?

2. The word translated *gentleness* in verse 5 (or *moderation*, KJV) encompasses the ideas of surrender and yieldedness. How can worship develop yieldedness in a person?

3. The phrase "The Lord is near" seems to be intentionally ambiguous, referring either to God's closeness to us or to the near return of Jesus (v. 5). Why would either meaning be an important assumption in worship and celebration?

   Which of the two ideas is more helpful to you in learning to be gentle (the first part of v. 5)? Why?

4. Celebration involves recollecting what God has done. How does that mitigate worry and anxiety?

5. How is this unexplainable "peace of God" different from "having peaceful feelings"?

6. How is worshiping God different from having worshipful feelings?

7. How is the process described in verse 8 likely to lead to worship and likely to flow from worship?

   During what in-between moments in life would it help you to focus on "excellent or praiseworthy" things? While driving? Doing yard work? Waiting in a doctor's office?

8. Think of a worship song that includes these two elements: (1) God being worshiped and praised, and (2) a person growing in character.

"Love is that ardent desire, continually nourished by devout hope, which inspires the constant practice of goodness in the expectation of the divine presence."

JEAN-PIERRE DE CAUSSADE

Read Philippians 4:10-13.

9. Monetary gifts are not always given and received with God-honoring attitudes. What words or phrases in verses 10-12 tell us that Paul and the Philippians had attitudes of giving God the glory about the monetary gift the Philippians sent him?

10. If you give money as an act of worship, you are responding to God. What helps people give in a mindset of worship?

11. The phrase "through him who gives me strength" expresses dependence on God. How might a sense of dependence on God flow from your making worship and celebration a part of your life?

"Let us desire

nothing else, wish

for nothing else,

and let nothing

please and delight

us except our

Creator and

Redeemer."

FRANCIS OF ASSISI

12. Which of the following outgrowths of worship and celebration do you see God currently building in you?

___ gentleness

___ surrender

___ recollecting the good God has done

___ giving glory to God

___ knowing the peace of God

___ trust instead of worry and anxiety

___ focusing on praiseworthy things

___ trusting God for strength

Transformation Exercises

Experiment with one or more of the following.

• Read several psalms, marking passages that speak of God's throne, God's reign, God's greatness and God's authority. (Hint: Psalms 89 and 132 are good places to start.) What effect might picturing these regularly have on a person?

• Look up Psalm 145. Underline all the phrases that describe the greatness of God (for example, "the glorious splendor of your majesty," v. 5). Circle the ones that describe our responses (for example, "I will meditate on your wonderful works," v. 5). Journal about how you would be different if you truly believed the truth in the phrases you underlined, such as "You open your hand and satisfy the desires of every living thing" (v. 16).

- Take a walk or run or bike ride and consider someone you need to forgive. Keep a worship song in mind, and then for a few minutes, practice trusting God to deal with that person justly so you can surrender your grudge.

- Think of a task you believe God wants you to do but you're afraid to do. Pick out a song that God can use to move you forward with courage to do that task.

STUDY NOTES FOR
WORSHIP AND CELEBRATION

Session 1. Longing for God

PSALM 63

FOCUS: David models a deep desire to connect with God, to behold God, to live life enthralled with God.

Question 2. David sensed God's presence even when he was cut off from the privileges of royal life, from the rhythm of Hebrew worship services and from the love of his son. He sensed God's presence even in a dry, weary, waterless land.

Question 3. Although certain forms of worship may make it easier for us to worship God, we regard "God rather than these forms as essential."[1]

When we're having a difficult time in personal worship, we may need to pause and journal about what's troubling us. In corporate worship, we may wish to pause and pray for the elements that trouble us, or even turn to this psalm and let God help us worship.

Question 4. Glorify, praise, lift up, sing, remember, think of God, stay close.

Question 5. David actively engaged his body in worship, moving his lips and lifting up his hands. The lifting of hands may indicate gratitude for past help or petition for future help, or both.

Question 6. You may wish to get them started with these ideas: My soul will be satisfied as with the most comfortable of beds, the most intriguing of books to read, the most beautiful, breathtaking views.

Question 9. Many people trust God only in the sense that they count on God to make their lives okay. When they have troubles, they become bitter. But others have learned to have confidence in God, to believe that God will do what is best and rescue us as needed. They believe in God's goodness and faithfulness. This makes the difference. Worship, at all times, helps build this confidence and faith.

Question 10. Even though David loved Absalom, he knew that those who opposed him were "fighting God" by seeking "to defeat the royal dynasty that has God's approval."[2] Yes, David may have praised God with great difficulty, but it shows how we often must remind ourselves of truth in the midst of emotional moments.

---

[1]H. C. Leupold, *Exposition of the Psalms* (Grand Rapids: Baker, 1972), p. 463.
[2]Ibid., p. 467.

Session 2. Responding in Worship

PSALM 104:31—105:5

FOCUS: While focusing on God's character, attributes and actions, we respond with worship practices such as giving thanks, setting forth God's remarkable character, honoring God's name, seeking God and remembering God's great deeds.

General note. You may want to go over the introduction to section eight on page 259 to review examples of God's character, attributes and actions.

Question 1. God is full of glory—that glowing divine essence. God has joy in this creative work (Psalm 104:31). God is holy (105:3). Don't be concerned if participants mix up character traits, attributes and actions. The important point is that they search and discover these things about God.

Question 2. God is powerful. The earth trembles as God looks at it (Psalm 104:31-32); God can be counted on to enact justice (104:35). God is strong (Psalm 105:4).

Question 3. God's work of creation (104:31-32); God has done wonders and miracles, made righteous judgments (105:5).

Question 4. Urge them to scour this passage for active verbs: singing (104:33), meditating (104:34), rejoicing (104:34), giving thanks (105:1), making known and telling about God's wonderful acts (105:1-2), giving glory to God's name, seeking God's face always (105:4).

Note that Psalm 104 before verse 31 has been reviewing God's wonders of creation—wildlife, natural wonders, celestial wonders—and how God feeds creation and sends the Spirit.

Question 5. It surprises some to read that God is indeed a joyous Being and rejoices easily. The reciprocal rejoicing in Psalm 104:31, 34 is interesting: God rejoices in humans (who are God's works) and humans rejoice in God. This is another indication of the back-and-forth relationship that can occur between God and people.

Question 6. This is not gloating over the extinction of the wicked but a plea that all may rightly praise God. Says Franz Delitzsch, "Those who take pleasure in wickedness . . . are contrary to the purpose of the good creation of God, they imperil its continuance, and mar the joy of His creatures."[3]

Question 7. Ask participants to look for clues in other versions, especially if they have *The Message* ("Honor his holy name with Hallelujahs") or the Contemporary English Version ("Celebrate and worship his holy name with all your heart"). Bible commentary writer Leupold translates the phrase as "Make your boast of His holy name" and interprets this as "in a wholesome sense being proud and happy of knowing what manner of reputation the Lord has attained among His saints."[4]

Question 9. Give participants a few minutes to think and ask them to write down their responses. Then explain that you'd like for them to offer their responses one at a time, going around the circle three times.

If you wish, plan a worship response after the last person speaks, but don't tell the group. Lead it yourself—it might be singing a song or clapping or saying "hallelujah" (all psalmic responses). Or if you wish, have them go around the circle only once, but after each person speaks, the entire group says, "His love endures forever" (as in Psalm 136).

Question 10. Bible study—diligent attention and focus on who God is and what God does—leads

---

[3]Franz Delitzsch, *Commentary on the Old Testament,* vol. 5, *Commentary on the Psalms* (Grand Rapids: Eerdmans, 1973), p. 136.
[4]Leupold, *Exposition of the Psalms,* p. 734.

to worship. Worship without study leads to fluff (see Romans 10:2); study without worship leads to pride. Study informs worship; worship completes study.

Session 3. Entering into Corporate Worship

1 CHRONICLES 16:1-36

FOCUS: Corporate worship brings the love and energy of many people to God. It trains us to make God the center of our personal life and our church life.

Question 1. They offered burnt offerings and fellowship offerings, which would have included sheep, goats and cattle (Exodus 20:24).

These worshipers did not sit back and watch others. They participated with great energy. They "entered into" it. A fellowship and burnt offering involved choosing an animal without defect, slaughtering it at the entrance to the Tent of Meeting and watching the priests sprinkle the blood against the altar on all sides. From this fellowship offering the individual brought certain parts of the animal to the priests to burn on the altar. This created a powerful aroma. The burnt offering symbolized "a person's total dedication to God," and the fellowship offering "expressed friendship or communion between the worshipper and God."[5]

Question 3. If you wish, ask participants to bring such an object for the next session. Then set them in the center and discuss them as participants arrive.

Question 5. Besides those who made petition, gave thanks and praised God, ten people played lyres, harps, cymbals and trumpets.

Question 7. Participants may want to flip through pages of previous chapters for ideas and notice headings to review Israelite history. The Israelites would give thanks (v. 8) for having a king in Jerusalem and an end to bloodshed between David and Saul and between the Israelites and the Philistines. "The nations" (v. 8) would include people who had bullied and blocked the Israelites' path to the Promised Land. God's wonders, miracles and judgments (v. 12) would include such things as Jacob's family's being saved from the famine, freedom from slavery through the ten plagues and the bringing of the ark of the covenant to Jerusalem.

Question 8. Some scholars think this psalm was composed for this event; others think it was borrowed from the psalter that existed then; still others think it was inserted in the text later by the "Chronicler." So it could have been an old favorite or a new tune.

Question 10. Singing, proclaiming, declaring God's glory, fearing God, ascribing to God glory and strength, bringing an offering, worshiping the Lord, trembling before God (vv. 23-30), giving thanks, crying out and praising God (vv. 34-36). The heavens were to rejoice, be glad and say among the nations, "The Lord reigns." Creation was also to respond (see vv. 32-33).

---

[5]J. A. Thompson, *Handbook of Life in Bible Times* (Downers Grove, Ill.: InterVarsity Press, 1986), p. 330.

Session 4. Celebrating the Life of God

LUKE 15:1-32

FOCUS: Celebration involves recollecting the ways God has benefited our lives and expressing this joy in outward ways.

Question 2. All three parables paint pictures of the determined and relentless love of God, who does outrageous acts for the people this great God *so loves.*[6] Notice also the shepherd carrying the sheep on his shoulder—a sign not only of tenderness but also of triumph.

Question 3. A shepherd owning a hundred sheep would have been in "very good circumstances,"[7] and so the rejoicing would be elaborate—drinking, eating, dancing. Since the shepherd has shown such extraordinary care of the found sheep, one wonders whether the sheep appears at the party as guest of honor instead of in the customary role of entrée. The woman's party would be more sparse, since she is obviously poor: "the original word for 'piece of silver' was 'drachma' and had the value of about sixteen or eighteen cents in our money."[8] These ten coins could have been her household budget for a time or they could have been her wedding dowry. Having that dowry broken by a lost coin would have been a bad omen about her marriage or her faithfulness to her husband, in which case her joy and thankfulness on finding the coin would be for more than monetary reasons.

Question 4. If time permits, ask participants how the finding something precious makes them want to respond. Worship and celebration are about responding.

Question 6. Dressy clothes and jewelry (best robe, ring) are not only festive but also symbols of what God has done in this boy's life. The robe may have been worn by the boy before he left, in which case this is a sign of reinstatement. The ring is a symbol of regained authority. Sandals were worn by freemen, not slaves. Usually only the master wore shoes in the house; servants went barefoot. The boy's full reinstatement is played out in his apparel.

For the feast, a specially fattened calf is roasted. The father makes a pronouncement about his son. It is followed by music and dancing.

Question 8. The father's words "you are always with me" imply that in the day-to-day, side-by-side victories at home there has been plenty to celebrate. Apparently the older son has not done so, for he says he has been "slaving" for his father (v. 29). The older son hasn't rejoiced even though the father's riches have been constantly at his disposal. Sure, the younger son gets the special-occasion calf, but the older son has been enjoying splendid meals day after day.

Daily celebration is important too. The disgruntled or overly serious person needs to choose to celebrate instead of keeping to himself while others celebrate. Celebration is about recollecting the good that has occurred, and negative folks need this!

Question 10. One possibility for more naturally celebrating within ourselves in a worship service is to celebrate God's graciousness every day. Then we will have worshiped all week and will already be deep in celebration when we participate in a worship service.

Question 11. Your body might bless God as you sing in the shower or cry out in delight at the sight of a bird you haven't seen in a while. Blessing food at meals can be a celebration. If it's not, try blessing your food *after* you eat!

---

[6]I. Howard Marshall, *Luke,* New International Greek Testament Commentary (Grand Rapids: Eerdmans, 1978), p. 601.
[7]Leo Boles, *A Commentary on the Gospel According to Luke* (Nashville: Gospel Advocate, 1972), p. 296.
[8]Ibid., p. 297.

Session 5. Coming to the Table

JOHN 6:47-58

FOCUS: Jesus asks us to partake of him; as we do so, he gives us eternal life, and we put ourselves in a position to let Christ transform our souls.

Question 1. They are those who believe (this concept involved putting one's full trust in so that one's heart and actions are deeply affected), who "eat of this bread" (v. 51), who "eat my flesh and drink my blood" (v. 54) and who "feed on this bread" (v. 58).

Question 2. Bread is a basic food that nourishes and sustains us. Often called the "staff of life," bread in some form is recognized this way by people throughout the world. Jesus nourishes and sustains our spiritual lives.

Question 3. People take in or experience Christ in many ways, such as seeing Christ's qualities in other people, taking in sunsets or taking a graduate level class that challenges them to think.

Question 6. Christ being the bread of life, which we ingest, suggests union with God and intimacy with Christ. It adds that dimension of Christ coming inside us to change us.

Question 7. Spend sufficient time on this question of great importance. You may even want to ask them if they want to write themselves a note to remind themselves to consider this the next time they take Communion.

Question 9. While Communion tends to be a reflective moment (which is appropriate), it's also a time to be thankful for Christ's love for us and redemption of the world (v. 51). It's a time to be thankful for Christ's desire that we form an intimate relationship with him by taking him in and experiencing him on a regular basis, as pictured by Communion.

Question 10. Feeding on Christ is our continual responsibility, privilege and joy. You may also wish to mention that the Greek verbs used in this passage ("eats my flesh, drinks my blood") are in present tense, indicating continued action.

Part of how God transforms our souls is in our relationships with other people. Communion can be a time to "recognize the body of the Lord," to look around and ask God to show us how to love others more, to have more gentleness and so on (1 Corinthians 11:29).

Session 6. Living in Transformation

PHILIPPIANS 4:4-13

FOCUS: While practicing the disciplines of worshiping and celebrating, we become full of joy, thankfulness, generosity and dependence on God, and our character changes.

General Note. You may want to review the section of the introduction titled "How We Get Spiritual Disciplines Wrong" (p. 9).

Question 1. You may want to have someone read Ephesians 5:19-20: "Speak to one another with psalms, hymns and spiritual songs. Sing and make music in your heart to the Lord, always giving thanks to God the Father for everything, in the name of our Lord Jesus Christ."

Question 2. Most of us are self-absorbed, insisting on our own way; worship draws us away from our own agenda toward the greatness of God.

Question 4. Recollecting is largely about thanksgiving (see v. 6) and praise. Such an optimistic focus leads us away from worry. Worship focuses on God, who is in control, which helps us not to worry about things over which we have no control.

Question 5. In study, the appropriate prelude to worship, we can learn about the deep peacefulness of God and who God is. Thus worship can be based on exulting in who God is, providing a substantive base for peace. (More is said about this in the section of the introduction titled "The Spiritual Disciplines of Worship and Celebration.") Peaceful feelings, however, may come and go.

Question 6. Worship consumes all of us, not just feelings. It consumes our thoughts (if it's based on substantive knowledge of who God is), our bodies (as we sing from the diaphragm or stand to honor God). We have a sense of God that includes our emotions, but we also have that deep inner knowing that wills us to move forward with God. We have a strong confidence in God's abilities.

Question 7. The verb used, "think about," is a favorite word for Paul; he is "exhorting them to consider [these qualities] seriously and shape their conduct by them.[9] Such serious intentionality creates worship from the heart that is weightier than a sentimental response to uplifting music. The intentional focus described in verse 8 is likely to lead someone to worship God even when life's circumstances go awry (as studied in session 1).

Question 8. You may want to use this as an example: "The Solid Rock" describes God as an unchanging, formidable being and also describes the growth of hope in a person's life. Listen to the group's suggestions and then pick one of these songs to sing.

Question 9. Paul "rejoice[d] greatly in the Lord"; he didn't rejoice greatly in the generosity of the Philippians. (In the same way, at church we do not give our offerings to people or to build a structure or to support Christian activities.) The gift grew out of the Philippians' "concern," not obligation or pretentious display. Paul hadn't sniveled or flattered to get the gift. He was content with whatever he had. We can follow this example by worshiping God alone when it would be easy to be distracted by abundance or lack (our own or others').

Question 10. It often helps if the person up front makes a disclaimer that resembles that of the apostle Paul (vv. 11-12): "We don't need your money to do what God wants us to do. Give only as God asks you to give. Give only what demonstrates your response to God's greatness and provision."

Question 11. Worship focuses on the infinite goodness, immense strength and boundless power of God, which makes us want to depend on God.

---

[9]Pat Edwin Harrell, *The Letter of Paul to the Philippians,* Living Word Commentary (Austin, Tex.: R. B. Sweet, 1971), p. 139.

APPENDIX

Guidelines for Leaders

MY GRACE IS SUFFICIENT FOR YOU.
2 CORINTHIANS 12:9

If leading a small group is something new for you, don't worry. These sessions are designed to be led easily. Because the Bible study questions flow from observation to interpretation to application, you may feel as if the studies lead themselves.

You don't need to be an expert on the Bible or a trained teacher to lead a small group discussion. As a leader, you can guide group members to discover for themselves what the Bible has to say and to listen for God's guidance. This method of learning will allow group members to remember much more of what is said than a lecture would.

This study guide is flexible. You can use it with a variety of groups—students, professionals, neighborhood or church folks. Each study takes forty-five to sixty minutes in a group setting.

It's true that getting people to discuss the Bible requires some thought. The suggestions listed below will help you encourage discussion by paying attention to group dynamics.

Preparing for the Study

1. Ask God to help you understand and apply the passage in your own life. Unless

this happens, you will not be prepared to lead others. Pray too for the various members of the group. Ask God to open your hearts to the message and motivate you to action.

2. Read the introduction to the entire guide to get an overview of the issues that will be explored.

3. As you begin each study, read and reread the assigned Scripture passage to familiarize yourself with it. Read also the focus statement at the beginning of the notes for that study, which appear after session six in each part.

4. This study guide is based on the New International Version of the Bible. It will help you and the group if you use this translation as the basis for your study and discussion.

5. Carefully work through each question in the study. Spend time in meditation and reflection as you consider how to respond.

6. Write your thoughts and responses in the space provided in the study guide. This will help you to express your understanding of the passage clearly.

7. It may help to have a Bible dictionary handy. Use it to look up any unfamiliar words, names or places. (For additional help on how to study a passage, see *How to Lead a LifeGuide Bible Study* from InterVarsity Press.)

8. Consider how you need to apply the Scripture to your life. Remember that the group members will follow your lead in responding to the studies. They will not go any deeper than you do.

Leading the Study

1. Begin the study on time. Open with prayer, asking God to help the group to understand and apply the passage.

2. Be sure that everyone in your group has a study guide. There are some questions and activities they will need to work through on their own before, during or after the study session.

3. At the beginning of your first session together, explain that these studies are meant to be discussions, not lectures. Encourage the members of the group to participate. However, do not put pressure on those who may be hesitant to speak during the first few sessions. You may want to suggest the following guidelines to your group.

   • Stick to the topic being discussed.

   • Base your response on the verses studied, not on outside authorities such as commentaries or speakers.

   • Focus on the passage of Scripture studied. Only rarely should you refer to other portions of the Bible. This allows for everyone to participate on equal ground and for in-depth study.

- Anything said in the group is considered confidential and will not be discussed outside the group unless specific permission is given to do so.

- Help everyone get involved by limiting your responses if you contribute a lot or by responding more if you're usually quiet. But don't feel forced to speak up.

- Listen attentively to each other and learn from one another.

- Pray for each other, especially if you feel that someone is struggling with an answer. Praying is better than interrupting.

4. Have a group member read aloud the introduction at the beginning of the discussion.

5. Every session begins with a "Turning Toward God" section. The questions or activities are meant to be used before the passage is read. These questions introduce the theme of the study and encourage group members to begin to open up. Encourage as many members as possible to participate, and be ready to get the discussion going with your own response.

6. Have one or more group members read aloud the passage to be studied.

7. As you ask the questions under "Hearing God Through the Word," keep in mind that they are designed to be used just as they are written. You may simply read them aloud. Or you may prefer to express them in your own words.

   There may be times when it is appropriate to deviate from the study guide. For example, a question may have already been answered. If so, move on to the next question. Or someone may raise an important question not covered in the guide. Take time to discuss it, but try to keep the group from going off on tangents.

8. Avoid answering your own questions. If necessary repeat or rephrase them until they are clearly understood. Or point out something you read in the leader's notes to clarify the context or meaning. An eager group quickly becomes passive and silent if members think the leader will do most of the talking.

9. Don't be afraid of silence in response to the discussion questions. People may need time to think about the question before formulating their answers. Count to twenty before rephrasing or commenting.

10. Don't be content with just one answer. Ask, "What do the rest of you think?" or "Anything else?" until several people have given answers to the question.

11. Acknowledge all contributions. Try to be affirming whenever possible. Never reject an answer. If it is clearly off-base, ask, "Which verse led you to that con-

clusion?" or again, "What do the rest of you think?"

12. Don't expect every answer to be addressed to you, even though this will probably happen at first. As group members become more at ease, they will begin to truly interact with each other. This is one sign of healthy discussion.

13. Don't be afraid of controversy. It can be very stimulating. If you don't resolve an issue completely, don't be frustrated. Explain that the group will move on and God may enlighten group members in later sessions.

14. Periodically summarize what the group has said about the passage. This helps to draw together the various ideas mentioned and gives continuity to the study. But don't preach.

15. Every session ends with "Transformation Exercises." At the end of the study, have a participant read them aloud. Then ask each participant to choose the one that fits them best, according to their personality or current needs. Ask them to tell the group which one that is and a time they could try it.

    Before the next session starts, ask whether any participants tried the transformation exercises. You might lead into this by telling about one you tried. So-called failures really are not failures. These things are a matter of skill building. You never learn to ride a bike unless you get on it the first time and keep trying.

16. Conclude your time together with conversational prayer. Ask for God's help in following through on the commitments you've made.

17. End on time.

Many more suggestions and helps can be found in *The Big Book on Small Groups* (from IVP Connect).

Using the Transformation Exercises in a Group

Because disciplines are as much "caught" as "taught," it's important for participants to tell each other their experiences in practicing the transformation exercises. Perhaps what you tried didn't work but you need to try what someone else in the group did.

End the first session by asking participants to look at the exercises and choose the one that best fits their personality and life habits. (Some may want to choose the one that most challenges them.) Encourage participants to change or modify the suggestions to fit them. If they're unsure about what to do, encourage them to ask God for ideas and seek God's guidance. To those who seem especially discouraged, ask, How are you already practicing these disciplines?

After the first meeting, use the opening moments to review how the experiments with the transformation exercises went. Allow at least ten minutes of your session time for this. (If you find there's not enough time to talk about transformation exercise experiences, it's okay to omit a few questions.) Be sure to use words such as "experiment" and "try it out."

Ask participants to focus on these questions:

- How did it help you connect with God?

- What worked?

- What didn't work?

- If you tried it again, what would you do differently?

You learn a great deal from having done an exercise that *didn't* work. The only way to fail is *not* to experiment.

Listen carefully and learn from each other. We often learn from the person most opposite from us. Honor any attempt to try the discipline. For example, practicing solitude and silence for only 15 minutes is good! Promote this approach: "progress, not perfection." We start small—we don't try to be martyrs. Apply this adage to the practice of all disciplines: "Pray as you can, not as you can't." Do what you can do and don't worry about what you can't do.

Publicizing the Studies for Groups

The term "spiritual disciplines" might scare some people so you might want to call them "exercises" or "practices" or "experiments" or "ways of connecting with God." When you explain the topic of a particular set of studies, you might want to describe instead the issues that trap us and are helped by the appropriate disciplines. For example:

- Solitude: Getting rid of busyness and hurry.

- Service: Following in the footsteps of Jesus and letting go of busywork.

- Community (or Confession): Do you know a lot of people, but don't have self-giving, transparent interaction with anyone?

These phrases describe not only what contemporary people are looking for but also Jesus and how Jesus lived.

As users of the studies ask questions, answers are posted on the website <www.janjohnson.org/spiritual_disciplines.html>.

SOURCES

INTRODUCTION

Henri Nouwen, *Making All Things New* (San Francisco: HarperSanFrancisco, 1981), p. 66.

Section 1: Solitude & Silence

SESSION 1

Sidebars

Dallas Willard, *The Divine Conspiracy* (San Francisco: HarperSanFrancisco, 1998), p. 355.

Elisabeth Elliot, "Turning Solitude into Prayer," *Cross Point,* Summer 1997, p. 7.

Jeanne Guyon, *Experiencing the Depths of Jesus Christ* (Beaumont, Tex.: SeedSowers, 1975), p. 60.

SESSION 2

Sidebars

Dallas Willard, *In Search of Guidance: Developing a Conversational Relationship with God* (San Francisco: HarperSanFrancisco, 1993), p. 78.

Anonymous, *The Cloud of Unknowing,* trans. William Johnston (New York: Doubleday, 1973), p. 55.

Henri Nouwen, "Deeper into Love," *Weavings,* September-October 1995, p. 25.

Transformation Exercise One

H. C. Leupold, *Exposition of Genesis* (Grand Rapids: Baker, 1976), 2:874.

SESSION 3

Sidebars

Anonymous, *The Cloud of Unknowing,* trans. William Johnston (New York: Doubleday, 1973), pp. 48, 47.

W. Phillip Keller "Solitude for Serenity and Strength," *Decision,* August-September 1981, p. 8, quoted in Joyce Huggett, *The Joy of Listening to God* (Downers Grove, Ill.: InterVarsity Press, 1986), p. 64.

John Baillie, *A Diary of Private Prayer* (London: Oxford University Press, 1956), p. 57.

Malcolm Muggeridge, *Something Beautiful for God: Mother Teresa of Calcutta* (San Francisco: Harper & Row, 1971), p. 40.

SESSION 4

Sidebars

Jeanne Guyon, *Experiencing the Depths of Jesus Christ* (Beaumont, Tex.: SeedSowers, 1975), p. 60.

Henri Nouwen, *The Genesee Diary: Report from a Trappist Monastery* (New York: Doubleday/Image, 1989), p. 133.

C. S. Lewis, *The Screwtape Letters* (New York: Macmillan, 1970), pp. 113-14.

SESSION 5

Sidebars

Oswald Chambers, *My Utmost for His Highest,* rev. ed. (Grand Rapids: Discovery House, 1992), February 13 entry, italics mine.

Bill Volkman, *Basking in His Presence* (Glen Ellyn, Ill.: UnionLife, 1996), p. 111.

SESSION 6

Sidebars

Thomas Merton, *New Seeds of Contemplation* (New York: New Directions, 1962), pp. 52-63, and Henri Nouwen, *Reaching Out: The Movements of the Spiritual Life* (New York: Doubleday, 1975), pp. 37-62, as developed and adapted by David Rensberger, "The Holiness of Winter," *Weavings,* November/December 1996, p. 40.

Henri Nouwen, *The Way of the Heart* (San Francisco: HarperSanFrancisco, 1991), p. 76.

Merton, *New Seeds of Contemplation,* p. 55.

Section 2: Service & Secrecy

Introduction

Richard Foster, *Celebration of Discipline* (San Francisco: Harper & Row, 1988), p. 134.

SESSION 1

Sidebars

Hildegard of Bingen, quoted by Robert Mulholland, *Invitation to a Journey* (Downers Grove, Ill.: InterVarsity Press, 1993), p. 99.

Oswald Chambers, *My Utmost for His Highest,* updated edition (Grand Rapids: Discovery House, 1992), October 3 entry.

SESSION 2

Introduction

Dallas Willard, *The Divine Conspiracy* (San Francisco: HarperSanFrancisco, 1998), p. 121.

Sidebars

Robert Mulholland, *Invitation to a Journey* (Downers Grove, Ill.: InterVarsity Press, 1993), p. 160.

Bob Pierce, quoted in Franklin Graham with Jeanette Lockerbie, *Bob Pierce: This One Thing I Do* (Waco, Tex.: Word, 1983), p. 77.

Hearing God Through the Word

The idea that the demons deceived Jesus comes from I. Howard Marshall's *Commentary on Luke,* New International Greek Testament Commentary (Grand Rapids: Eerdmans, 1978), p. 340. The suggestion that the stampede helped confirm that the exorcism was not a hoax comes from Ray Summers, *Commentary on Luke* (Waco, Tex.: Word, 1972), p. 100.

SESSION 3

Hearing God Through the Word

The information about a slave being expected to wash the master's feet but not vice versa comes from J. N. Sanders and B. A. Mastin, *The Gospel According to St. John* (London: Adam and Charles Black, 1977), p. 309.

Sidebars

Thelma Hall, *Too Deep for Words: Rediscovering Lectio Divina* (New York: Paulist, 1988), p. 13.

Henri Nouwen, *The Genesee Diary: Report from a Trappist Monastery* (New York: Doubleday/ Image, 1989), p. 177.

Richard Foster, *Celebration of Discipline* (San Francisco: Harper & Row, 1988), p. 130.

SESSION 4

Sidebars

R. C. H. Lenski, *The Interpretation of St. Matthew's Gospel* (Minneapolis: Augsburg, 1943), p. 903.

John Baillie, *A Diary of Private Prayer* (London: Oxford University Press, 1956), p. 37 (8th day, morning).

Robert Mulholland, *Invitation to a Journey* (Downers Grove, Ill.: InterVarsity Press, 1993), p. 42.

Transformation Exercise One

John Baillie, *A Diary of Private Prayer* (London: Oxford University Press, 1956), p. 75.

SESSION 5

Introduction

Elaine Prevallet, "Through an Autumn Lens," *Weavings,* May-June 1991, pp. 23-24.

Sidebars

Oswald Chambers, *My Utmost for His Highest,* updated ed. (Grand Rapids: Discovery House, 1992), January 7 entry.

Dallas Willard, *The Divine Conspiracy* (San Francisco: HarperSanFrancisco, 1998), p. 200.

SESSION 6

Sidebars

Frank Laubach, *Man of Prayer,* Heritage Collection (Syracuse, N.Y.: Laubach Literacy International, 1990), p. 47.

Oswald Chambers, *My Utmost for His Highest,* updated ed. (Grand Rapids: Discovery House, 1992), February 25 entry.

Ibid., November 15 entry.

Section 3: Prayer & Listening

Introduction

Oswald Chambers, *My Utmost for His Highest,* updated ed. (Grand Rapids.: Discovery House, 1992), August 28 entry.

SESSION 1

Sidebars

Jean-Nicholas Grou, *How to Pray* (Cambridge: James Clarke, 1955), p. 15.

Dallas Willard, *The Divine Conspiracy* (San Francisco: HarperSanFrancisco, 1998), p. 194.

Thelma Hall, *Too Deep for Words: Rediscovering Lectio Divina* (New York: Paulist, 1988), p. 32.

SESSION 2

Sidebars

Dom Chapman, quoted in Thelma Hall, *Too Deep for Words: Rediscovering Lectio Divina* (New York: Paulist, 1988), p. 40.

Roberta Bondi, "The Paradox of Prayer," *Weavings*, March-April 1989, p. 7.

C. S. Lewis, *Letters to Malcolm: Chiefly on Prayer* (New York: Harcourt Brace, 1964), p. 82.

Transformation Exercises

Henri Nouwen, in *Eerdmans' Book of Famous Prayers,* ed. Veronica Zundel (Grand Rapids: Eerdmans, 1983), p. 106.

SESSION 3

Introduction

Dallas Willard, *The Divine Conspiracy* (San Francisco: HarperSanFrancisco, 1998), p. 194.

Sidebars

John Mogabgab, "Editor's Introduction," *Weavings*, July-August 1996, p. 2.

Oswald Chambers, *My Utmost for His Highest,* updated ed. (Grand Rapids: Discovery House, 1992), August 6 entry.

Question Four

Evelyn Underhill, *The Soul's Delight: Selected Writings of Evelyn Underhill,* ed. Keith

Beasley-Topliffe, Upper Room Spiritual Classics (Nashville: Upper Room, 1998), pp. 23-24.

Ibid., p. 24.

William Barclay, *The Gospel of Matthew* (Philadelphia: Westminster Press, 1958), 1:206.

Transformation Exercises

Francis of Assisi, in *The Riches of Simplicity: Selected Writings of Francis and Clare,* ed. Keith Beasley-Topliffe, Upper Room Spiritual Classics (Nashville: Upper Room, 1998), pp. 34-35.

SESSION 4

Introduction

Mary Geegh, *God Guides* (Holland, Mich.: Missionary, 1995), pp. 2-3, 9, 18-19.

Douglas Steere, *On Listening to Another,* ed. Glenn Hinson, Doubleday Devotional Classics (Garden City, N.Y.: Doubleday, 1978), pp. 211, 213, with my annotations.

Sidebars

Wendy Wright, "Desert Listening," *Weavings*, May-June 1994, pp. 7, 14.

Amy Carmichael, *A Very Present Help,* ed. Judith Couchman (Ann Arbor, Mich.: Servant, 1996), p. 60.

Jean-Pierre de Caussade, *The Sacrament of the Present Moment* (San Francisco: Harper & Row, 1982), p. 80.

SESSION 5

Sidebars

Hannah Hurnard, *God's Transmitters* (Wheaton, Ill.: Tyndale House, 1981), p. 12, quoted in Dallas Willard, *In Search of Guidance: Developing a Conversational Relationship with God* (San Francisco: HarperSanFrancisco, 1993), p. 155.

Oswald Chambers, *My Utmost for His Highest,* updated ed. (Grand Rapids: Discovery House, 1992), December 13 entry.

Douglas Steere, "Intercession: Caring for Souls," *Weavings,* March-April 1989, p. 21.

Question Two

Ray Summers, *Commentary on Luke* (Waco, Tex.: Word, 1972), p. 280.

SESSION 6

Introduction

Douglas Steere, introduction to Brother Lawrence, *The Practice of the Presence of God,* Great Devotional Classics (Nashville: Upper Room, 1961), p. 7.

A. W. Tozer, *The Pursuit of God* (Camp Hill, Penn.: Christian Publications, 1982), p. 126.

Sidebars

Augustine, *Early Will I Seek You,* ed. David Hazard (Minneapolis: Bethany House, 1991), p. 81.

Brother Lawrence, *The Practice of the Presence of God,* ed. Douglas Steere, Great Devotional Classics (Nashville: Upper Room, 1961), pp. 27-28.

Frank Laubach, *Channels of Spiritual Power* (Westwood, N.J.: Fleming H. Revell, 1954), p. 96.

Section 4: Study & Meditation

Introduction

Chart content taken from Jan Johnson, *Listening to God* (Colorado Springs: NavPress, 1997).

SESSION 1

Sidebars

A. W. Tozer, *The Pursuit of God* (Camp Hill, Penn.: Christian Publications, 1982), pp. 81-82.

Dallas Willard, unpublished manuscript.

SESSION 2

Sidebars

Philipp Jakob Spener, "The Necessary and Useful Reading of the Holy Scriptures," quoted in *The Spiritual Formation Bible, NRSV* (Grand Rapids: Zondervan, 1999), p. 925.

Enzo Bianchi, *Praying the Word* (Kalamazoo, Mich.: Cistercian Publications, 1998), p. 23.

William Law, *A Serious Call to a Devout and Holy Life* (London: J. Richardson, 1720), p. 200, as quoted in *Spiritual Formation Bible,* p. 670.

Transformation Exercise Three

C. F. Keil, *Commentary on the Old Testament,* vol. 3, *I and II Kings, I and II Chronicles, Ezra, Nehemiah, Esther* (Grand Rapids: Eerdmans, 1973), p. 232.

SESSION 3

Introduction

J. Steven Harper, "Meeting God in Scripture," in *The Spiritual Formation Bible, NRSV* (Grand Rapids: Zondervan, 1999), p. 1089.

Sidebars

Richard Foster, *Celebration of Discipline* (San Francisco: Harper & Row, 1988), p. 64.

Question Seven

Franz Delitzsch, *Commentary on the Old Testament,* vol. 7, *Biblical Commentary on the Prophecies of Isaiah* (Grand Rapids: Eerdmans, 1969), 1:284.

SESSION 4

Sidebars

Enzo Bianchi, *Praying the Word* (Kalamazoo, Mich.: Cistercian Publications, 1998), p. 50.

Jeanne Guyon, *Experiencing the Depths of Jesus Christ* (Beaumont, Tex.: SeedSowers, 1975), p. 11.

Robert Mulholland, *Shaped by the Word* (Nashville: Upper Room, 2000), p. 57.

SESSION 5

Sidebars

Enzo Bianchi, *Praying the Word* (Kalamazoo, Mich.: Cistercian Publications, 1998), p. 52.

Dallas Willard, *The Divine Conspiracy* (San Francisco: HarperSanFrancisco, 1998), pp. 88-89.

Robert Mulholland, *Shaped by the Word* (Nashville: Upper Room, 2000), p. 57.

SESSION 6

Introduction

C. S. Lewis, introduction to George MacDonald, *Phantastes* (Grand Rapids: Eerdmans, 2000), p. xi.

Sidebars

Oswald Chambers, *My Utmost for His Highest,* updated ed., ed. James Reimann (Grand Rapids: Discovery House, 1992), January 3 entry.

Robert Mulholland, *Shaped by the Word* (Nashville: Upper Room, 2000), p. 56.

Thelma Hall, *Too Deep for Words: Rediscovering Lectio Divina* (New York: Paulist, 1988), p. 37.

Transformation Exercise Two

This and other intriguing ideas are included in Anne Broyles, *Journaling: A Spirit Journey* (Nashville: Upper Room, 1988), pp. 45-46.

Section 5: Community & Submission

INTRODUCTION

Norvene Vest, *Gathered in the Word* (Nashville: Upper Room, 1996), p. 43.

SESSION 1

Introduction

Dallas Willard, *Renovation of the Heart* (Colorado Springs: NavPress, 2002), p. 184.

Sidebars

C. S. Lewis, *They Stand Together: The Letters of C. S. Lewis to Arthur Greeves (1914-1963)* (New York: Macmillan, 1979), p. 514.

Robert Mulholland, *Invitation to a Journey* (Downers Grove, Ill. InterVarsity Press, 1993), p. 154.

Dietrich Bonhoeffer, *Life Together* (New York: Harper & Row, 1954), p. 23.

Question Six

William Lane, *The Gospel According to Mark,* New International Commmentary on the New Testament (Grand Rapids Eerdmans, 1975), p. 518.

Question Eleven

Henri Nouwen, *Making All Things New* (San Francisco: HarperSanFrancisco, 1981), pp. 81-82, 87.

Transformation Exercise One

Kristin Henderson and Margery Larrabee, "Spiritual Friendship: Deepening Your Relationship with God Through Intentional Friendship," paper delivered at the Yearly Meeting of the Religious Society of Friends, Baltimore, May 1998, pp. 6, 8.

SESSION 2

Introduction

C. S. Lewis, *God in the Dock* (Grand Rapids: Eerdmans, 1999), pp. 61-62.

C. S. Lewis, *Letters of C. S. Lewis,* December 7, 1950, p. 224, quoted in *The Quotable Lewis,* ed. Wayne Martindale and Jerry Root (Wheaton, Ill.: Tyndale House, 1989), quote 203, pp. 105-6.

Sidebars

Dietrich Bonhoeffer, *Life Together* (New York: Harper & Row, 1954), pp. 26-27.

The Rule of St. Benedict in English, ed. Timothy Fry (Collegeville, Minn.: Liturgical Press, 1982), 58.18, 23, as paraphrased by Esther de Waal, "Woven Together in Love," *Weavings,* July-August 1988, p. 12.

Henri Nouwen, *Making All Things New* (San Francisco: HarperSanFrancisco, 1981), pp. 86-87.

SESSION 3

Introduction

Oswald Chambers, *My Utmost for His Highest,* updated ed. (Grand Rapids: Discovery House, 1992), February 25 entry.

Sidebars

Marjorie Thompson, review of *Why We Live in Community* by Eberhard Arnold, *Weavings,* September-October 1996, p. 46.

Richard Foster, *Celebration of Discipline* (San Francisco: Harper & Row, 1988), p. 111.

Henri Nouwen "Power, Powerlessness and Power," *Weavings,* January-February 1995, p. 35.

Question Eleven

Richard Foster, *The Challenge of the Disciplined Life* (San Francisco: Harper & Row, 1985), pp. 201-6.

Transformation Exercise Three

These ideas come from John C. Wagner, "Spirituality and Administration: The Sign of Integrity," *Weavings,* July-August 1988, p. 19.

Transformation Exercise Four

Chambers, *My Utmost for His Highest,* July 19 entry.

SESSION 4

Sidebars

Dietrich Bonhoeffer, *Life Together* (New York: Harper & Row, 1954), p. 76.

Richard Foster, *Celebration of Discipline* (San Francisco: Harper & Row, 1988), p. 117.

Ibid., p. 124.

SESSION 5

Introduction

Dietrich Bonhoeffer, *Life Together* (New York: Harper & Row, 1954), p. 97.

Ibid., p. 98.

Turning Toward God

Ibid., p. 78.

Sidebars

Ibid., pp. 98-99.

Ibid., p. 98.

Mary Rose O'Reilley, "Deep Listening: An Experimental Friendship," *Weavings,* May-June 1994, p. 22.

Transformation Exercise Three

Thomas Merton, *The Wisdom of the Desert* (Norfolk, Conn.: New Directions, 1960), p. 30.

SESSION 6

Introduction

Gerrit S. Dawson, "Feasts in the Desert and Other Unlikely Places," *Weavings,* January-February 1994, p. 33.

Sidebars

Dallas Willard, *Renovation of the Heart* (Colorado Springs: NavPress, 2002), p. 183.

Michael E. Williams, "Voices from Unseen Rooms: Storytelling and Community," *Weavings,* July-August 1990, p. 21.

Susan Mangram, "Open the Door!" *Weavings,* January-February 1994, p. 27.

Section 6: Reflection & Confession

SESSION 1

Sidebars

Frederick Buechner, *Wishful Thinking* (San Francisco: HarperSanFrancisco, 1993), p. 18.

Marjorie Thompson, *Soul Feast* (Louisville, Ky.: Westminster John Knox, 1995), p. 98.

Jeanne Guyon, *Experiencing the Depths of Jesus Christ* (Beaumont, Tex.: SeedSowers, 1975), p. 76.

SESSION 2

Sidebars

Jeanne Guyon, *Experiencing the Depths of Jesus Christ* (Beaumont, Tex.: SeedSowers, 1975), p. 73.

Marjorie Thompson, *Soul Feast* (Louisville, Ky.: Westminster John Knox, 1995), p. 85.

Tad Dunne, *Spiritual Mentoring* (San Francisco: HarperSanFrancisco, 1991), pp. 99-100.

Transformation Exercises

Adapted from ibid., pp. 93, 97.

SESSION 3

Sidebars

Richard Foster, *Prayer: Finding the Heart's True Home* (San Francisco: HarperSanFrancisco, 1992), p. 29.

Jeanne Guyon, *Experiencing the Depths of Jesus Christ* (Beaumont, Tex.: SeedSowers, 1975), p. 74.

Marjorie Thompson, *Soul Feast* (Louisville, Ky.: Westminster John Knox, 1995), p. 85.

SESSION 4

Sidebars

Dietrich Bonhoeffer, *Life Together* (New York: Harper & Row, 1954), p. 112.

Ibid., pp. 113-15.

SESSION 5

Introduction

Deborah Smith Douglas, "The Examen Re-examined," *Weavings,* March-April 1995, p. 37.

Sidebars

Richard Foster, *Prayer: Finding the Heart's True Home* (San Francisco: HarperSan-Francisco, 1992), p. 28.

Douglas, "Examen Re-examined," p. 36.

Question Eleven

The questions have been adapted from a handout by retreat leader Linda Douty, Memphis, Tennessee.

Transformation Exercise Two

The list of Ignatian elements comes from W. H. Longridge, *The Spiritual Exercises of Ignatius of Loyola* (London: A. R. Mowbray, 1950), p. 50.

SESSION 6

Introduction

Madeleine L'Engle, *Walking on Water: Reflections on Faith and Art* (Wheaton, Ill.: Harold Shaw, 1980), p. 137.

Sidebars

Ibid.

Anne Broyles, "One More Door into God's Presence: Journaling as a Spiritual Discipline," *Weavings,* May-June 1987, p. 34.

John Baillie, *A Diary of Private Prayer* (London: Oxford University Press, 1956), p. 75.

Transformation Exercise Two

These steps are mentioned in Marjorie Thompson, *Soul Feast* (Louisville, Ky.: Westminster John Knox, 1995), p. 88. Similar processes are described in twelve-step books.

Section 7: Simplicity & Fasting

SESSION 1

Sidebars

Mary Conrow Coelho, "Participating in the New Creation," *Weavings,* March-April 1987, p. 17.

Os Guinness, as quoted in Dallas Willard, *The Divine Conspiracy* (San Francisco: HarperSanFrancisco, 1998), p. 190.

Richard Foster, "Fasting, Twentieth Century Style," cassette tape (Renovaré, n.d.); permission granted to quote.

Question Six

Richard Foster, *Freedom of Simplicity* (San Francisco: Harper & Row, 1981), p. 35.

SESSION 2

Introduction

Jean-Nicholas Grou, *How to Pray,* trans. Joseph Dalby (Cambridge: James Clarke, 1955), p. 72.

Sidebars

Evelyn Underhill, *Great Devotional Classics: Selections from the Writings of Evelyn Underhill,* ed. Douglas Steere (Nashville: Upper Room, 1961), p. 10.

Marjorie Thompson, *Soul Feast* (Louisville, Ky.: Westminster John Knox, 1995), p. 73.

Dallas Willard, *The Spirit of the Disciplines* (San Francisco: Harper & Row, 1988), p. 168.

Question Eight

Dallas Willard, *The Divine Conspiracy* (San Francisco: HarperSanFrancisco, 1998), p. 205.

SESSION 3

Introduction

Dallas Willard, *The Spirit of the Disciplines* (San Francisco: Harper & Row, 1988), p. 165.

Sidebars

R. C. H. Lenski, *The Interpretation of St. Matthew's Gospel* (Minneapolis: Augsburg, 1943), p. 238.

Richard Foster, *Freedom of Simplicity* (San Francisco: Harper & Row, 1981), p. 142.

William Penn, quoted in James Gilchrist Lawson, *Deeper Experiences of Famous Christians* (Anderson, Ind.: Warner, 1911), p. 100.

SESSION 4

Sidebars

Robert Mulholland, *Invitation to a Journey* (Downers Grove, Ill.: InterVarsity Press, 1993), p. 119.

Dallas Willard, *The Spirit of the Disciplines* (San Francisco: Harper & Row, 1988), p. 166.

Robert Morris, "Holy and Glorious Flesh: The Transfiguration of Desire," *Weavings,* July-August 1999, p. 29.

Chart

"Doubts" and "weaknesses" are modified from *Life Application Bible* (Wheaton, Ill.: Tyndale House, 1991), p. 1649.

"Desires" are listed in Henri J. M. Nouwen, *The Way of the Heart* (San Francisco: HarperSanFrancisco, 1981), p. 25.

SESSION 5

Sidebars

Marjorie Thompson, *Soul Feast* (Louisville, Ky.: Westminster John Knox, 1995), p. 71.

Dallas Willard, *The Kingdom as a Basis of Death to Self,* tape 2, "Living Like Jesus: How to Do It" (Chatsworth, Calif.: Sower's Yield Tape Ministry).

Frederica Mathewes-Green, *The Illumined Heart* (Brewster, Mass.: Paraclete, 2001), p. 42, 45, 44.

SESSION 6

Introduction

Richard Foster, "Fasting, Twentieth Century Style," cassette tape (Renovaré, n.d.); permission granted to quote.

Sidebars

Arthur Wallis, *God's Chosen Fast* (Fort Washington, Penn.: Christian Literature Crusade, 1977), p. 28.

Marjorie Thompson, *Soul Feast* (Louisville, Ky.: Westminster John Knox, 1995), p. 72.

Wallis, *God's Chosen Fast,* p. 37.

Question Three

Arthur Wallis, *God's Chosen Fast* (Fort Washington, Penn.: Christian Literature Crusade, 1977), pp. 32-33.

Section 8: Worship & Celebration

INTRODUCTION

Dallas Willard, *The Spirit of the Disciplines* (San Francisco: Harper & Row, 1988), p. 177.

SESSION 1

Hearing God Through the Word

Franz Delitzsch, *Commentary on the Old Testament*, vol. 5, *Commentary on the Psalms* (Grand Rapids: Eerdmans, 1973), p. 213.

H. C. Leupold, *Exposition of the Psalms* (Grand Rapids: Baker, 1972), p. 463.

Sidebars

John Baillie, *A Diary of Private Prayer* (London: Oxford University Press, 1956), p. 41 (9th day, morning).

Dallas Willard, *The Divine Conspiracy* (San Francisco: HarperSanFrancisco, 1998), p. 321.

SESSION 2

Sidebars

John Baillie, *A Diary of Private Prayer* (London: Oxford University Press, 1956), p. 73 (17th day, morning).

Augustine, *Early Will I Seek You*, ed. David Hazard (Minneapolis: Bethany House, 1991), p. 77.

C. S. Lewis, *Reflections on the Psalms,* large print ed. (New York: Walker, 1985), p. 130.

Transformation Exercise Four

Adapted from Jack R. Taylor, *The Hallelujah Factor* (Nashville: Broadman, 1983), p. 17.

SESSION 3

Introduction

K. C. Ptomey (quoting loosely from Kierkegaard, not cited), "The Work of the People," in *Communion, Community and Commonweal Readings for Spiritual Leadership,* ed. John Mogabgab (Nashville: Upper Room, 1995), p. 93.

Sidebars

Robert Webber, "Let's Put *Worship* into the Worship Service," *Christianity Today,* February 17, 1984, p. 52.

Robert Mulholland, *Invitation to a Journey* (Downers Grove, Ill.: InterVarsity Press, 1993), p. 117.

Jack R. Taylor, *The Hallelujah Factor* (Nashville: Broadman, 1983), pp. 24-25.

Transformation Exercises One and Three

Adapted from Taylor, *Hallelujah Factor,* pp. 25, 110.

SESSION 4

Introduction

Dallas Willard, *The Spirit of the Disciplines* (San Francisco: Harper & Row, 1988), p. 179.

Sidebars

C. S. Lewis, *Reflections on the Psalms,* large print ed. (New York: Walker, 1985), p. 132.

Brother Lawrence, *The Practice of the Presence of God* (Old Tappan, N.J.: Fleming H. Revell, 1958), pp. 20-21.

C. S. Lewis, *Letters to Malcolm: Chiefly on Prayer* (New York: Harcourt Brace, 1964), pp. 91, 93.

SESSION 5

Sidebars

R. C. H. Lenski, *The Interpretation of St. John's Gospel* (Minneapolis: Augsburg, 1943), p. 483.

C. S. Lewis, *Letters to Malcolm: Chiefly on Prayer* (New York: Harcourt Brace, 1964), p. 103.

SESSION 6

Sidebars

Robert Mulholland, *Invitation to a Journey* (Downers Grove, Ill.: InterVarsity Press, 1993), p. 117.

Jean-Pierre de Caussade, *The Sacrament of the Present Moment* (San Francisco: Harper & Row, 1982), p. 35.

Francis of Assisi, *Selections from the Writings of St. Francis of Assisi,* Great Devotional Classics, ed. J. Minton Batted (Nashville: Upper Room, 1952), p. 23.